ANALYSIS OF ECONOMIC DATA

ANALYSIS OF ECONOMIC DATA

Third Edition

by

Gary Koop

University of Strathclyde, UK

A John Wiley & Sons, Ltd., Publication

Other Wiley Editorial Offices

John Wiley & Sons Inc., 111 River Street, Hoboken, NJ 07030, USA

Jossey-Bass, 989 Market Street, San Francisco, CA 94103-1741, USA

Wiley-VCH Verlag GmbH, Boschstr. 12, D-69469 Weinheim, Germany

John Wiley & Sons Australia Ltd, 42 McDougall Street, Milton, Queensland 4064, Australia

John Wiley & Sons (Asia) Pte Ltd, 2 Clementi Loop #02-01, Jin Xing Distripark, Singapore 129809

John Wiley & Sons Canada Ltd, 6045 Freemont Blvd. Mississauga, Ontario, L5R 4J3 Canada

Wiley also publishes its books in a variety of electronic formats. Some content that appears in print may not
be available in electronic books.

Library of Congress Cataloging-in-Publication Data

Koop, Gary.
Analysis of economic data / by Gary Koop.—3rd ed.
     p. cm.
  Includes bibliographical references and index.
  ISBN 978-0-470-71389-1 (pbk.)
1. Econometrics. I. Title.

HB141.K644 2009
330.01'5195—dc22

               2008049827

British Library Cataloguing in Publication Data
A catalogue record for this book is available from the British Library

ISBN 978-0-470-71389-1 (P/B)

Typeset in 11/13 pt Garamond Monotype by SNP Best-set Typesetter Ltd, Hong Kong
Printed and bound in Great Britain by CPI Antony Rowe, Chippenham, Wiltshire

Contents

Preface to the Third Edition

I am happy to say that in the years since the second edition was published, *Analysis of Economic Data* has continued to be moderately successful. In writing the third edition I have tried to build upon this success. I have made no major changes in style or content in the new edition. This book is still intended to teach the basic tools of the applied economist without involving complicated econometric theory. However, I have made numerous minor changes. More empirical examples have been added (including more empirical project topics) and here and there new important methods have been added (for example, the Johansen test for cointegration has been added to Chapter 11). Most of the changes to the previous edition have arisen out of the realization that, although the book has been used primarily in economics courses, it is also being used in an increasing number of business and finance courses. This has motivated many of the changes and, in particular, the addition of substantial new material on financial volatility (including ARCH and GARCH models).

In the prefaces to previous editions I thanked many people, including students, colleagues, reviewers and all the people at Wiley. I would like to thank them all again for their assistance.

Preface to the
Second Edition

When writing the new edition of my book, I tried to take into account the comments of many colleagues who used the first edition, the reviewers (some anonymous) who Wiley persuaded to evaluate my proposal for a new edition as well as my personal experience. With regards to the last, I have used the first edition of the book at three different universities (Edinburgh, Glasgow and Leicester) at three different levels. I have used it for a third-year course (for students who were not specialist economists and had little or no background in statistics), for a second-year course (for students with a fair amount of economics training, but little or no training in statistics) and for a first-year course (for students facing economic data analysis for the first time). Based on student performance and feedback, the book can successfully be used at all these levels. Colleagues have told me that the book has also been used successfully with business students and MBAs.

The second edition has not deleted anything from the first edition (other than minor corrections or typos and editorial changes). However, substantial new material has been added. Some of this is to provide details of the (minimal) mathematical background required for the book. Some of this provides more explanation of key concepts such as index numbers. And some provides more description of data sources. Throughout, I have tried to improve the explanation so that the concepts of economic data analysis can be easily understood. In light of the book's use in business courses, I have also added a bit more material relevant for business students, especially those studying finance.

I still believe in all the comments I made in the preface for the first edition, especially those expressing gratitude to all the people who have helped me by offering perceptive comments. To the list of people I thank in that preface, I would like to add the names Julia Darby, Kristian Skrede Gleditsch and Hilary Lamaison and all my students from the Universities of Edinburgh, Glasgow and Leicester.

Preface to the First Edition

This book aims to teach econometrics to students whose primary interest is not in econometrics. These are the students who simply want to apply econometric techniques sensibly in the context of real-world empirical problems. This book is aimed largely at undergraduates, for whom it can serve either as a stand-alone course in applied data analysis or as an accessible alternative to standard econometric textbooks. However, students in graduate economics and MBA programs requiring a crash-course in the basics of practical econometrics will also benefit from the simplicity of the book and its intuitive bent.

This book grew out of a course I teach at the University of Edinburgh entitled "Analysis of Economic Data." Before this course was created, all students were required to take a course in probability and statistics in their first or second year. Students specializing in economics were also required to take an econometrics course in their third or fourth year. However, nonspecialist students (e.g. economics and politics or economics and business students) were not required to take econometrics, with the consequence that they entered their senior undergraduate years, and eventually the job market, with only a basic course in probability and statistics. These students were often ill-prepared to sensibly analyze real economic data. Since this is a key skill for undergraduate projects and dissertations, for graduate school, as well as for most careers open to economists, it was felt that a new course was needed to provide a firm practical foundation in the tools of economic data analysis. There was a general consensus in the department that the following principles should be adhered to in designing the new course:

1. It must cover most of the tools and models used in modern econometric research (e.g. correlation, regression and extensions for time series methods).
2. It must be largely nonmathematical, relying on verbal and graphical intuition.

3. It must contain extensive use of real data examples and involve students in hands-on computer work.

4. It must be short. After all, students, especially those in joint degrees (e.g. economics and business or economics and politics) must master a wide range of material. Students rarely have the time or the inclination to study econometrics in depth.

This book follows these basic principles. It aims to teach students reasonably sophisticated econometric tools, using simple nonmathematical intuition and practical examples. Its unifying themes are the related concepts of regression and correlation. These simple concepts are relatively easy to motivate using verbal and graphical intuition and underlie many of the sophisticated models and techniques (e.g. cointegration and unit roots) in economic research today. If a student understands the concepts of correlation and regression well, then he/she can understand and apply the techniques used in advanced econometrics and statistics.

This book has been designed for use in conjunction with a computer. I am convinced that practical hands-on computer experience, supplemented by formal lectures, is the best way for students to learn practical data-analysis skills. Extensive problem sets are accompanied by different data sets in order to encourage students to work as much as possible with real-world data. Every theoretical point in the book is illustrated with practical economic examples that the student can replicate and extend using the computer. It is my strong belief that every hour a student spends in front of the computer is worth several hours spent in a lecture.

This book has been designed to be accessible to a variety of students, and thus, contains minimal mathematical content. Aside from some supplementary material in appendices, it assumes no mathematics beyond the pre-university level. For students unfamiliar with these basics (e.g. the equation of a straight line, the summation operator, logarithms), a wide variety of books are available that provide sufficient background.

I would like to thank my students and colleagues at the University of Edinburgh for their comments and reactions to the lectures that formed the foundation of this book. Many reviewers also offered numerous helpful comments. Most of these were anonymous, but Denise Young, Craig Heinicke, John Hutton, Kai Li and Jean Soper offered numerous invaluable suggestions that were incorporated in the book. I am grateful, in particular, to Steve Hardman at John Wiley for the enthusiasm and expert editorial advice he gave throughout this project. I would also like to express my deepest gratitude to my wife, Lise, for the support and encouragement she provided while this book was in preparation.

Introduction

Several types of professional economists are working in the world today. Academic economists in universities often derive and test theoretical models of various aspects of the economy. Economists in the civil service often study the merits and demerits of policies under consideration by government. Economists employed by a central bank often give advice on whether or not interest rates should be raised and, in the private sector, economists often predict future variables such as exchange-rate movements and their effect on company exports.

For all of these economists, the ability to work with data is an important skill. To decide between competing theories, to predict the effect of policy changes or to forecast what may happen in the future it is necessary to appeal to facts. In economics we are fortunate in having at our disposal an enormous number of facts (in the form of "data") that we can analyze in various ways to shed light on many economic issues.

The purpose of this book is to present the basics of data analysis in a simple, non-mathematical way, emphasizing graphical and verbal intuition. It focuses on the tools that economists apply in practice (primarily regression) and develops computer skills that are necessary in virtually any career path that the economics student may choose to follow.

To explain further what this book does, it is perhaps useful to begin by discussing what it does *not* do. *Econometrics* is the name given to the study of quantitative tools for analyzing economic data. The field of econometrics is based on probability and statistical theory; it is a fairly mathematical field. This book does not attempt to teach

Jim employs — but with Mauricio this idea

probability and statistical theory, nor does it contain much mathematical content. In both of these respects it represents a clear departure from traditional econometrics textbooks. Yet it aims to teach most of the practical tools used by applied econometricians today.

Books that merely teach the student which buttons to press on a computer without providing an understanding of what the computer is doing, are commonly referred to as "cookbooks." The present book is *not* a cookbook. Some econometricians may interject at this point: "But how can a book teach the student to use the tools of econometrics, without teaching the basics of probability and statistics?" My answer is that much of what the econometrician does in practice can be understood intuitively, without resorting to probability and statistical theory. Indeed, this book contends that most of the tools econometricians use can be mastered simply through a thorough understanding of the concept of correlation, and its generalization, regression. If a student understands correlation and regression well, then he/she can understand most of what econometricians do. In the vast majority of cases, it can be argued that regression will reveal most of the information in a data set. Furthermore, correlation and regression are fairly simple concepts that can be understood through verbal intuition or graphical methods. They provide the basis of explanation for more difficult concepts, and can be used to analyze many types of economic data.

This book focuses on the *analysis* of economic data. That is, *it is not a book about collecting economic data*. With some exceptions, it treats the data as given, and does not explain how they are collected or constructed. For instance, it does not explain how national accounts are created or how labor surveys are designed. It simply teaches the reader to make sense out of the data that has been gathered.

Statistical theory usually proceeds from the formal definition of general concepts, followed by a discussion of how these concepts are relevant to particular examples. The present book attempts to do the opposite—*it attempts to motivate general concepts through particular examples*. In some cases formal definitions are not even provided. For instance, P-values and confidence intervals are important statistical concepts, providing measures relating to the accuracy of a fitted regression line (see Chapter 5). The chapter uses examples, graphs and verbal intuition to demonstrate how they might be used in practice. But no formal definition of a P-value or derivation of a confidence interval is ever given. It would require the introduction of probability and statistical theory, which is not necessary for using these techniques sensibly in practice. For the reader wishing to learn more about the statistical theory underlying the techniques, many books are available—for instance Wonnacott and Wonnacott (1990). For those interested in how statistical theory is applied in econometric modeling, Hill, Griffiths and Judge (1997) provide a useful introduction.

This book reflects my belief that the use of concrete examples is the best way to teach data analysis. Appropriately, each chapter presents several examples as a means

Principles:
(1) Time Series view when appropriate
(2) Simple graphical views
(3) Include fishbone?

of illustrating key concepts. One risk with such a strategy is that some students might interpret the presence of so many examples to mean that a myriad of concepts must be mastered before they can ever hope to become adept at the practice of econometrics. This is not the case. There are only a few basic concepts at the heart of this book and they appear repeatedly in a variety of different problems and data sets. The best approach for teaching introductory econometrics, in other words, is to illustrate its specific concepts over and over again in a variety of contexts.

Use well documented do files with students executing
small pieces to get acquainted with Stata & Analysis

Organization of the Book   *require input from students —*

follow pattern & extend

In organizing the book, I have attempted to adhere to the general philosophy outlined above. Each chapter covers a topic and includes a general discussion. However, much of the chapter is devoted to empirical examples that illustrate and, in some cases, introduce important concepts. Exercises that further illustrate these concepts are included in the text. Data required for working through the empirical examples and exercises can be found in the web site that accompanies this book. By including real-world data it is hoped that students will not only replicate the examples but will feel comfortable extending and/or experimenting with the data in a variety of ways. Exposure to real-world data sets is essential if students are to master the conceptual material and apply the techniques covered in this book.

The empirical examples in this book are mostly done using the computer package Excel. The web site associated with the book contains Excel files. Excel is a simple and common software package. It is also one that students are likely to use in their economic careers. However, the data can be analyzed using many other computer software packages, not just Excel. Many of these packages recognize Excel files and the data sets can be imported directly into them. Alternatively, the web site also contains all of the data files in ASCII text form. An appendix at the end of the book provides more detail about the data.

Mathematical material has been kept to a minimum throughout. In some cases, a little bit of mathematics will provide additional intuition. For students familiar with mathematical techniques, appendices have been included at the end of some chapters. However, students can choose to omit this material without any detriment to their understanding of the basic concepts. The content of the book breaks logically into two parts. Chapters 1–7 cover all the basic material relating to graphing, correlation and regression. A very short course would cover only this material. Chapters 8–12 emphasize time series topic and analyze some of the more sophisticated econometric models in use today. The focus on the underlying intuition behind regression means that this material should be easily accessible to students. Nevertheless, students will probably find that these latter chapters are more difficult than Chapters 1–7.

Useful Background

As mentioned, this book assumes very little mathematical background beyond the pre-university level. Of particular relevance are:

- Knowledge of simple equations. For instance, the equation of a straight line is used repeatedly in this book.
- Knowledge of simple graphical techniques. For instance, this book is full of graphs that plot one variable against another (standard XY graphs).
- Familiarity with the summation operator is useful occasionally.
- In a few cases logarithms are used.

For the reader unfamiliar with these topics, the appendix at the end of this chapter provides a short introduction. These topics are also discussed elsewhere, in many introductory mathematical textbooks.

The book also has a large computer component and much of the computer material is explained in the text. A myriad of computer packages could be used to implement the procedures described in this book. In the places where I write directly about computer programs I will use the language of the spreadsheet and, particularly, that most common of spreadsheets, Excel. I do this largely because the average student is more likely to have knowledge of and access to a spreadsheet rather than a specialized statistics or econometrics package such as E-views, Stata or Microfit.[1] I assume that the students know the basics of Excel (or whatever computer software package they are using). In other words, students should understand the basics of spreadsheet terminology, be able to open data sets, cut, copy and paste data, and so forth. If this material is unfamiliar to the student, simple instructions can be found in Excel's online documentation. For computer novices (and those who simply want to learn more about the computing side of data analysis) Judge (2000) is an excellent place to start.

Appendix 1.1: Mathematical Concepts Used in this Book

This book uses very little mathematics, relying instead on intuition and graphs to develop an understanding of key concepts (including understanding how to interpret the numbers produced by computer programs such as Excel). For most students, previous study of mathematics at the pre-university level should give you all the background knowledge you need. However, here is a list of the concepts used in this book along with a brief description of each.

The equation of a straight line

Economists are often interested in the relationship between two (or more) variables. Examples of variables include house prices, gross domestic product (GDP) and interest rates. In our context a variable is something that economists find interesting and can collect data on. I use capital letters (such as Y or X) to denote variables. A very general way of denoting a relationship is through the concept of a function. A common mathematical notation for a function of X is $f(X)$. So, for instance, if economists are interested in the factors that explain why some houses are worth more than others, they may think that the price of a house depends on the size of the house. In mathematical terms, he/she would then let Y denote the variable "price of the house" and X denote the variable "size of the house" and the fact the Y depends on X is written using the notation:

$$Y = f(X).$$

This notation should be read "Y is a function of X" and captures the idea that the value for Y depends on the value of X. There are many functions that one could use, but in this book I will usually focus on linear functions. Hence, I will not use this general "$f(X)$" notation in this book.

The equation of a straight line (what was called a "linear function" above) is used throughout this book. Any straight line can be written in terms of an equation:

$$Y = \alpha + \beta X.$$

where α and β are *coefficients* which determine a particular line. So, for instance, setting $\alpha = 1$ and $\beta = 2$ defines one particular line while $\alpha = 4$ and $\beta = -5$ defines a different line.

It is probably easiest to understand straight lines by using a graph (and it might be worthwhile for you to sketch one at this stage). In terms of an XY graph (one that measures Y on the vertical axis and X on the horizontal axis) any line can be defined by its intercept and slope. In terms of the equation of a straight line α is the intercept and β the slope. The intercept is the value of Y when $X = 0$ (point at which the line cuts the Y axis). The slope is a measure of how much Y changes when X is changed. Formally, it is the amount Y changes when X changes by one unit. For the student with a knowledge of calculus, the slope is the first derivative, $\dfrac{dY}{dX}$.

Summation notation

At several points in this book, subscripts are used to denote different observations from a variable. For instance, a labor economist might be interested in the wage of every one of 100 people in a certain industry. If the economist uses Y to denote this variable, then he/she will have a value of Y for the first individual, a value of Y for the second individual and so forth. A compact notation for this is to use subscripts so that Y_1 is the wage of the first individual, Y_2 the wage of the second individual, and so forth. In some contexts, it is useful to speak of a generic individual and refer to this individual as the ith. We can then write, Y_i for $i = 1, \ldots, 100$ to denote the set of wages for all individuals.

With the subscript notation established, summation notation can now be introduced. In many cases we want to add up observations (for example, when calculating an average you add up all the observations and divide by the number of observations). The Greek symbol, Σ, is the summation (or "adding-up") operator and superscripts and subscripts on Σ indicate the observations that are being added up. So, for instance

$$\sum_{i=1}^{100} Y_i = Y_1 + Y_2 + \ldots + Y_{100}$$

adds up the wages for all of the 100 individuals. Other examples are:

$$\sum_{i=1}^{3} Y_i,$$

which adds up the wages for the first three individuals and

$$\sum_{i=47}^{48} Y_i,$$

which adds up the wages for the 47th and 48th individuals.

Sometimes, where it is obvious from the context (usually when summing over all individuals), the subscript and superscript will be dropped and I will simply write:

$$\sum Y_i.$$

Logarithms

For various reasons (which are explained later on), in some cases the researcher does not work directly with a variable but with a transformed version of this variable. Many such transformations are straightforward. For instance, in comparing the incomes of different countries the variable GDP per capita is used. This is a transformed version of the variable GDP. It is obtained by dividing GDP by population.

One particularly common transformation is the logarithmic one. The logarithm (to the base B) of a number, A, is the power to which B must be raised to give A. The notation for this is: $\log_B(A)$. So, for instance, if $B = 10$ and $A = 100$ then the logarithm is 2 and we write $\log_{10}(100) = 2$. This follows since $10^2 = 100$. In economics, it is common to work with the so-called natural logarithm which has $B = e$ where $e \approx 2.71828$. We will not explain where e comes from or why this rather unusual-looking base is chosen. The natural logarithm operator is denoted by ln (i.e. $\ln(A) = \log_e(A)$).

In this book, you do not really have to understand the material in the previous paragraph. The key thing to note is that the natural logarithmic operator is a common one (for reasons explained later on) and it is denoted by $\ln(A)$. In practice, it can be easily calculated in a spreadsheet such as Excel (or on a calculator).

Endnote

1. I expect that most readers of this book will have access to Excel (or a similar spreadsheet or statistics software package) through their university computing labs or on their home computers. However, computer software can be expensive and, for the student who does not have access to Excel and is financially constrained, there are an increasing number of free statistics packages designed using open-source software such as R. Zelig, which is available at http://gking.harvard.edu/zelig/ (accessed 3 November 2008), is a good example of such a package.

References

Hill, C., Griffiths, W. and Judge, G. (1997) *Undergraduate Econometrics*, John Wiley & Sons, Ltd, Chichester.

Judge, G. (2000) *Computing Skills for Economists*, John Wiley & Sons, Ltd, Chichester.

Wonnacott, T. and Wonnacott, R. (1990) *Introductory Statistics for Business and Economics*, 4th edn, John Wiley & Sons, Ltd, Chichester.

CHAPTER 2

Basic Data Handling

This chapter introduces the basics of economic data handling. It focuses on four important areas:

- the types of data that economists often use
- a brief discussion of the sources from which economists obtain data[1]
- an illustration of the types of graphs that are commonly used to present information in a data set
- a discussion of simple numerical measures, or descriptive statistics, often presented to summarize key aspects of a data set.

Types of Economic Data

This section introduces common types of data and defines the terminology associated with their use.

Time series data

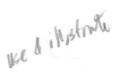

Macroeconomic data measure phenomena such as real gross domestic product (GDP), interest rates and the money supply. These data are collected at specific points in time (for example, yearly). Financial data measure phenomena such as changes in the price of stocks. Such data are sometimes collected more frequently than the above, for instance, every day or even every hour. In all of these examples, the data are ordered by time and are referred to as *time series* data. The underlying phenomenon that we are measuring (such as GDP or wages or interest rates) is referred to as a *variable*. Time series data can be observed at many *frequencies*. Commonly used frequencies are: *annual* (if a variable is observed every year), *quarterly* (four times a year), *monthly, weekly* or *daily*.

In this book, we will use the notation, Y_t, to indicate an observation on variable Y (for example, real GDP) at time t. A series of data runs from period $t = 1$ to $t = T$. "T" is used to indicate the total number of time periods covered in a data set. To give an example, if we were to use post-war annual real GDP data from 1946–98—a period of 53 years—then $t = 1$ would indicate 1946, $t = 53$ would indicate 1998 and $T = 53$ the total number of years. Hence, Y_1 would be real GDP in 1946, Y_2 real GDP for 1947 and so forth. Time series data are typically presented in chronological order.

Working with time series data often requires some special tools, which are discussed in Chapters 8–11.

Cross-sectional data *use & illustrate*

In contrast to the above, microeconomists and labor economists often work with data that are characterized by individual *units*. These units might refer to people, companies or countries. A common example is data pertaining to many different people within a group, such as the wage of every person in a certain company or industry. With such *cross-sectional* data, the ordering of the data typically does not matter (unlike time series data).

In this book, we use the notation, Y_i, to indicate an observation on variable Y for individual i. Observations in a cross-sectional data set run from individual $i = 1$ to N. By convention, "N" indicates the number of cross-sectional units (such as the number of people surveyed). For instance, a labor economist might wish to survey $N = 1,000$ workers in the steel industry, asking each individual questions such as how much they make or whether they belong to a union. In this case, Y_1 will be equal to the wage (or union membership) reported by the first worker, Y_2 the wage (or union membership) reported by the second worker, and so on.

Similarly, a microeconomist may ask $N = 100$ representatives from manufacturing companies about their profit figures in the last month. In this case, Y_1 will equal the profit reported by the first company, Y_2 the profit reported by the second company, through to Y_{100}, the profit reported by the 100th company.

The distinction between qualitative and quantitative data

The previous data sets can be used to illustrate an important distinction between types of data. The microeconomist's data on profits will have a number corresponding to each firm surveyed (for example, last month's profits in the first company surveyed were £20,000). These are referred to as *quantitative* data.

The labor economist, when asking whether or not each surveyed employee belongs to a union, receives either a Yes or a No answer. These answers are referred to as *qualitative* data. Such data often arise in economics when choices are involved (for example, the choice to buy or not buy a product, to take public transport or a private car, to join or not to join a club).

Economists will usually convert these qualitative answers into numeric data. For instance, the labor economist might set Yes = 1 and No = 0. Hence, $Y_1 = 1$ means that the first individual surveyed does belong to a union, $Y_2 = 0$ means that the second individual does not. When variables can take on only the values 0 or 1, they are referred to as *dummy (or binary) variables*. Working with such variables is a topic that will be discussed in detail in Chapter 7.

Panel data

Some data sets will have both a time series and a cross-sectional component. These data are referred to as *panel* data. Economists working on issues related to growth often make use of panel data. For instance, GDP data are available for many countries for many years. A panel data set on Y = GDP for 30 countries in the Organisation for Economic Co-operation and Development (OECD) would contain the GDP value for each country in 1970 (N = 30 observations), followed by the GDP for each country in 1971 (another N = 30 observations), and so on. Over a period of T years, there would be $T \times N$ observations on Y. Alternatively, labor economists often work with large panel data sets created by asking many individuals questions such as how much they make every year for several years.

We will use the notation Y_{it} to indicate an observation on variable Y for unit i at time t. In the economic growth example, Y_{11} will be GDP in country 1, year 1, Y_{12} GDP for country 1 in year 2, etc. In the labor economics example, Y_{11} will be the wage of the first individual surveyed in the first year, Y_{12} the wage of the first individual surveyed in the second year, etc.

Data transformations: levels versus growth rates

In this book, we will mainly assume that the data of interest, Y, is directly available. However, in practice, you may be required to take raw data from one source, and then transform it into a different form for your empirical analysis. For instance, you may take raw time series data on the variables W = total consumption expenditure, and X = expenditure on food, and create a new variable: Y = the proportion of expenditure devoted to food. Here the transformation would be $Y = \dfrac{X}{W}$. The exact nature of the transformations required depends on the problem at hand, so it is hard to offer any general recommendations on data transformation. Some special cases are considered in later chapters. Here it is useful to introduce one common transformation that econometricians use with time series data.

To motivate this transformation, suppose we have annual data on real GDP for 1950–98 (i.e. 49 years of data) denoted by Y_t for t = 1 to 49. In many empirical projects, this might be the variable of primary interest. We will refer to such series as the *level* of real GDP. However, people are often more interested in how the economy is growing over time, or in real GDP *growth*. A simple way to measure growth is to take the real GDP series and calculate a percentage change for each year. The percentage change in real GDP between period t and $t + 1$ is calculated according to the formula:[2]

$$\text{Percentage change} = \frac{(Y_{t+1} - Y_t)}{Y_t} \times 100.$$

The percentage change in real GDP is often referred to as the *growth* of GDP or the *change* in GDP. Time series data will be discussed in more detail in Chapters 8–11. It is sufficient for you to note here that we will occasionally distinguish between the level of a variable and its growth rate, and that it is common to transform levels data into growth rate data.

Index numbers

Many variables that economists work with come in the form of *index numbers*. Appendix A, at the end of this chapter, provides a detailed discussion of what these are and how they are calculated. However, if you just want to use an index number in your empirical work, a precise knowledge of how to calculate indices is probably unnecessary. Having a good intuitive understanding of how an index number is interpreted is sufficient. Accordingly, here in the body of the text we provide only an informal intuitive discussion of index numbers.

Suppose you are interested in studying a country's inflation rate, which is a measure of how prices change over time. The question arises as to how we measure "prices" in a country. The price of an individual good (such as milk, oranges, electricity, a particular brand of car or a pair of shoes) can be readily measured, but often interest centers not on individual goods, but on the *price level* in the country as a whole. The latter concept is usually defined as the price of a "basket" containing the sorts of goods that a typical consumer might buy. The price of this basket is observed at regular intervals over time in order to determine how prices are changing in the country as a whole. But the price of the basket is usually not directly reported by the government agency that collects such data. After all, if you are told the price of an individual good (for example, an orange costs 35 pence), you have been told something informative, but if you are told "the price of a basket of representative goods" is £10.45, that statement is not very informative. To interpret this latter number, you would have to know what precisely was in the basket and in what quantities. Given the millions of goods bought and sold in a modern economy, far too much information would have to be given.

In light of such issues, data often come in the form of a price *index*. Indices may be calculated in many ways, and it would distract from the main focus of this chapter to talk in detail about how they are constructed (see Appendix A for more details). However, the following points are worth noting at the outset. Firstly, indices almost invariably come as time series data. Secondly, one time period is usually chosen as a base year and the price level in the base year is set to 100.[3] Thirdly, price levels in other years are measured in percentages relative to the base year.

An example will serve to clarify these issues. Suppose a price index for four years exists, and the values are: $Y_1 = 100$, $Y_2 = 106$, $Y_3 = 109$ and $Y_4 = 111$. These numbers can be interpreted as follows: The first year has been selected as a base year and, accordingly, $Y_1=100$. The figures for other years are all relative to this base year and allow for a simple calculation of how prices have changed since the base year. For instance, $Y_2=106$ means that prices have risen from 100 to 106—a 6% rise since the first year. It can also be seen that prices have risen by 9% from year 1 to year 3 and by 11% from year 1 to year 4. Since the percentage change in prices is the definition of inflation, the price index allows the person looking at the data to easily see what inflation is. In other words, you can think of a price index as a way of presenting price data that is easy to interpret and understand.

A price index is very good for measuring *changes* in prices over time, but should not be used to talk about the *level* of prices. For instance, it should not be interpreted as an indicator of whether prices are "high" or "low." A simple example illustrates why this is the case.

The US and Canada both collect data on consumer prices. Suppose that both countries decide to use 1988 as the base year for their respective price indices. This means that the price index in 1988 for both countries will be 100. *It does not mean that prices were identical in both countries in 1988*. The choice of 1988 as a base year is arbitrary; if Canada were to suddenly change its choice of base year to 1987 then the indices in 1988 would no longer be the same for both countries. Price indices for the two countries cannot be used to make statements such as: "prices are higher in Canada than the US." But they can be used to calculate inflation rates. This allows us to make statements of the type: "inflation (the change in prices) is higher in Canada than the US."

Finance is another field where price indices often arise since information on stock prices is often presented in this form. That is, commonly reported measures of stock market activity such as the Dow Jones Industrial Average, the FTSE index, the S&P500 are all price indexes.

In our discussion, we have focused on price indices, and these are indeed by far the most common type of index numbers. Note that other types of indices (such as quantity indices) exist and should be interpreted in a similar manner to price indices. That is, they should be used as a basis for measuring how phenomena have changed from a given base year.

This discussion of index numbers is a good place to mention another transformation, which is used to deal with the effects of inflation. As an example, consider the most common measure of the output of an economy: gross domestic product (GDP). This can be calculated by adding up the value of all goods produced in the economy. However, in times of high inflation, simply looking at how GDP is changing over time can be misleading. If inflation is high, the prices of goods will be rising and thus their value will be rising over time, even if the actual amount of goods produced is not increasing. Since GDP measures the value of all goods, it will be rising in high inflation times even if production is stagnant. This leads researchers to want to correct for the *Do it* effect of inflation. The way to do this is to divide the GDP measure by a price index.[4] Gross domestic product transformed in this way is called *real* GDP. The original GDP variable is referred to as *nominal* GDP. This distinction between real and nominal variables is important in many fields of economics. The key things you should remember is that a real variable is a nominal variable divided by a price variable (usually a price index) and that real variables have the effects of inflation removed from them.

The case where you wish to correct a growth rate for inflation is slightly different. In this case, creating the real variable involves subtracting the change in the price index from the nominal variable. So, for instance, real interest rates are nominal interest rates minus inflation (where inflation is defined as the change in the price index).

Obtaining Data *— see Jim list how to include? or are?*

All of the data you need in order to understand the basic concepts and to carry out the simple analyses covered in this book can be downloaded from the web site associated with this book. However, in the future you may need to gather your own data for an essay, dissertation or report. Economic data come from many different sources and it is hard to offer general comments on the collection of data. Below are a few key points that you should note about common data sets and where to find them.

Most macroeconomic data are collected through a system of national accounts, made available in printed and increasingly, digital, form in university and government libraries.

Microeconomic data are usually collected by surveys of households, employment and businesses, which are often available from the same sources.

It is becoming increasingly common for economists to obtain their data over the Internet and many relevant web sites now exist from which data can be downloaded. You should be forewarned that the Web is a rapidly growing and changing place, so that the information and addresses provided here might soon be outdated. Appropriately, this section is provided only to give an indication of what can be obtained over the Internet. As such it is far from complete.

Before you begin searching, you should also note that some sites allow users to access data free while others charge for their data sets. Many will provide free data to noncommercial (for example, university) users, the latter requiring that you register before being allowed access to the data.

An extremely useful American site is "Resources for Economists on the Internet" (http://rfe.org/, accessed 3 November 2008). This site contains all sorts of interesting material on a wide range of economic topics. You should take the time to explore it. This site also provides links to many different data sources. For instance, on this site you can also find links to Journal Data Archives. Many journals encourage their authors to make their data publicly available and, hence, in some cases you can get data from published academic papers through Journal Data Archives.

Another site with useful links is the National Bureau of Economic Research (http://www.nber.org/, accessed 3 November 2008). One good data source available through this site is the Penn World Table (PWT), which gives macroeconomic data for over 100 countries for many years. We will refer to the PWT below.

In the United Kingdom, MIMAS (Manchester Information and Associated Services) is a useful gateway to many data sets (http://mimas.ac.uk, accessed 3 November 2008).

For financial data, there are many excellent databases of stock prices and accounting information for all sorts of companies for many years. Unfortunately, these tend to be very expensive and, hence, you should see whether your university has a subscription to a financial database. Two of the more popular ones are DataStream by Thompson Financial (http://www.datastream.com/, accessed 3 November 2008) and Wharton Research Data Services (http://wrds.wharton.upenn.edu/, accessed 3 November 2008). With regards to free data, a more limited choice of financial data is available through popular Internet portals such as Yahoo! (http://yahoo.finance.com, accessed 3 November 2008). The Federal Reserve Bank of St Louis also maintains a free database with a wide variety of data, including some financial time series (http://research.stlouisfed.org/fred2/, accessed 3 November 2008). The Financial Data Finder (http://www.cob.ohio-state.edu/fin/osudata.htm, accessed 3 November 2008), provided by the Fisher College of Business at the Ohio State University is also a useful source. Many academics also make the data sets they have used available on their web sites. For instance, Robert Shiller at Yale University has a web site that provides links to many different interesting financial data sets (http://aida.econ.yale.edu/%7Eshiller/index.html, accessed 3 November 2008).

The information listed in this section barely scratches the surface of what is available on the Web. The general advice I want to give here is that spending some time searching the Web can often be very fruitful.

Working with Data: Graphical Methods

Once you have your data, it is important for you to summarize it. After all, anybody who reads your work will not be interested in the dozens—or more likely—hundreds or more observations contained in the original raw data set. Indeed, you can think of the whole field of econometrics as one devoted to the development and dissemination of methods whereby information in data sets is summarized in informative ways. Charts and tables are very useful ways of presenting your data. There are many different types (e.g. bar chart, pie chart, etc.). A useful way to learn about the charts is to experiment with the graphing options of whatever spreadsheet and computer software package you are using. In this section, we will illustrate a few of the commonly used types of charts.

Since most economic data is either in time series or cross-sectional form, we will briefly introduce simple techniques for graphing both types of data.

Time series graphs

Monthly time series data from January 1947 through October 1996 on the UK pound/ US dollar exchange rate in Figure 2.1.[5] Such charts are commonly referred to as *time series graphs*. The data set contains 598 observations—far too many to be presented as raw numbers for a reader to comprehend. However, a reader can easily capture the main features of the data by looking at the chart. One can see, for instance, the attempt by the UK government to hold the exchange rate fixed until the end of 1971 (apart from large devaluations in September 1949 and November 1967) and the gradual depreciation of the pound as it floated downward through the middle of the 1970s.

Histograms

With time series data, a chart that shows how a variable evolves over time is often very informative. However, in the case of cross-sectional data, such methods are not appropriate and we must summarize the data in other ways.

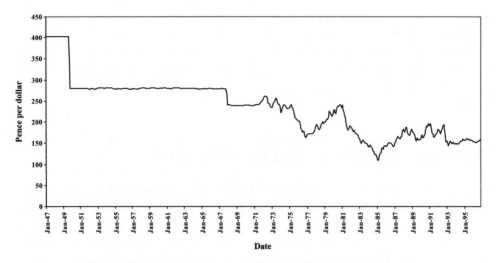

Figure 2.1   Time Series Graph of UK pound/US dollar Exchange rate.

Exercise 2.1

(a) Recreate Figure 2.1.
(b) File INCOME.XLS contains data on the natural logarithm of personal income and consumption in the US from 1954Q1 to 1994Q2.[6] Make one time series graph that contains both of these variables.
(c) Transform the logged personal income data to growth rates. Note that the percentage change in personal income between period $t-1$ and t is approximately $100 \times [\ln(Y_t) - \ln(Y_{t-1})]$ and the data provided in INCOME.XLS is already logged. Make a time series graph of the series you have created.

The file GDPPC.XLS is available on the web site associated with this book. It contains cross-sectional data on real GDP per capita in 1992 for 90 countries from the PWT. Real GDP per capita in every country has been converted into US dollars using purchasing power parity exchange rates. This allows us to make direct comparisons across countries.

One convenient way of summarizing this data is through a *histogram*. To construct a histogram, begin by constructing *class intervals* or *bins* that divide the countries into groups based on their GDP per capita. In our data set, GDP per person varies from $408 in Chad to $17,945 in the US. One possible set of class intervals is 0–2,000,

2,001–4,000, 4,001–6,000, 6,001–8,000, 8,001–10,000, 10,001–12,000, 12,001–14,000, 14,001–16,000 and 16,001 and over (where all figures are in US dollars).

Note that each class interval (with the exception of the 16,001 + category) is $2,000 wide. In other words, the *class width* for each of our bins is 2,000. For each class interval we can count up the number of countries that have GDP per capita in that interval. For instance, there are seven countries in our data set with real GDP per capita between $4,001 and $6,000. The number of countries lying in one class interval is referred to as the *frequency*[7] of that interval. A histogram is a bar chart that plots frequencies against class intervals.[8]

Below is a histogram of our cross-country GDP per capita data set that uses the class intervals specified in the previous paragraph. Note that, if you do not wish to specify class intervals, most computer software packages will do it automatically for you. They will also typically create a *frequency table*, which is located next to the histogram.

The frequency table indicates the number of countries belonging to each class interval (or bin). The numbers in the column labeled "Bin" indicate the upper bounds of the class intervals. For instance, we can read that there are 33 countries with GDP per capita less than $2,000; 22 countries with GDP per capita above $2,000 but less than $4,000 and so on. The last row says that there are four countries with GDP per capita above $16,000.

This same information is graphed in a simple fashion in the histogram. Graphing allows for a quick visual summary of the cross-country *distribution* of GDP per capita. We can see from the histogram that many countries are very poor, but that there is also a "clump" of countries that are quite rich (for example, 19 countries have GDP per capita greater than $12,000). There are relatively few countries in between these poor and rich groups (few countries fall in the bins labeled 8,000, 10,000 and 12,000).

Growth economists often refer to this clumping of countries into poor and rich groups as the "twin peaks" phenomenon. In other words, if we imagine that the histogram is a mountain range, we can see a peak at the bin labeled 2,000 and a smaller peak at 14,000. These features of the data can be seen easily from the histogram, but would be difficult to comprehend simply by looking at the raw data.

Exercise 2.2

(a) Recreate the histogram in Figure 2.2.
(b) Create histograms using different class intervals. For instance, begin by letting your software package choose default values and see what you get, then try values of your own.

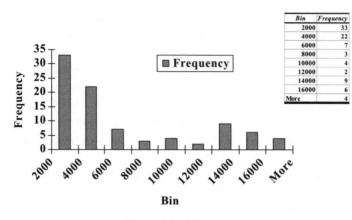

Bin	Frequency
2000	33
4000	22
6000	7
8000	3
10000	4
12000	2
14000	9
16000	6
More	4

Figure 2.2 Histogram.

XY-plots

Economists are often interested in the nature of the relationships between two or more variables. For instance, questions such as "Are higher education levels and work experience associated with higher wages among workers in a given industry?" "Are changes in the money supply a reliable indicator of inflation changes?" "Do differences in capital investment explain why some countries are growing faster than others?" All involve two or more variables.

The techniques described previously are suitable for describing the behavior of only one variable; for instance, the properties of real GDP per capita across countries in Figure 2.2. They are not, however, suitable for examining relationships between pairs of variables.

Once we are interested in understanding the nature of the relationships between two or more variables, it becomes harder to use graphs. Future chapters will discuss regression analysis, which is the prime tool used by applied economists working with many variables. However, graphical methods can be used to draw out some simple aspects of the relationship between two variables. *XY-plots* (also called *scatter diagrams*) are particularly useful in this regard.

Below you will find a graph of data[9] on deforestation (the average annual forest loss over the period 1981–90 expressed as a percentage of total forested area) for 70 tropical countries, along with data on population density (number of people per thousand hectares). It is commonly thought that countries with a high population density will likely deforest more quickly than those with low population densities, because high population density may increase the pressure to cut down forests for fuel wood or for agricultural land required to grow more food.

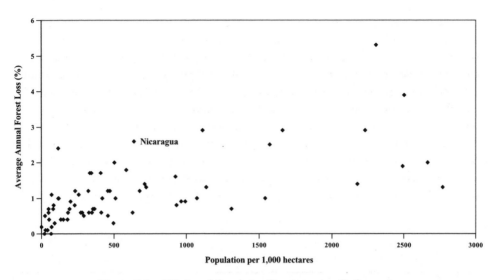

Figure 2.3 *XY*-plot of Population Density against Deforestation.

Figure 2.3 is an *XY*-plot of these two variables. Each point on the chart represents a particular country. Reading up the *Y*-axis (the vertical one) gives us the rate of deforestation in that country. Reading across the *X*-axis (the horizontal one) gives us population density. It is certainly possible to label each point with its corresponding country name. We have not done so here, since labels for 70 countries would clutter the chart and make it difficult to read. However, one country, Nicaragua, has been labeled. Note that this country has a deforestation rate of 2.6% per year ($Y = 2.6$) and a population density of 640 people per thousand hectares ($X = 640$).

The *XY*-plot can be used to give a quick visual impression of the relationship between deforestation and population density. An examination of this chart indicates some support for the idea that a relationship between deforestation and population density does exist. For instance, if we look at countries with a low population density, (less than 500 people per hectare, say), almost all of them have very low deforestation rates (less than 1% per year). If we look at countries with high population densities, (for example, over 1,500 people per thousand hectares), almost all of them have high deforestation rates (more than 2% per year). This indicates that there may be a *positive relationship* between population density and deforestation (high values of one variable tend to be associated with high values of the other; and low values, associated with low values). It is also possible to have a *negative relationship*. This would occur, for instance, if we substituted urbanization for population density in an *XY*-plot. In this case, high levels of urbanization might be associated with low levels of deforestation since expansion of cities would possibly reduce population pressures in rural areas where forests are located.

It is worth noting that the positive or negative relationships found in the data are only *tendencies*, and as such, do not hold necessarily for every country. That is, there may be exceptions to the general pattern of high population density's association with high rates of deforestation. For example, on the XY-plot we can observe one country with a high population density of roughly 1,300 and a low deforestation rate of 0.7%. Similarly, low population density can also be associated with high rates of deforestation, as evidenced by one country with a low population density of roughly 150 but a high deforestation rate of almost 2.5%! As economists, we are usually interested in drawing out *general patterns or tendencies in the data*. However, we should always keep in mind that exceptions (in statistical jargon *outliers*) to these patterns typically exist. *In some cases, finding out which countries don't fit the general pattern can be as interesting as the pattern itself.*

Exercise 2.3

The file FOREST.XLS contains data on both the percentage increase in cropland from 1980 to 1990 and on the percentage increase in permanent pasture over the same period. Construct and interpret XY-plots of these two variables (one at a time) against deforestation. Does there seem to be a positive relationship between deforestation and expansion of pasture land? How about between deforestation and the expansion of cropland?

Working with Data: Descriptive Statistics

Graphs have an immediate visual impact that is useful for livening up an essay or report. However, in many cases it is important to be numerically precise. Later chapters will describe common numerical methods for summarizing the relationship between several variables in greater detail. Here we discuss briefly a few *descriptive statistics* for summarizing the properties of a single variable. By way of motivation, we will return to the concept of distribution introduced in our discussion on histograms.

In our cross-country data set, real GDP per capita varies across the 90 countries. This variability can be seen by looking at the histogram in Figure 2.2, which plots the distribution of GDP per capita across countries. Suppose you wanted to summarize the information contained in the histogram numerically. One thing you could do is to present the numbers in the frequency table in Figure 2.2. However, even this table may

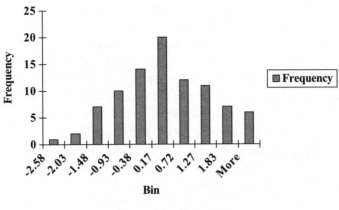

Figure 2.4 Histogram.

provide too many numbers to be easily interpretable. Instead it is common to present two simple numbers called the *mean* and *standard deviation*.

The *mean* is the statistical term for the average. The mathematical formula for the mean is given by:

$$\bar{Y} = \frac{\sum_{i=1}^{N} Y_i}{N}$$

where N is the *sample size* (i.e. number of countries) and Σ is the summation operator (i.e. it adds up real GDP per capita for all countries). In our case, mean GDP per capita is $5,443.80. Throughout this book, we will place a bar over a variable to indicate its mean ($\bar{Y}$ is the mean of the variable Y, $\bar{X}$ is the mean of X, and so forth).

The concept of the mean is associated with the middle of a distribution. For example, if we look at the previous histogram, $5,443.80 lies somewhere in the middle of the distribution. The cross-country distribution of real GDP per capita is quite unusual, having the twin peaks property described earlier. It is more common for distributions of economic variables to have a single peak and to be bell shaped. Figure 2.4 is a histogram that plots just such a bell-shaped distribution. For such distributions, the mean is located precisely in the middle of the distribution, under the single peak.

Of course, the mean or average figure hides a great deal of variability across countries. Other useful summary statistics, which shed light on the cross-country variation in GDP per capita, are the minimum and maximum. For our data set, minimum GDP per capita is $408 (Chad) and maximum GDP is $17,945 (US). By looking at the distance between the maximum and minimum we can see how *dispersed* the distribution is.

The concept of dispersion is quite important in economics and is closely related to the concepts of variability and inequality. For instance, real GDP per capita in 1992 in our data set varies from $408 to $17,945. If poorer countries were, in the near future, to grow quickly, and richer countries to stagnate, then the dispersion of real GDP per capita in, say, 2012, might be significantly less. It may be the case that the poorest country at this time will have real GDP per capita of $10,000 while the richest country will remain at $17,945. If this were to happen, then the cross-country distribution of real GDP per capita would be more equal (less dispersed, less variable). Intuitively, the notions of dispersion, variability and inequality are closely related.

The minimum and maximum, however, can be unreliable guidelines to dispersion. For instance, what if, with the exception of Chad, all the poor countries experienced rapid economic growth between 1992 and 2012, while the richer countries did not grow at all? In this case, cross-country dispersion or inequality would decrease over time. However, since Chad and the US did not grow, the minimum and maximum would remain at $408 and $17,945, respectively.

A more common measure of dispersion is the *standard deviation*. Its mathematical formula is given by:

$$s = \sqrt{\frac{\sum_{i=1}^{N}(Y_i - \bar{Y})^2}{N-1}},$$

although in practice you will probably never have to calculate it by hand as computer software will do it for you.[10] The square of the standard deviation is known as the *variance*.

The standard deviation has little direct intuition. In our cross-country GDP data set, the standard deviation is $5,369.496 and it is difficult to get a direct feel for what this number means in an *absolute* sense. However, the standard deviation can be interpreted in a *comparative* sense. That is, if you compare the standard deviations of two different distributions, the one with the smaller standard deviation will always exhibit less dispersion. In our example, if the poorer countries were to suddenly experience economic growth and the richer countries to stagnate, the standard deviation would decrease over time.

Exercise 2.4

Construct and interpret descriptive statistics for the pasture change and cropland change variables in FOREST.XLS.

Appendices 2.2 and 2.3 at the end of this chapter contain a discussion of more advanced topics relating to descriptive statistics.

Chapter Summary

1. Economic data come in many forms. Common types are time series, cross-sectional and panel data.
2. Economic data can be obtained from many sources. The Internet is becoming an increasingly valuable repository for many data sets.
3. Simple graphical techniques, including histograms and XY-plots, are useful ways of summarizing the information in a data set.
4. Many numerical summaries can be used. The most important are the mean, a measure of the location of a distribution, and the standard deviation, a measure of how spread out or dispersed a distribution is.

Appendix 2.1: Index Numbers

To illustrate the basic ideas in constructing a price index, we use the data in Table 2.1 on the price of various fruits in various years.

Calculating a banana price index *Do it*

We begin by calculating a price index for a single fruit, bananas, before proceeding to the calculation of a fruit price index. As described in the text, calculating a price index involves first selecting a base year. For our banana price index, let us choose the year 2000 as the base year (although, it should be stressed that any year can be chosen). By definition, the value of the banana price index is 100 in this base year. How did we transform the price of bananas in the year 2000 to obtain the price index value of 100?

Table 2.1   Prices of different fruits in different years ($£$/kg).

	Bananas	Apples	Kiwi fruit
1999	0.89	0.44	1.58
2000	0.91	0.43	1.66
2001	0.91	0.46	1.90
2002	0.94	0.50	2.10
2003	0.95	0.51	2.25

Table 2.2 Calculating a banana price index.

	Price of bananas	Transformation	Price index
1999	0.89	× 100 ÷ 0.91	97.8
2000	0.91	× 100 ÷ 0.91	100
2001	0.91	× 100 ÷ 0.91	100
2002	0.94	× 100 ÷ 0.91	103.3
2003	0.95	× 100 ÷ 0.91	104.4

It can be seen that this transformation involved taking the price of bananas in 2000 and dividing by the price of bananas in 2000 (dividing the price by itself) and multiplying by 100. To maintain comparability, this same transformation must be applied to the price of bananas in every year. The result is a price index for bananas (with the year 2000 as the base year). This is illustrated is Table 2.2

From the banana price index, it can be seen that between 2000 and 2003 the price of bananas increased by 4.4% and in 1999 the price of bananas was 97.8% as high as in 2000.

Calculating a fruit price index

When calculating the banana price index (a single good), all we had to look at were the prices of bananas. However, if we want to calculate a fruit price index (involving several goods), then we have to combine the prices of all fruits together somehow. One thing you could do is simply average the prices of all fruits together in each year (and then construct a price index in the same manner as for the banana price index). However, this strategy is usually inappropriate since it implicitly weights all goods equally to one another (a simple average just would add up the prices of the three fruits and divide by three). In our example (and most real world applications), this equal weighting is unreasonable.[11] An examination of Table 2.1 reveals that the prices of bananas and apples are going up only slightly over time (and, in some years, their prices are not changing or even dropping). However, the price of kiwi fruit is going up rapidly over time. Bananas and apples are common fruit purchased frequently by many people, whereas kiwi fruits are an obscure exotic fruit, rarely purchased by a tiny minority of people. In light of this, it is unreasonable to weight all three fruits equally when calculating a price index. A fruit price index that was based on a simple average would reveal the fruit prices were growing at a fairly rapid rate (combining the slow growth of banana and apple prices with the very fast growth of kiwi fruit prices would yield a fruit price index, which indicates moderately fast growth). However, if the government were to use such a price index to report "fruit prices are increasing at a fairly rapid rate" the vast majority of people would find this report inconsistent with their own experience. That is, the vast majority of people only buy bananas and apples and the prices of these fruits are growing only slowly over time.

The line of reasoning in the previous paragraph suggests that a price index that weights all goods equally will not be a sensible one. It also suggests how one might construct a sensible fruit price index: use a weighted average of the prices of all fruits to construct an index where the weights are chosen so as to reflect the importance of each good. In our fruit price index, we would want to attach more weight to bananas and apples (the common fruits) and little weight to the exotic kiwi fruit.[12] There are many different ways of choosing such weights. Here we shall describe two common choices based on the idea that the weights should reflect the amount of each fruit that is purchased. Of course, the amount of each fruit purchased can vary over time and it is with regards to this issue that our two price indices differ.

Do this?,

The Laspeyres price index (using base year weights)

The Laspeyres price index uses the amount of each fruit purchased in the base year (2000 in our example) to construct weights. In words, to construct the Laspeyres price index, you calculate the average price of fruit in each year *using a weighted average where the weights are proportional to amount of each fruit purchased in 2000*. You then use this average fruit price to construct an index in the same manner as for the banana price index (see Table 2.2).

Intuitively, if the average consumer spends 100 times more on bananas than kiwi fruit in 2000, then banana prices will receive 100 times as much weight as kiwi fruit prices in the Laspeyres price index. The Laspeyres price index can be written in terms of a mathematical formula. Let P denote the price of a good, Q denote the quantity of the good purchased and subscripts denote the good and year with bananas being good 1, apples good 2 and kiwi fruit good 3. Thus, for instance, $P_{1,2000}$, is the price of bananas in the year 2000, $Q_{3,2002}$ is the quantity of kiwi fruit purchased in 2002 and so forth. See the appendix to Chapter 1 if you are having trouble understanding this subscripting notation or the summation operator used below.

With this notational convention established, the Laspeyres price index (LPI) in year t (for $t = 1999, 2000, 2001, 2002$ and 2003) can be written as:

$$LPI_t = \frac{\sum_{i=1}^{3} P_{it} Q_{i,2000}}{\sum_{i=1}^{3} P_{i,2000} Q_{i,2000}} \times 100.$$

Note that the numerator of this formula takes the price of each fruit and multiplies it by the quantity of that fruit purchased in the year 2000. This ensures that bananas

Table 2.3 Quantities purchased of fruits (thousands of kg).

	Bananas	Apples	Kiwi fruit
1999	100	78	1
2000	100	82	1
2001	98	86	3
2002	94	87	4
2003	96	88	5

and apples receive much more weight in the Laspeyres price index. We will not explain the denominator other than to note that it is necessary to ensure that the Laspeyres price index is a valid index with a value of 100 in the base year. For the more mathematically inclined, the denominator ensures that the weights in the weighted average sum to one (which is necessary to ensure that it is a proper weighted average).

Note also that the definition of the Laspeyres price index above has been written for our fruit example involving three goods with a base year of 2000. In general, the formula above can be extended to allow for any number of goods and any base year by changing the "3" and 2000 as appropriate.

The calculation of the Laspeyres price index requires us to know the quantities purchased of each fruit. Table 2.3 presents these quantities.

The Laspeyres fruit price index can be interpreted in the same way as the banana price index. For instance, we can say that, between 2000 and 2003, fruit prices rose by 8.7 per cent.

Do this?

The Paasche price index (using current year weights)

The Laspeyres price index used base year weights to construct an average fruit price from the prices of the three types of fruit. However, it is possible that the base year weights (in our example, the base year was 2000) may be inappropriate if fruit consumption patterns are changing markedly over time. In our example, bananas and apples are the predominant fruits and, in all years, there are few kiwi fruit eaters. Our Laspeyres price index (sensibly) weighted the prices of bananas and apples much more heavily in the index than kiwi fruit. But what would have happened if, in 2001, there was a health scare indicating that eating apples was unhealthy and people stopped eating apples and ate many more kiwi fruit instead. The Laspeyres price index would keep on giving a low weight to kiwi fruit and a high weight to apples even though people were now eating more kiwi fruit. The Paasche price index is an index that attempts to surmount this problem by using current year purchases to weight the individual fruits in the index.

Table 2.4 Calculating the Laspeyres fruit price index.

	Numerator $= \sum_{i=1}^{3} P_{it} Q_{i,2000}$	Denominator $= \sum_{i=1}^{3} P_{i,2000} Q_{i,2000}$	Laspeyres price index
1999	126.64	127.92	99.0
2000	127.92	127.92	100
2001	130.62	127.92	102.1
2002	137.1	127.92	107.2
2003	139.07	127.92	108.7

In words, to construct the Paasche price index, you calculate the average price of fruit in each year *using a weighted average where the weights are proportional to the amount of each fruit purchased in the current year.* You then use this average fruit price to construct an index in the same manner as we did for the banana price index (see Table 2.2).

The mathematical formula for the Paasche price index (PPI) in year t (for $t = 1999$, 2000, 2001, 2002 and 2003) can be written as:

$$PPI_t = \frac{\sum_{i=1}^{3} P_{it} Q_{it}}{\sum_{i=1}^{3} P_{i,2000} Q_{it}} \times 100.$$

Table 2.5 Calculating the Paasche fruit price index.

	Numerator $= \sum_{i=1}^{3} P_{it} Q_{it}$	Denominator $= \sum_{i=1}^{3} P_{i,2000} Q_{it}$	Paasche price index
1999	124.90	126.20	99.0
2000	127.92	127.92	100
2001	134.44	131.14	102.5
2002	140.26	129.59	108.2
2003	147.33	133.50	110.4

Note that PPI is the same as LPI except that Q_{it} appears in the PPI formula where $Q_{i,2000}$ appeared in the LPI formula. Thus, the two indexes are the same except for the fact that PPI is using current year purchases instead of base year purchases.

Table 2.5 shows the calculation of the Paasche price index using the fruit price data of Table 2.1 and the data on quantity of fruit purchased in Table 2.3.

Note that, since the Paasche price index does not weight the prices in the same manner as the Laspeyres price index, we do not get exactly the same results in Tables 2.4 and 2.5. For instance, the Paasche price index says that, between 2000 and 2003, fruit prices rose by 10.4% (whereas the Laspeyres price index said 8.7%).

Table 2.6 Splicing together an index when the base year changes.

	Old index with base year 1995	New index with base year 2001	Transformation to old index	Spliced index with base year 2001
1995	100		× 95 ÷ 107	88.8
1996	102		× 95 ÷ 107	90.6
1997	103		× 95 ÷ 107	91.5
1998	103		× 95 ÷ 107	91.5
1999	105		× 95 ÷ 107	93.2
2000	107	95		95
2001		100		100
2002		101		101
2003		105		105

The Paasche and Laspeyres price indices are merely two out of a myriad of possibilities. We will not discuss any of the other possibilities. However, it is important to note that indices arise in many places in economics and finance. For instance, measures of inflation reported in the newspapers are based on price indices. In the economy, there are thousands of goods that people buy and price indices such as the consumer price index (CPI) or retail price index (RPI) are weighted averages of the prices of these thousands of goods. Information about stock markets is often expressed in terms of stock price indices.

There is one other issue that sometimes complicates empirical studies, especially involving macroeconomic data. Government statistical agencies often update the base year they use in calculating their price index. So, when collecting data, you will sometimes face the situation where the first part of your data uses one base year and the last part a different one. This problem is not hard to fix if you have one overlap year where you know the value of the index in terms of both base years. Table 2.6 provides an illustration of how you can splice an index together when the base year changes in this manner. The statistical office has constructed a price index using 1995 as a base year, but discontinued it after the year 2000. This is in the column labeled "Index with base year 1995." In 2001, the statistical office started constructing the index using 2001 as the base year, but also went back and worked out the year 2000 value for this index using the new base year. This new index is listed in the column labeled "Index with Base Year 2001." Note that we have one overlapping year: 2000. In order to make the 2000 value for the old index and the new the same we have to take the old index value, multiply it by 95 and divide it by 107. In order to be consistent we must apply this same transformation to all values of the old index. The result of transforming all values of the old index in this manner is given in the last column of Table 2.6. This spliced index can now be used for empirical work as now the entire index has the same base year of 2001.

Appendix 2.2: Advanced Descriptive Statistics

The mean and standard deviation are the most common descriptive statistics but many others exist. The mean is the simplest *measure of location* of a distribution. The word "location" is meant to convey the idea of the center of the distribution. The mean is the average. Other common measures of location are the *mode* and *median*.

To distinguish between the mean, mode and median, consider a simple example. Seven people report their respective incomes in pounds sterling per year as: £18,000, £15,000, £9,000, £15,000, £16,000 £17,000 and £20,000. The mean, or average, income of these seven people is £15,714.

The *mode* is the most common value. In the present example, two people have reported incomes of £15,000. No other income value is reported more than once. Hence, £15,000 is the modal income for these seven people.

The *median* is the middle value. That is, it is the value that splits the distribution into two equal halves. In our example, it is the income value at which half the people have higher incomes and half the people have lower incomes. Here the median is £16,000. Note that three people have incomes less than the median and three have incomes higher than it.

The mode and median can also be motivated through consideration of Figures 2.2 and 2.4, which plot two different histograms or distributions. A problem with the mode is that there may not be a most common value. For instance, in the GDP per capita data set (GDPPC.XLS), no two countries have precisely the same values. So there is no value that occurs more than once. For cases like this, the mode is the highest point of the histogram. A minor practical problem with defining the mode in this way is that it can be sensitive to the choice of class intervals. In Figure 2.2, the histogram is highest over the class interval labeled 2,000. Remember, we are labeling Figure 2.2 so that the label 2,000 means that the class interval runs from 0 to 2,000. Hence, we could say that "the class interval 0 to 2,000 is the modal (or most likely) value." Alternatively, it is common to report the middle value of the relevant class interval as the mode. In this case, we could say, "the mode is $1,000." The mode is probably the least commonly used of the three measures of location introduced here.

To understand the median, imagine that all the area of the histogram is shaded. The median is the point on the X-axis that divides this shaded area precisely in half. For Figure 2.4 the highest point (i.e. the mode) is also the middle point that divides the distribution in half (the median). It turns out it is also the mean. However, in Figure 2.2 the mean ($5,443.80), median ($3,071.50) and mode ($1,000) are quite different.

Other useful summary statistics are based on the notion of a *percentile*. Consider our GDP per capita data set. For any chosen country, say Belgium, you can ask "how many countries are poorer than Belgium?" or, more precisely, "what proportion of countries are poorer than Belgium?" When we ask such questions we are asking what percentile Belgium is at. Formally, the Xth percentile is the data value (for example, a GDP per capita figure) such that X% of the observations (for example, countries) have lower data values. In the cross-country GDP data set, the 37th percentile is $2,092. This is the GDP per capita figure for Peru. Thirty-seven percent of the countries in our data set are poorer than Peru.

Several percentiles relate to concepts that we have discussed before. The 50th percentile is the median. The minimum and maximum are the 0th and 100th percentile. The percentile divides the data range up into hundredths, whereas other related concepts use other basic units. *Quartiles* divide the data range up into quarters. Hence, the first quartile is equivalent to the 25th percentile, the second quartile, the 50th percentile (the median) and the third quartile, the 75th percentile. *Deciles* divide the data up into tenths. In other words, the first decile is equivalent to the 10th percentile, the second decile, the 20th percentile and so forth.

After the standard deviation, the second most common measure of dispersion is the *interquartile range*. As its name suggests, it measures the difference between the third and first quartiles. For the cross-country data set, 75% of countries have GDP per capita less than $9,802 and 25% have GDP per capita less than $1,162. In other words, $1,162 is the first quartile and $9,802 is the third quartile. The interquartile range is $9,802 − $1,162 = $8,640.

Appendix 2.3: Expected Values and Variances

In the previous section we talked about means and variances. If this were a statistics textbook, we would actually have called them *sample means* and *sample variances*. The word "sample" is added to emphasize that they are calculated using an actual "sample" of data. For instance, in our cross-country GDP data set we took the data we had and calculated exact numbers for $\overline{Y}$ and s. We found these to be $5,443.80 and $5,369.496, respectively. These are the sample mean and standard deviation calculated using the data set at hand.

As another example, suppose we have collected data on the return to holding stock in a company for the past 100 months. We can use this data to calculate the mean and variance. However, these numbers are calculated based on the historical performance of the company's stock. In finance, we are often interested in predicting future stock returns. By definition we do not know exactly what these will be, so we cannot calculate sample means and variances as we did above. But a potential investor would be interested in some similar measures. That is, this investor would be interested in the typical return that she might expect. She might also be interested in the risk involved in purchasing the stock. The concept of a typical expected value sounds similar to the ideas we discussed relating to the mean. The concept of riskiness sounds similar to the idea of a variance we discussed above. In short, we need concepts like the sample mean and variance, but for cases when we do not actually have data to calculate them. The relevant concepts are the *population mean* and *population variance*.

If this were a statistics book, we would now get into a long discussion of the distinction between population and sample concepts involving probability theory and many equations. However, for the student who is interested in analyzing economic data, it is enough to provide some intuition and definitions.

A conventional statistics textbook might begin motivating population and sample concepts through an example. Consider, for instance, the height of every individual in the USA. In the population as a whole there is some average height (the population mean height) and some variance of heights (the population variance). This population mean and variance will be unknown, unless someone actually went out and measured the height of every person in the USA.

However, a researcher might have data on the actual heights of 100 people (for example, a medical researcher might measure the height of each of 100 patients). Using the data for 100 people, the researcher could calculate $\bar{Y}$ and s^2. These are the sample mean and variance. These will be actual numbers. The medical researcher could then use these numbers as estimates (or approximations) for what is going on in the country as a whole (sample means and variances can be used as estimates for population means and variances). However, despite these relationships it is important to stress that sample and population concepts are different with the former being actual numbers calculated using the data at hand and the latter being unobserved.

Perhaps the previous two paragraphs are enough to intuitively motivate the distinction between sample and population means and variances. To see why economists need to know this distinction (and to introduce some notation), let us use as an example an investor interested in the potential return she might make from buying a stock. Let Y denote next month's return on this stock. From the investor's point of view, Y is unknown. The typical return she might expect is measured by the population mean and is referred to as the *expected value*. We use the notation $E(Y)$ to denote the expected return. Its name accurately reflects the intuition for this statistical concept. The "expected value" sheds light on what we expect will occur.

However, the return on a stock is rarely exactly what is expected (rarely will you find Y to turn out to be exactly $E(Y)$). Stock markets are highly unpredictable, sometimes the return on stocks could be higher than expected, sometimes it could be lower than expected. In other words, there is always risk associated with purchasing a stock. A potential investor will be interested in a measure of this risk. Variance is a common way of measuring this risk. We use the notation var(Y) for this.

To summarize, in the previous section on descriptive statistics we motivated the use of the sample mean and variance, $\overline{Y}$ and s^2, to give the researcher an idea of the average value and dispersion, respectively, in a data set. In this section, we have motivated their population counterparts, $E(Y)$ and var(Y), as having similar intuition but being relevant for summarizing information about an uncertain outcome (for example, the return on a stock next month). This is probably enough intuition about the mean and variance operator for you to master the concepts and techniques used in this book. However, for the reader interested in how $E(Y)$ and var(Y) are calculated, we provide the following example.

Suppose you are an investor trying to decide whether to buy a stock based on its return next month. You do not know what this return will be. You are quite confident (say, 70% sure) that the markets will be stable, in which case you will earn a 1% return. But you also know there is a 10% chance the stock market will crash, in which case the stock return will be −10%. There is also a 20% probability that good news will boost the stock markets and you will get a 5% return on your stock.

Let us denote this information in terms of three possible outcomes (good, normal, bad) which we label as 1, 2, 3. So, for instance, $Y_1 = 0.05$ will denote the 5% return if good times occur. We will use the symbol "P" for probability and the same subscripting convention. Thus, $P_3 = 0.10$ will denote a 10% probability of a stock market crash. We can now define the expected return as a weighted average of all the possible outcomes:

$$E(Y) = P_1 Y_1 + P_2 Y_2 + P_3 Y_3 = 0.20 \times 0.05 + 0.70 \times 0.01 + 0.10 \times (-0.10) = 0.007$$

In words, the expected return on the stock next month is 0.7% (a bit less than 1%).

In our example, we have assumed that there are only three possible outcomes next month. In general, if there are K possible outcomes, the formula for the expected value is:[13]

$$E(Y) = \sum_{i=1}^{K} P_i Y_i.$$

The formula for var(Y) is similar to that for s^2 presented in this chapter. It also has a similar lack of intuition and, hence, we shall not discuss it in detail. For the case where we have K possible outcomes, the variance of Y is defined as:

$$\text{var}(Y) = \sum_{i=1}^{K} P_i [Y_i - E(Y)]^2.$$

The key thing to remember is that var(Y) is a measure of the dispersion of the possible outcomes that could occur and, thus, is closely related to the concept of risk.

Endnotes

1. As emphasized in Chapter 1, this is not a book about collecting data. Nevertheless, it is useful to offer a few brief pointers about how to look for data sets.
2. As will be discussed in later chapters, it is sometimes convenient to take the natural logarithm, or ln(.), of variables. The definition and properties of logarithms can be found in virtually any introductory mathematics textbook (see also the appendix to Chapter 1). Using the properties of logarithms, it can be shown that the percentage change in a variable is approximately $100 \times [\ln(Y_t) - \ln(Y_{t-1})]$. This formula is often used in practice and relates closely to ideas in nonstationary time series (see Chapters 9 and 10).
3. Some indices set the base year value to 1.00 instead of 100.
4. In the case of GDP, the name given to the price index is the *GDP deflator*.
5. This data is located in Excel file EXRUK.XLS.
6. 1954Q1 means the first quarter (January, February and March) of 1954.
7. Note that the use of the word "frequency" here as meaning "the number of observations that lie in a class interval" is somewhat different from the use of the word "frequency" in time series analysis (see the discussion of time series data above).
8. Excel creates the histogram using the Histogram command (in Tools/Data Analysis). It simply plots the bins on the horizontal axis and the frequency (or number of observations in a class) on the vertical axis. Note that most statistics books plot class intervals against frequencies divided by class width. This latter strategy corrects for the fact that class widths may vary across class intervals.
9. These data are available in Excel file FOREST.XLS.
10. In some textbooks, a slightly different formula for calculating the standard deviation is given, where the $N - 1$ in the denominator is replaced by N.
11. An exception to this is the Dow Jones Industrial Average, which does equally weight the stock prices of all companies included in making the index.
12. For the student of finance interested in following up the stock price example of the previous endnote, it should be mentioned that the S&P500 is a price index that weights stock prices by the size of the company.
13. The case where there is a continuity of possible outcomes has similar intuition to the case with K outcomes, but is mathematically more complicated. We are only interested in providing intuition so we will not discuss this case.

Correlation

Often economists are interested in investigating the nature of the relationship between different variables, such as the education level of workers and their wages or interest rates and inflation. Correlation is an important way of numerically quantifying the relationship between two variables. A related concept, introduced in future chapters is regression, which is essentially an extension of correlation to cases of three or more variables. As you will quickly find as you read through this chapter and those that follow, it is no exaggeration to say that correlation and regression are the most important unifying concepts of this book.

In this chapter we will first describe the theory behind correlation and then work through a few examples designed to think intuitively about the concept in different ways.

Understanding Correlation

Let X and Y be two variables (for example, population density and deforestation, respectively) and let us also suppose that we have data on $i = 1, \dots , N$ different units (for example, countries). The *correlation* between X and Y is denoted by the small letter, r, and its precise mathematical formula is given in the appendix to this chapter. Of course, in practice, you will never actually have to use this formula directly. Any spreadsheet or econometrics software package will do it for you. The variables to which r

refs are usually clear from the context. However, in some cases we will use subscripts to indicate that r_{XY} is the correlation between variables X and Y, r_{XZ} the correlation between variables X and Z, etc.

Once you have calculated the correlation between two variables you will obtain a number (for example, $r = 0.55$). It is important that you know how to interpret this number. In this section, we will try to develop some intuition about correlation. First, however, let us briefly list some of the numerical properties of correlation.

Properties of correlation

Correlation has the following properties:

- r always lies between -1 and 1, which may be written as $-1 \leq r \leq 1$
- positive values of r indicate a positive correlation between X and Y. Negative values indicate a negative correlation; $r = 0$ indicates that X and Y are uncorrelated
- larger positive values of r indicate stronger positive correlation; $r = 1$ indicates perfect positive correlation; larger negative values[1] of r indicate stronger negative correlation; $r = -1$ indicates perfect negative correlation;
- the correlation between Y and X is the same as the correlation between X and Y;
- the correlation between any variable and itself (for example, the correlation between Y and Y) is 1.

Understanding correlation through verbal reasoning

Statisticians use the word correlation in much the same way as the layperson does. The following continuation of the deforestation/population density example from Chapter 2 will serve to illustrate verbal ways of conceptualizing the concept of correlation.

Example: The Correlation between Deforestation and Population Density

Let us suppose that we are interested in investigating the relationship between deforestation and population density. Remember that Excel file FOREST.XLS contains data on these variables (and others) for a cross-section of 70 tropical countries. Using Excel, we find that the correlation between deforestation (Y) and population density (X) is 0.66. Being greater than zero, this number allows us to make statements of the following form:

1. There is a positive relationship (or positive association) between deforestation and population density.
2. Countries with high population densities tend to have high deforestation rates. Countries with low population densities tend to have low deforestation rates. Note that we use the word "tend" here. *A positive correlation does not mean that every country with a high population density necessarily has a high deforestation rate, but rather, that this is the general tendency. It is possible that a few individual countries do not follow this pattern* (see the discussion of outliers in Chapter 2).
3. Deforestation rates vary across countries as do population densities (this is the reason we call them "variables"). Some countries have high deforestation rates, others have low rates. This high/low cross-country variance in deforestation rates tends to "match up" with the observed high/low variance in population densities.

   All that the preceding statements require is for r to be positive. If r were negative, the opposite of these statements would hold. For instance, *high* values of X would be associated with *low* values of Y, etc.

   It is somewhat more difficult to get an intuitive feel for the exact number of the correlation (for example, how is the correlation 0.66 different from 0.26?). The XY-plots discussed below offer some help, but here we will briefly note an important point to which we shall return when we discuss regression:
4. The degree to which deforestation rates vary across countries can be measured numerically using the formula for the variance discussed in Chapter 2. As mentioned in point 3 above, the fact that deforestation and population density are positively correlated means that their patterns of cross-country variability tend to match up. The correlation squared (r^2) measures the proportion of the cross-country variability in deforestation that matches up with, or is explained by, the variance in population density. In other words, correlation is a numerical measure of the degree to which patterns in X and Y correspond. In our population/deforestation example, since $0.66^2 = 0.44$, we can say that 44% of the cross-country variance in deforestation can be explained by the cross-country variance in population density.

Exercise 3.1

(a) Using the data in FOREST.XLS, calculate and interpret the mean, standard deviation, minimum and maximum of deforestation and population density.
(b) Verify that the correlation between these two variables is 0.66.

Example: House Prices in Windsor, Canada

The Excel file HPRICE.XLS contains data relating to $N = 546$ houses sold in Windsor, Canada in the summer of 1987. It contains the selling price (in Canadian dollars) along with many characteristics for each house. We will use this data set extensively in future chapters, but for now let us focus on just a few variables. In particular, let us assume that $Y =$ the sales price of the house and $X =$ the size of its lot in square feet.[2] The correlation between these two variables is $r_{XY} = 0.54$.

The following statements can be made about house prices in Windsor:

1. Houses with large lots tend to be worth more than those with small lots.
2. There is a positive relationship between lot size and sales price.
3. The variance in lot size accounts for 29% ($0.54^2 = 0.29$) of the variability in house prices.

Now let us add a third variable, $Z =$ number of bedrooms. Calculating the correlation between house prices and number of bedrooms, we obtain $r_{YZ} = 0.37$. This result says, as we would expect, that houses with more bedrooms tend to be worth more than houses with fewer bedrooms.

Similarly, we can calculate the correlation between number of bedrooms and lot size. This correlation turns out to be $r_{XZ} = 0.15$, and indicates that houses with larger lots also tend to have more bedrooms. However, this correlation is very small and quite unexpectedly, perhaps, suggests that the link between lot size and number of bedrooms is quite weak. In other words, you may have expected that houses on larger lots, being bigger, would have more bedrooms than houses on smaller lots. But the correlation indicates that there is only a weak tendency for this to occur.

The above example allows us to motivate briefly an issue of importance in econometrics, namely, that of *causality*. Indeed, economists are often interested in finding out whether one variable "causes" another. We will not provide a formal definition of causality here but instead will use the word in its everyday meaning. In this example, it is sensible to use the positive correlation between house price and lot size to reflect a causal relationship. That is, lot size is a variable that directly influences (or causes) house prices. However, house prices do not influence (or cause) lot size. In other words, the direction of causality flows from lot size to house prices, not the other way around.

Another way of thinking about these issues is to ask yourself what would happen if a homeowner were to purchase some adjacent land and thereby increase the lot size of his/her house. This action would tend to increase the value of the house (an increase in lot size would cause the price of the house to increase).

However, if you reflect on the opposite question: "will increasing the price of the house cause lot size to increase?" you will see that the opposite causality does not hold (house price increases do not cause lot size increases). For instance, if house prices in Windsor were suddenly to rise for some reason (for example, due to a boom in the economy) this would not mean that houses in Windsor suddenly got bigger lots.

The discussion in the previous paragraph could be repeated with "lot size" replaced by "number of bedrooms." That is, it is reasonable to assume that the positive correlation between Y = house prices and Z = number of bedrooms is due to Z's influencing (or causing) Y, rather than the opposite. Note, however, that it is difficult to interpret the positive (but weak) correlation between X = lot size and Z = number of bedrooms as reflecting causality. That is, there is a tendency for houses with many bedrooms to occupy large lots, but this tendency does not imply that the former causes the latter.

One of the most important things in empirical work is knowing how to interpret your results. The house example illustrates this difficulty well. It is not enough just to report a number for a correlation (for example, $r_{XY} = 0.54$). Interpretation is important too. Interpretation requires a good intuitive knowledge of what a correlation is in addition to a lot of common sense about the economic phenomenon under study. Given the importance of interpretation in empirical work, the following section will present several examples to show why variables are correlated and how common sense can guide us in interpreting them.

Exercise 3.2

(a) Using the data in HPRICE.XLS, calculate and interpret the mean, standard deviation, minimum and maximum of Y = house price (labeled "sale price" in HPRICE.XLS), X = lot size and Z = number of bedrooms (labeled "#bedroom").

(b) Verify that the correlation between X and Y is the same as given in the example. Repeat for X and Z then for Y and Z.

(c) Now add a new variable, W = number of bathrooms (labeled "#bath"). Calculate the mean of W.

(d) Calculate and interpret the correlation between W and Y. Discuss to what extent it can be said that W causes Y.

(e) Repeat part (d) for W and X and then for W and Z.

Understanding Why Variables Are Correlated

In our deforestation/population density example, we discovered that deforestation and population density are indeed correlated positively, indicating a positive relationship between the two. But what exact form does this relationship take? As discussed above, we often like to think in terms of causality or influence and it may indeed be the case that correlation and causality are closely related. For instance, the finding that population density and deforestation are correlated could mean that the former directly causes the latter. Similarly, the finding of a positive correlation between education levels and wages could be interpreted as meaning that more education does directly influence the wage one earns. However, as the following examples demonstrate, the interpretation that correlation implies causality is not always necessarily an accurate one.

Example: Correlation Does Not Necessarily Imply Causality

It is widely accepted that cigarette smoking causes lung cancer. Let us assume that we have collected data from many people on a) the number of cigarettes each person smokes per week (X) and b) on whether they have ever had or now have lung cancer (Y). As smoking causes cancer we would undoubtedly find $r_{XY} > 0$; that is, that people who smoked tend to have higher rates of lung cancer than nonsmokers. Here the positive correlation between X and Y indicates direct causality.

Now suppose that we also have data on the same people, measuring the amount of alcohol they drink in a typical week. Let us call this variable Z. In practice, heavy drinkers also tend to smoke and, hence, $r_{XZ} > 0$. This correlation does not mean that cigarette smoking also causes people to drink. Rather it probably reflects some underlying social attitudes. It may reflect the fact, in other words, that people who smoke do not worry about their nutrition, or that their social lives revolve around the pub, where drinking and smoking often go hand in hand. In either case, the positive correlation between smoking and drinking probably reflects some underlying cause (such as social attitude), which in turn causes both. Thus, a correlation between two variables does not necessarily mean that one causes the other. It may be the case that an underlying third variable is responsible.

Now consider the correlation between lung cancer and heavy drinking. Since people who smoke tend to get lung cancer more, and people who smoke also tend to drink more, it is reasonable to expect that lung cancer rates will be higher among heavy drinkers ($r_{YZ} > 0$). Note that this positive correlation does not imply that alcohol consumption causes lung cancer. Rather, it is cigarette smoking that causes cancer, but smoking and drinking are related to some underlying social attitude. This example serves to indicate the kind of complicated patterns of causality that occur in practice and how care must be taken when trying to relate the concepts of correlation and causality.

Example: Direct versus Indirect Causality

Another important distinction is that between *direct* (or immediate) and *indirect* (or proximate) causality. Recall that in our deforestation/population density example, population density (X) and deforestation (Y) were found to be positively correlated ($r_{XY} > 0$). One reason for this positive correlation is that high population pressures in rural areas cause farmers to cut down forests to clear new land in order to grow food. It is this latter ongoing process of agricultural expansion that directly causes deforestation. If we calculated the correlation between deforestation and agricultural expansion (Z) we would find $r_{YZ} > 0$. In this case population density would be an indirect cause, and agricultural expansion, a direct cause of deforestation. In other words, we can say that X (population pressures) causes Z (agricultural expansion), which in turn causes Y (deforestation). Such a pattern of causality is consistent with $r_{XY} > 0$ and $r_{ZY} > 0$.

In our house price example, however, it is likely that the positive correlations we observed reflect direct causality. For instance, having a larger lot is considered by most people to be a good thing in and of itself, so that increasing the lot size should directly increase the value of a house. There is no other intervening variable here, and hence we say that the causality is direct.[3]

The general message that should be taken from these examples is that *correlations can be very suggestive but cannot on their own establish causality*. In the smoking/cancer example above, the finding of a positive correlation between smoking and lung cancer, in conjunction with medical evidence on the manner in which substances in cigarettes trigger changes in the human body, have convinced most people that smoking causes cancer. In the house price example, common sense tells us that the variable, number of bedrooms, directly influences house prices. In economics, the concept of correlation can be used in conjunction with common sense or a convincing economic theory to establish causality.

Exercise 3.3

People with a university education tend to hold higher paying jobs than those with fewer educational qualifications. This could be due to the fact that a university education provides important skills that employers value highly. Alternatively, it could be the case that smart people tend to go to university and that employers want to hire these smart people (in other words, a university degree is of no interest in and of itself to employers).

Suppose you have data on Y = income, X = number of years of schooling and Z = the results of an intelligence test of many people,[4] and that you have calculated r_{XY}, r_{XZ} and r_{YZ}. In practice, what signs would you expect these correlations to have? Assuming the correlations do have the signs you expect, can you tell which of the two stories in the paragraph above is correct?

Understanding Correlation through XY-plots

Intuition about the meaning of correlations can also be obtained from the XY-plots described in Chapter 2. Recall that in Chapter 2 we discussed positive and negative relationships based on whether the XY-plots exhibited a general upward or downward slope.[5] If two variables are correlated, then an XY-plot of one against the other will also exhibit such patterns. For instance, the XY-plot of population density against deforestation exhibits an upward sloping pattern (see Figure 2.3). This plot implies that these two variables should be positively correlated, and we find that this is indeed the case from the correlation, $r = 0.66$. The important point here is that *positive correlation is associated with upward-sloping patterns in the XY-plot and negative correlation is associated with downward-sloping patterns*. All the intuition we developed about XY-plots in the previous chapter can now be used to develop intuition about correlation.

Figure 3.1 uses the Windsor house price data set (HPRICE.XLS) to produce an XY-plot of X = lot size against Y = house price. Recall that that the correlation between these two variables was calculated as $r_{XY} = 0.54$, which is a positive number. This positive (upward sloping) relationship between lot size and house price can clearly be seen in Figure 3.1. That is, houses with small lots (small X-axis values) also tend to have small prices (small Y-axis values). Conversely, houses with large lots tend to have high prices.

The previous discussion relates mainly to the sign of the correlation. However, XY-plots can also be used to develop intuition about how to interpret the magnitude of a correlation, as the following examples illustrate.

Figure 3.2 is an XY-plot of two perfectly correlated variables ($r = 1$). Note that they do not correspond to any actual economic data, but were simulated on the computer. All the points lie exactly on a straight line.

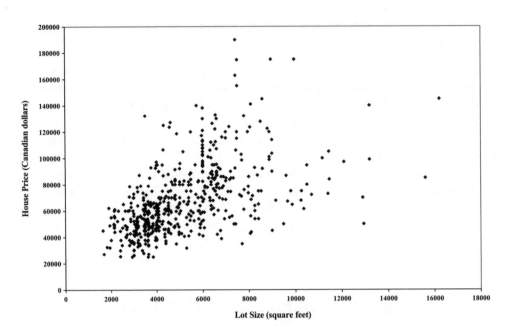

Figure 3.1 *XY*-plot of House Price vs. Lot Size.

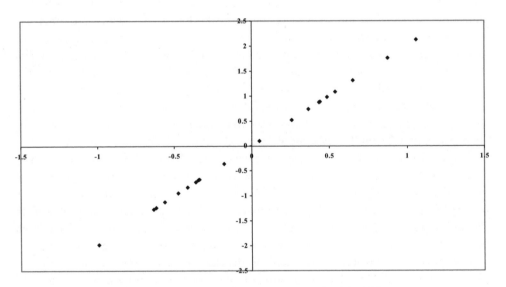

Figure 3.2 *XY*-plot of Two Perfectly Correlated Variables.

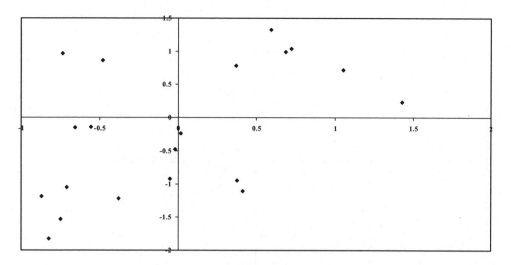

Figure 3.3 *XY*-plot of Two Positively Correlated Variables (*r* = 0.51).

Figure 3.3 is an *XY*-plot of two variables which are positively correlated (*r* = 0.51), but not perfectly correlated. Note that the *XY*-plot still exhibits an upward sloping pattern, but that the points are much more widely scattered.

Figure 3.4 is an *XY*-plot of two completely uncorrelated variables (*r* = 0). Note that the points seem to be randomly scattered over the entire plot.

Plots for negative correlation exhibit downward sloping patterns, but otherwise the same sorts of patterns noted above hold for them. For instance, Figure 3.5 is an *XY*-plot of two variables that are negatively correlated (*r* = −0.58).

These figures illustrate one way of thinking about correlation: Correlation indicates how well a straight line can be fit through an *XY*-plot. Variables that are strongly correlated fit on or close to a straight line. Variables that are weakly correlated are more scattered in an *XY*-plot.

Exercise 3.4

The file EX34.XLS contains four variables: *Y*, *X*1, *X*2 and *X*3.

(a) Calculate the correlation between *Y* and *X*1. Repeat for *Y* and *X*2 and for *Y* and *X*3.

(b) Create an *XY*-plot involving *Y* and *X*1. Repeat for *Y* and *X*2 and for *Y* and *X*3.

(c) Interpret your results for (a) and (b).

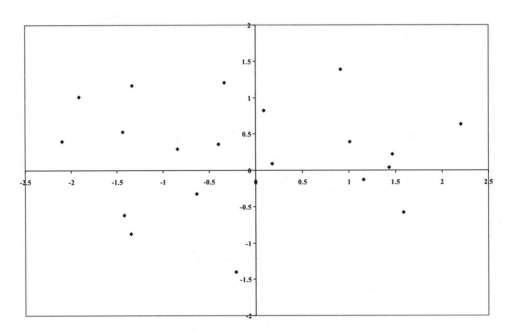

Figure 3.4 *XY*-plot of Two Uncorrelated Variables.

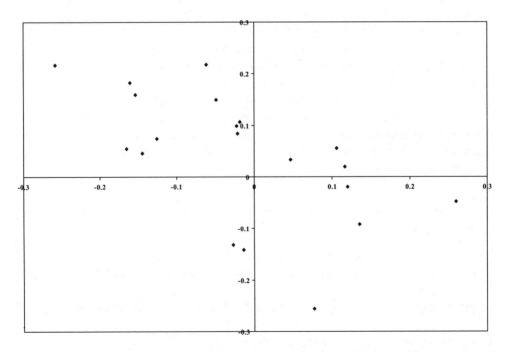

Figure 3.5 *XY*-plot of Two Negatively Correlated Variables ($r = -0.58$).

Correlation between Several Variables

Correlation is a property that relates two variables together. Frequently, however, economists must work with several variables. For instance, house prices depend on the lot size, number of bedrooms, number of bathrooms and many other characteristics of the house. As we shall see in subsequent chapters, regression is the most appropriate tool for use if the analysis contains more than two variables. Yet it is also not unusual for empirical researchers, when working with several variables, to calculate the correlation between each pair. This calculation is laborious when the number of variables is large. For instance, if we have three variables, X, Y and Z, then there are three possible correlations (i.e. r_{XY}, r_{XZ} and r_{YZ}). However, if we add a fourth variable, W, the number increases to six (i.e. r_{XY}, r_{XZ}, r_{XW}, r_{YZ}, r_{YW} and r_{ZW}). In general, for M different variables there will be $M \times (M-1)/2$ possible correlations. A convenient way of ordering all these correlations is to construct a matrix or table, as illustrated by the following example.

CORMAT.XLS contains data on three variables labeled X, Y and Z. X is in the first column, Y the second and Z the third. We can create the following correlation matrix for these variables.

	Column 1	Column 2	Column 3
Column 1	1		
Column 2	0.318237	1	
Column 3	−0.13097	0.096996	1

The number 0.318237 is the correlation between the variable in the first column (X), and that in the second column (Y). Similarly, −0.13097 is the correlation between X and Z, and 0.096996, the correlation between Y and Z. Note that the 1s in the correlation matrix indicate that any variable is perfectly correlated with itself.

Exercise 3.5

(a) Using the data in FOREST.XLS, calculate and interpret a correlation matrix involving deforestation, population density, change in pasture and change in cropland.

(b) Repeat part (a) using the following variables in the data set HPRICE.XLS: house price, lot size, number of bedrooms, number of bathrooms and number of stories. How many individual correlations have you calculated?

Chapter Summary

1. Correlation is a common way of measuring the relationship between two variables. It is a number that can be calculated using Excel or any spreadsheet or econometric software package.
2. Correlation can be interpreted in a common sense way as a numerical measure of a relationship or association between two variables.
3. Correlation can also be interpreted graphically by means of XY-plots. That is, the sign of the correlation relates to the slope of a best fitting line through an XY-plot. The magnitude of the correlation relates to how scattered the data points are around the best fitting line.
4. Correlations can arise for many reasons. However, correlation does not necessarily imply causality between two variables.

Appendix 3.1: Mathematical Details

The *correlation* between X and Y is referred to by the small letter r and is calculated as:

$$r = \frac{\sum_{i=1}^{N}(Y_i - \bar{Y})(X_i - \bar{X})}{\sqrt{\sum_{i=1}^{N}(Y_i - \bar{Y})^2}\sqrt{\sum_{i=1}^{N}(X_i - \bar{X})^2}},$$

where $\bar{X}$ and $\bar{Y}$ are the means of X and Y (see Chapter 2). To provide some intuition, note that if we were to divide the numerator and denominator of the previous expression by $N-1$, then the denominator would contain the product of the standard deviations of X and Y, and the numerator, the covariance between X and Y. Covariance is a concept that we have not defined here but you might come across it in the future, particularly if you are interested in developing a deeper understanding of the statistical theory underlying correlation.

Endnotes

1. By "larger negative values" we mean more negative. For instance, −0.9 is a larger negative value than −0.2.
2. Lot size is the area occupied by the house itself plus its garden or yard.

3. An alternative explanation is that good neighborhoods tend to have houses with large lots. People are willing to pay extra to live in a good neighborhood. Thus, it is possible that houses with large lots tend also to have higher sales prices, not because people want large lots but because they want to live in good neighborhoods. In other words, "lot size" may be acting as a proxy for the "good neighborhood" effect. We will discuss such issues in more detail in later chapters on regression. You should merely note here that the interpretation of correlations can be quite complicated and a given correlation pattern may be consistent with several alternative stories.

4. It is a controversial issue among psychologists and educators as to whether intelligence tests really are meaningful measures of intelligence. For the purposes of answering this question, avoid this controversy and assume that they are indeed an accurate reflection of intelligence.

5. We will formalize the meaning of "upward-" or "downward"-sloping patterns in the XY-plots when we come to regression. To aid in interpretation, think of drawing a straight line through the points in the XY-plot that best captures the pattern in the data (the best fitting line). The upward or downward slope discussed here refers to the slope of this line.

4

An Introduction to Simple Regression

Regression is the most important tool that applied economists use to understand the relationship between two or more variables. It is particularly useful for the common case where there are many variables (for example, unemployment and interest rates, the money supply, exchange rates and inflation) and the interactions between them are complex.

To give an example: in the summer of 1998 a great deal of attention in the UK media focused on the proper level at which interest rates should be set. In particular, the manufacturing sector complained that interest rates were too high. They argued that high interest rates encouraged foreigners to invest their money in the UK, which, in turn, caused the pound to appreciate. A higher pound made it difficult for UK firms to export their products, resulting in falling sales, increased layoffs and rising unemployment.

But this is only part of the story. Still others believed that interest rates were too low, and argued that higher interest rates were necessary to choke off inflationary pressures due to a relationship between inflation and interest rates. Thus, an important economic question (interest rate determination) was at stake, and a large number of variables— interest rates, exchange rates, inflation, manufacturing output, exports, unemployment—must be considered in arriving at an answer to the problem. All these variables (and more) shaped the discussion of what the relevant interest rate should be.

As a second example, consider the problem of trying to explain the price of houses. The price of a house depends on many characteristics (for example, number of bedrooms, number of bathrooms, location of house, or size of lot). Many variables must be included in a model seeking to explain why some houses are more expensive than others.

These two examples are common. Most problems in economics are of a similar level of complexity. Unfortunately, the basic tool you have encountered so far—simple correlation analysis—cannot handle such complexity. For these more complex cases—that is, those involving more than two variables—regression is the tool to use.

Regression as a Best Fitting Line

As a way of understanding regression, let us begin with just two variables (Y and X). We refer to this case as simple regression. Multiple regression, involving many variables, will be discussed in Chapter 6. Beginning with simple regression makes sense since graphical intuition can be developed in a straightforward manner and the relationship between regression and correlation can be illustrated quite easily.

Let us return to the XY-plots used previously (for example, in Figure 2.3, which plots population density against deforestation, or Figure 3.1 which plots lot size against house price). We have discussed in Chapters 2 and 3 how an examination of these XY-plots can reveal a great deal about the relationship between X and Y. In particular, a straight line drawn through the points on the XY-plot provides a convenient summary of the relationship between X and Y. In regression analysis, we formally analyze this relationship.

To start with, we assume that a linear relationship exists between Y and X. As an example, you might consider Y to be the house price variable and X to be the lot size variable from data set HPRICE.XLS. Remember that this data set contained the sales prices of 546 houses in Windsor, Canada, along with several characteristics for each house. It is sensible to assume that the size of the lot affects the price at which a house sells.

We can express the linear relationship between Y and X mathematically as:

$$Y = \alpha + \beta X,$$

where α is the intercept of the line and β is the slope. This equation is referred to as the *regression line*. If in actuality we knew what α and β were, then we would know what the relationship between Y and X was. In practice, of course, we do not have this information. Furthermore, even if our *regression model*, which posits a linear relationship between Y and X, were true, in the real world we would never find that our data points lie precisely on a straight line. Factors such as measurement error mean that individual data points might lie close to but not exactly on a straight line.

For instance, suppose the price of a house (Y) depends on the lot size (X) in the following manner: $Y = 34{,}000 + 7X$ (i.e. $\alpha = 34{,}000$ and $\beta = 7$). If X were 5,000 square feet, this model says the price of the house should be $Y = 34{,}000 + 7 \times 5{,}000 = \$69{,}000$. But, of course, not every house with a lot size of 5,000 square feet will have a sales price of precisely \$69,000. No doubt in this case, the regression model is missing some important variables (for example, number of bedrooms) that may affect the price of a house. Furthermore, the price of some houses might be higher than they should be (for example, if they were bought by irrationally exuberant buyers). Alternatively, some houses may sell for less than their true worth (for example, if the sellers have to relocate to a different city and must sell their houses quickly). For all these reasons, even if $Y = 34{,}000 + 7X$ is an accurate description of a straight line relationship between Y and X, it will not be the case that every data point lies exactly on the line.

Our house price example illustrates a truth about regression modeling: *the linear regression model will always be only an approximation of the true relationship.* The truth may differ in many ways from the approximation implicit in the linear regression model. In economics, the most probable source of error is due to missing variables, usually because we cannot observe them. In our previous example, house prices reflect many variables for which we can easily collect data (for example, number of bedrooms and number of bathrooms). But they will also depend on many other factors for which it is difficult if not impossible to collect data (for example, the number of loud parties held by neighbors, the degree to which the owners have kept the property well maintained, the quality of the interior decoration of the house). The omission of these variables from the regression model will mean that the model makes an error.

We call all such errors e. The regression model can now be written as:

$$Y = \alpha + \beta X + e.$$

In the regression model, Y is referred to as the *dependent* variable, X the *explanatory* variable, and α and β, *coefficients*. It is common to assume implicitly that the explanatory variable "causes" Y, and the coefficient β measures the influence of X on Y. In light of the comments made in the previous chapter about how correlation does not necessarily imply causality, you may want to question the assumption that the explanatory variable causes the dependent variable. There are three responses that can be made to this statement.

First, note that we talk about the regression *model*. A model specifies how different variables interact. For instance, models of land use posit that population pressures cause rural farmers to expand their lands by cutting down forests, thus causing deforestation. Such models have the causality "built in" and the purpose of a regression involving $Y =$ deforestation and $X =$ population density is to measure the magnitude of the effect of population pressures only (i.e. the causality assumption may be reasonable and we do not mind assuming it). Secondly, we can treat the regression purely as a technique for generalizing correlation and interpret the numbers that the regression model produces purely as reflecting the association between variables. (In other words, we can drop the causality assumption if we wish). Thirdly, we can acknowledge that the implicit assumption of causality can be a problem and develop new methods. This issue will be discussed briefly in the last chapter of this book.[1]

In light of the error, e, and the fact that we do not know what α and β are, the first problem in regression analysis is how we can make a sensible guess at, or *estimate*, what α and β are. It is standard practice to refer to the estimates of α and β as $\hat{\alpha}$ and $\hat{\beta}$ (i.e. $\hat{\alpha}$ and $\hat{\beta}$ are actual numbers that the computer calculates, for instance, $\hat{\alpha} = 34,316$ and $\hat{\beta} = 6.599$, which are estimates of the unknown true values $\alpha = 34,000$ and $\beta = 7$). In practice, the way we find estimates is by drawing a line through the points on an XY-plot that fits best. Hence, we must define what we mean by "best fitting line."

Before we do this, it is useful to make a distinction between *errors* and *residuals*. The error is defined as the distance between a particular data point and the *true regression line*. Mathematically, we can rearrange the regression model to write $e_i = Y_i - \alpha - \beta X_i$. This is the *error* for the ith observation. However, if we replace α and β by their estimates $\hat{\alpha}$ and $\hat{\beta}$, we get a straight line, which is generally a little different from the true regression line. The deviations from this *estimated regression line* are called *residuals*. We will use the notation "u" when we refer to residuals. That is, the residuals are given by $u_i = Y_i - \hat{\alpha} - \hat{\beta} X_i$. If you find the distinction between errors and residuals confusing, you can probably ignore it in the rest of this book and assume errors and residuals are the same thing. However, if you plan on further study of econometrics, this distinction becomes crucial.

If we return to some basic geometry, note that we can draw one (and only one) straight line connecting any two distinct points. Thus, in the case of two points, there is no doubt about what the best fitting line through an XY-plot is. However, typically we have many points—for instance, our deforestation/population density example has 70 different countries and the XY-plots 70 points—and there is ambiguity about what is the "best fitting line." Figure 4.1 plots three data points (A, B and C) on an XY graph. Clearly, there is no straight line that passes through all three points. The line I have drawn does not pass through any of them; each point, in other words, is a little bit off the line. To put it another way: the line drawn implies residuals that are labeled u_1, u_2 and u_3. The residuals are the vertical difference between a data point and the line. A good fitting line will have small residuals.

The usual way of measuring the size of the residuals is by means of the sum of squared residuals (*SSR*), which is given by:

$$SSR = \sum_{i=1}^{N} u_i^2,$$

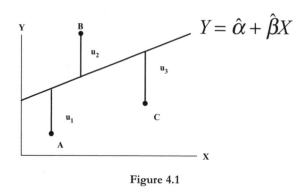

Figure 4.1

for $i = 1, \ldots, N$ data points. We want to find the best fitting line that minimizes the sum of squared residuals. For this reason, estimates found in this way are called *least squares* estimates (or ordinary least squares—*OLS*—to distinguish them from more complicated estimators which we will not discuss until the last chapter of this book).

In practice, software packages such as Excel can automatically find values for $\hat{\alpha}$ and $\hat{\beta}$ which will minimize the sum of squared residuals. The exact formulae for $\hat{\alpha}$ and $\hat{\beta}$ can be derived using simple calculus, but we will not derive them here (see the appendix to this chapter for more details).

Example: The Regression of Deforestation on Population Density

Consider again the data set FOREST.XLS, which contains data on population density and deforestation for 70 tropical countries. It makes sense to assume that population density influences deforestation rather than the other way around. Thus we choose deforestation as the dependent variable (Y = deforestation) and population as the explanatory variable (X = population density). Running the regression using OLS, we obtain $\hat{\alpha} = 0.60$ and $\hat{\beta} = 0.000842$. To provide some more jargon, note that when we estimate a regression model it is common to say that "we run a regression of Y on X."

Note also that it is very easy to calculate these numbers in most statistical software packages. The more important issue is: how do we interpret these numbers.

Example: Cost of Production in the Electric Utility Industry

The file ELECTRIC.XLS contains data on the costs of production (measured in millions of dollars) for 123 electric utility companies in the US in 1970. Interest centers on understanding the factors that affect costs. Hence, Y = cost of production is the dependent variable. The costs incurred by an electric utility company can potentially depend on many factors. One of the most important of these is the output (measured as thousands of kilowatt hours of electricity produced) of the company. We would expect companies that are producing more electricity will also be incurring higher costs (for example, because they have to buy more fuel to generate the electricity). Hence, X = output is a plausible explanatory variable. If we run the regression of costs on output, we obtain $\hat{\alpha} = 2.19$ and $\hat{\beta} = 0.005$.

Example: The Effect of Advertising on Sales

The file ADVERT.XLS contains data on annual sales and advertising expenditures (both measured in millions of dollars) for 84 companies in the US A company executive might be interested in trying to quantify the effect of advertising on sales. This suggests running a regression with dependent variable Y = sales and explanatory variable X = advertising expenditures. Doing so, we obtain the value $\hat{\alpha} = 502.02$ and $\hat{\beta} = 0.218$, which is indicative of a positive relationship between advertising and sales.

Interpreting OLS Estimates

In the previous examples, we obtained OLS estimates for the intercept and slope of the regression line. The question now arises: how should we interpret these estimates? The intercept in the regression model, α, usually has little economic interpretation so we will not discuss it here. However, β is typically quite important. This coefficient is the slope of the best fitting straight line through the XY-plot. In the deforestation/ population density example, $\hat{\beta}$ was positive. Remembering the discussion on how to interpret correlations in the previous chapter, we note that since $\hat{\beta}$ is positive X and Y are positively correlated. However, we can go further in interpreting $\hat{\beta}$ if we differentiate the regression model and obtain:

$$\frac{dY}{dX} = \beta.$$

Even if you do not know calculus, the verbal intuition of the previous expression is not hard to provide. Derivatives measure how much Y changes when X is changed by a small (marginal) amount. Hence, β can be interpreted as the *marginal effect* of X on Y and is a measure of how much X influences Y. To be more precise, we can interpret β as a measure of how much Y tends to change when X is changed by one unit.[2] The definition of "unit" in the previous sentence depends on the particular data set being studied and is best illustrated through examples. Before doing this, it should be stressed that regressions measure tendencies in the data (note the use of the word "tends" in the explanation of β above). It is not necessarily the case that every observation (for example, country or house) fits the general pattern established by the other observations. In Chapter 2 we called such unusual observations outliers and argued that, in some cases, examining outliers could be quite informative. In the case of regression, outliers are those with residuals that stand out as being unusually large so examining the residuals from a regression is a common practice.

Example: The Regression of Deforestation on Population Density (Continued)

In the deforestation/population density example we obtained $\hat{\beta} = 0.000842$. This is a measure of how much deforestation tends to change when population density changes by one unit. Since population density is measured in terms of the number of people per 1,000 hectares and deforestation as the percentage forest loss per year, this figure implies that if we add one more person per 1,000 hectares (a change of one unit in the explanatory variable) deforestation will tend to increase by 0.000842%.

Alternatively, we could present this information as follows. The population density varies quite a bit across countries: from below 100 people to over 2,500 people per 1,000 hectares. Hence it is not surprising that a change of one person per hectare will have little effect on deforestation. We could multiply everything by 100 and say that "increasing population density by 100 people per thousand hectares will tend to increase deforestation by 0.0842%." Even the latter number may seem insignificant but note that an increase of annual deforestation rates by 0.0842% per year will result in a country losing an extra 5% of its forest over 50 years. In the long run and over a large area—the spatial and time scales in which environmental economists are accustomed to thinking—this degree of forest loss can be substantial.

Example: Cost of Production in the Electric Utility Industry (Continued)

In the regression of company costs on output, we obtained $\hat{\beta} = 0.005$. Remember that β units is the effect on the dependent variable of a one unit change in the explanatory variable. Since output is measured in thousands of kWh, a one-unit change in the explanatory variable is 1,000 kWh. Costs are measured in millions of dollars, so β units are β million dollars. Combining these facts we can say that "increasing output by one thousand Kwh tends to increase costs by \$5,000 $(0.005 \times 1,000,000 = 5,000)$."

Of course, we could also express this in terms of a decrease of one unit. That is, we could say, "decreasing output tends to decrease costs by \$5,000."

Example: The Effect of Advertising on Sales (Continued)

Both advertising and sales are measured in millions of dollars and we found $\hat{\beta} = 0.218$. Following the same line of reasoning as above, we can say that a one million dollar increase in advertising tends to be associated with a \$218,000 increase in sales $(1,000,000 \times 0.218 = 218,000)$. This result would seem to indicate that spending on advertising is rather counterproductive since an extra \$1,000,000 spent on advertising would only translate into an extra \$218,000 in sales.

Does this mean that the company executive running this regression should decide to reduce advertising expenditures? Possibly, but not necessarily. The reason for this uncertainty relates to the issue of causality and the question of how correlation or regression results can be interpreted (see Chapter 3 or earlier in this chapter). That is, if the regression truly is a causal one (if it is the case that advertising has a direct influence on sales) then we can interpret the \$218,000 figure as indicative of what the effect of a change in advertising will be. However, if it is not causal, then it is risky to use the regression result to provide strategic advice to a company. Indeed, it is possible that larger companies tend to have egomaniacs as bosses and egomaniacs enjoy seeing their companies advertised. If this (possibly implausible) story is true then we would expect to see larger companies advertising more—exactly what our regression has found. Such an interpretation would imply that it is possible that advertising is not directly influencing sales. The apparent positive relationship between advertising and sales from the regression analysis may be due solely to the behavior of the bosses of large companies.

Deciding whether it is reasonable to assume that a regression model captures a causal relationship in which one variable directly influences another is very difficult, and it is hard to offer any general rules on the subject. Perhaps the best advice is to draw on common sense and economic theory to guide you in interpretation.

Exercise 4.1

The Excel data set FOREST.XLS contains data on $Y =$ deforestation, $X =$ population density, $W =$ change in cropland and $Z =$ change in pasture land.

(a) Run a regression of Y on X and interpret the results.
(b) Run a regression of Y on W and one of Y on Z and interpret the results.
(c) Create a new variable, V, by dividing X by 100. What are the units in terms of which V is measured?
(d) Run a regression of Y on V. Compare your results to those for (a). How do you interpret your coefficient estimate of β? How does $\hat{\alpha}$ differ between (a) and (d)?
(e) Experiment with scaling dependent and explanatory variables (by dividing them by a constant) and see what effect this has on your coefficient estimates.

Fitted Values and R^2: Measuring the Fit of a Regression Model

In the preceding discussion we learned how to calculate and interpret regression coefficients, $\hat{\alpha}$ and $\hat{\beta}$. Furthermore, we explained that regression finds the "best fitting" line in the sense that it minimizes the *SSR*. However, it is possible that the "best" fit is not a very good fit at all. Appropriately, it is desirable to have some measure of fit (or a measure of how good the best fitting line is). The most common measure of fit is referred to as the R^2. It relates closely to the correlation between Y and X. In fact, for the simple regression model (but not the multiple regression model), it is the correlation squared. This provides the formal statistical link between regression and correlation. This and the previous discussion should make the link between correlation and regression clear. Both are interested in quantifying the degree of association between different variables and both can be interpreted in terms of fitting lines through XY-plots.

To derive and explain R^2, we will begin with some background material. We start by clarifying the notion of a *fitted value*. Remember that regression fits a straight line through an XY-plot, but does not pass precisely through each point on the plot. For each data point an error is made. In the case of our deforestation/population density example, this meant that individual countries did not lie on the regression line. The fitted value for observation *i* is the value that lies on the regression line corresponding to the X_i value for that particular observation (for example, house or country). In other words, if you draw a straight vertical line through a particular point in the *XY*-plot, the intersection of this vertical line and the regression line is the fitted value corresponding to the point you chose.

Alternatively, we can think of the idea of a fitted value in terms of the formula for the regression model:

$$Y_i = \alpha + \beta X_i + e_i.$$

Remember that adding *i* subscripts (such as Y_i) indicates that we are referring to a particular observation (for example the ith country or the ith house). If we ignore the error, we can say that the model's prediction of Y_i should be equal to $\alpha + \beta X_i$. If we replace α and β by the OLS estimates $\hat{\alpha}$ and $\hat{\beta}$, we obtain a so-called "fitted" or "predicted" value for Y_i:

$$\hat{Y}_i = \hat{\alpha} + \hat{\beta} X_i.$$

Note that we are using the value of the explanatory variable and the OLS estimates to predict the dependent variable. By looking at actual (Y_i) versus fitted ($\hat{Y}_i$) values we can gain a rough impression of the "goodness of fit" of the regression model. Most software packages allow you to print out the actual and fitted values for each observation. An examination of these values not only gives you a rough measure of how well the regression model fits, they allow you to examine individual observations to determine which ones are close to the regression line and which are not. Since the regression line captures general patterns or tendencies in your data set, you can see which observations conform to the general pattern and which do not.

Exercise 4.2

Using the data in FOREST.XLS (see Exercise 4.1), run a regression of Y on X and compare the actual observations to the fitted values.

We have defined the residual made in fitting our best fitting line previously. Another way to express this residual is in terms of the difference between the actual and fitted values of Y. That is:

$$u_i = Y_i - \hat{Y}_i.$$

Software packages such as Excel can also plot or list the residuals from a regression model. These can be examined in turn to give a rough impression of the goodness of fit of the regression model. We emphasize that unusually big residuals are outliers and sometimes these outliers are of interest.

Exercise 4.3

(a) Using the data in FOREST.XLS (see Exercise 4.1) run a regression of Y on X and obtain the residuals. How would you interpret the residuals? Are there any outliers?

(b) Repeat question (a) for the other variables, W and Z, in this data set.

To illustrate the kind of information that residual analysis can provide, take a look at your computer output from Exercise 4.3 (a). It can be seen that observation 39 has a fitted value of 2.93 and a residual of −1.63. By adding these two figures together (or by looking at the original data), you can see that the actual deforestation rate for this country is 1.3. What do all these numbers imply? Note that the regression model is predicting a much higher value (2.93) for deforestation than actually occurred (1.3) in this country. This means that this country may be doing much better at protecting its forests than the regression model implies, and, consequently, is making better efforts at forest conversation than are other countries. This kind of information may be important to policymakers in other countries, particularly as this outlier country may provide useful lessons that can be applied to them.

The ideas of a residual and a fitted value are important in developing an informal understanding of how well a regression model fits. However, we still lack a formal numerical measure of fit. At this stage, we can now derive and motivate such a measure: R^2.

Recall that variance is the measure of dispersion or variability of a variable. Here we define a closely related concept, the total sum of squares or *TSS*:

$$TSS = \sum (Y_i - \bar{Y})^2.$$

Note that the formula for the variance of Y is $TSS/(N-1)$ (see Chapter 2). Loosely speaking, the $N-1$ term will cancel out in our final formula for R^2 and, hence, we ignore it. So think of *TSS* as being a measure of the variability of Y. The regression model seeks to explain the variability in Y through the explanatory variable X. It can be shown that the total variability in Y can be broken into two parts as:

$$TSS = RSS + SSR,$$

where *RSS* is the regression sum of squares, a measure of the explanation provided by the regression model. *RSS* is given by:

$$RSS = \sum (\hat{Y}_i - \bar{Y})^2.$$

Remembering that *SSR* is the sum of squared residuals and that a good fitting regression model will make the *SSR* very small, we can combine the equations above to yield a measure of fit:

$$R^2 = 1 - \frac{SSR}{TSS}$$

or, equivalently

$$R^2 = \frac{RSS}{TSS}.$$

Intuitively, the R^2 measures the proportion of the total variance of Y that can be explained by X. Note that TSS, RSS and SSR are all sums of squared numbers and, hence, are all non-negative. This implies that $TSS \geq RSS$ and $TSS \geq SSR$. Using these facts, it can be seen that $0 \leq R^2 \leq 1$.

Further intuition about this measure of fit can be obtained by noting that small values of SSR indicate that the regression model is fitting well. A regression line that fits all the data points perfectly in the XY-plot will have no errors and hence $SSR = 0$ and $R^2 = 1$. Looking at the formula above, you can see that values of R^2 near 1 imply a good fit and that $R^2 = 1$ implies a perfect fit. In sum, high values of R^2 imply a good fit and low values a bad fit.

An alternative source of intuition is provided by the RSS. This measures how much of the variation in Y the explanatory variables explain. If RSS is near TSS, then the explanatory variables account for almost all of the variability in the dependent variable and the fit will be a good one. Looking at the previous formula you can see that R^2 is near 1 in this case.

Example: Cost of Production in the Electric Utility Industry (Continued)

In the regression of Y = cost of production on X = output for the 123 electric utility companies, $R^2 = 0.92$. This is a number that is quite high and close to one, indicating that the fit of the regression line is quite good. Put another way, 92% of the variation in costs across companies can be explained by the variation in output. Note that if you simply calculate the correlation between output and cost you obtain $r_{XY} = 0.96$. This correlation squared is exactly equal to R^2 ($0.96^2 = 0.92$).

This example highlights the close relationship between correlation and regression. Notice that the R^2 from the regression of Y on X is exactly equal to the square of the correlation between Y and X. Regression is really just an extension of correlation. Yet, regression also provides you with an explicit expression for the marginal effect (β), which is often important for policy analysis.

> **Example: The Effect of Advertising on Sales (Continued)**
>
> The R^2 from the regression of sales on advertising expenditures using data set ADVERT.XLS is 0.09. This relatively small number indicates that variations in advertising expenditures across companies account for only a small proportion of the variation in sales. This finding is probably reasonable, in that you would expect factors other than advertising (for example product quality or pricing) to play a very important role in explaining the sales of a company.

Exercise 4.4

(a) Using the data in FOREST.XLS (see Exercise 4.1) run a regression of Y on X. What is the R^2?

(b) Calculate the correlation between Y and X.

(c) Discuss the relationship between your answers in (a) and (b).

(d) Redo (a) for various regressions involving the variables W, X, Y and Z in the data set. Comment on the fit of each of these regressions.

Nonlinearity in Regression

So far, we have used the linear regression model and fit a straight line through XY-plots. However, this may not always be appropriate. Consider the XY-plot in Figure 4.2.

It looks like the relationship between Y and X is not linear. If we were to fit a straight line through the data, it might give a misleading representation of the relationship between Y and X. In fact, we have artificially generated this data by assuming the relationship between Y and X is of the form:

$$Y_i = 6X_i^2,$$

such that the true relationship is quadratic. A cursory glance at the XY-plots can often indicate whether fitting a straight line is appropriate or not.

What should you do if a quadratic relationship rather than a linear relationship exists? The answer is surprisingly simple: rather than regressing Y on X, regress Y on X^2 instead.

Of course, the relationship revealed by the XY-plot may be found to be neither linear nor quadratic. It may appear that Y is related to $\ln(X)$ or $1/X$ or X^3 or any other

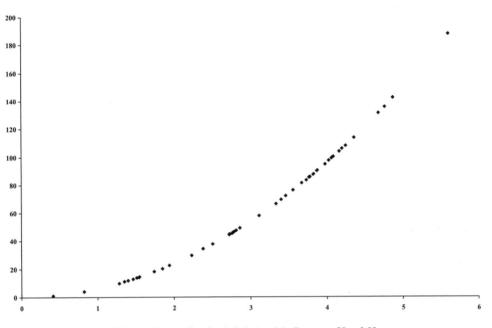

Figure 4.2 A Quadratic Relationship Between X and Y.

transformation of X. However, the same general strategy holds: transform the X variable as appropriate and then run a regression of Y on the transformed variable. You can even transform Y if it seems appropriate.

A very common transformation, of both the dependent and explanatory variables, is the logarithmic transformation. Even if you are not familiar with logarithms, they are easy to work with in any spreadsheet or econometric software package. Often economists work with natural logarithms, for which the symbol is ln. In this book, we will always use natural logarithms and simply refer to them as "logs" for short. It is common to say that: "we took the log of variable X" or that "we worked with log X." The mathematical notation is $\ln(X)$. One thing to note about logs is that they are only defined for positive numbers. So if your data contains zeros or negative numbers, you cannot take logs (i.e. the software will display an error message).

Why is it common to use $\ln(Y)$ as the dependent variable and $\ln(X)$ as the explanatory variable? First, the expressions will often allow us to interpret results quite easily. Second, in practice data transformed in this way often does appear to satisfy the linearity assumption of the regression model.

To fully understand the first point, we need some background in calculus, which is beyond the scope of this book. Fortunately, the intuition can be stated verbally. In the following regression:

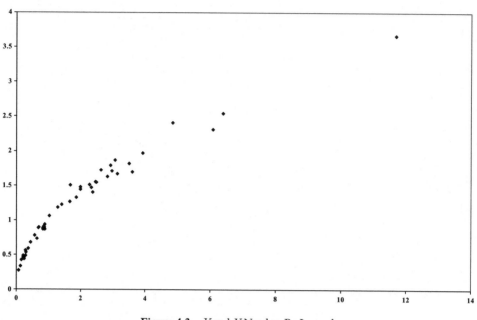

Figure 4.3 X and Y Need to Be Logged.

$$\ln(Y) = \alpha + \beta \ln(X) + e,$$

β can be interpreted as an *elasticity*. Recall that, in the basic regression without logs, we said that "Y tends to change by β *units* for a one *unit* change in X." In the regression containing both logged dependent and explanatory variables, we can now say that "Y tends to change by β *percent* for a one *percent* change in X." That is, instead of having to worry about units of measurements, regression results using logged variables are always interpreted as elasticities. Logs are convenient for other reasons too. For instance, as discussed in Chapter 2, when we have time series data, the percentage change in a variable is approximately $100 \times [\ln(Y_t) - \ln(Y_{t-1})]$. This transformation will turn out to be useful in later chapters in this book which discuss time series data.

The second justification for the log transformation is purely practical. With many data sets, if you take the logs of dependent and explanatory variables and make an *XY*-plot the resulting relationship will look linear. This is illustrated in Figures 4.3 and 4.4. Figure 4.3 is an *XY*-plot of two data series, Y and X, neither of which has been transformed in any way. Figure 4.4 is an *XY*-plot of $\ln(X)$ and $\ln(Y)$. Note that the points in the first figure do not seem to lie along a straight line. Rather the relationship is one of a steep-sloped pattern for small values of X that gradually flattens out as X increases. This is a typical pattern for data which should be logged. Figure 4.4 shows that, once the data is logged, the *XY*-plot indicates a linear pattern. An OLS regression will fit a straight line with a high degree of accuracy in Figure 4.4. However, fitting an accurate

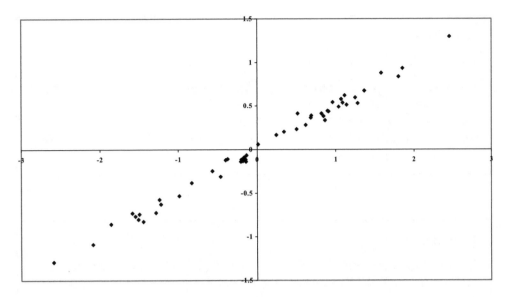

Figure 4.4 $\ln(X)$ vs. $\ln(Y)$.

straight line through Figure 4.3 is a very difficult thing (and probably not the best thing) to do.

On what basis should you log your data (or for that matter take any other transformation)? There is no simple rule that can be given. Examining XY-plots of the data transformed in various ways is often instructive. For instance, begin by looking at a plot of X against Y. This may look roughly linear. If so, just go ahead and run a regression of Y on X. If the plot does not look linear, it may exhibit some other pattern that you recognize (for example, the quadratic form of Figure 4.2 or the logarithmic form of Figure 4.3). If so, create an XY-plot of suitable transformed variables (e.g. $\ln(Y)$ against $\ln(X)$) and see if it looks linear. Such a strategy will likely work well in a simple regression containing only one explanatory variable. In Chapter 6, we will move on to cases with several explanatory variables. In these cases, the examination of XY-plots may be quite complicated since there are so many possible XY-plots that could be constructed but other strategies for detecting nonlinearity will be introduced there.

Exercise 4.5

Using the data in FOREST.XLS, examine different XY-plots involving the variables X, Y, W and Z (see Exercise 4.1 for a definition of these variables). Does there seem to be a nonlinear relationship between any pair of variables? Repeat the exercise using the data in the advertising example (ADVERT.XLS).

Exercise 4.6

Data set EX46.XLS contains two variables, labeled Y and X.

(a) Make an XY-plot of these two variables. Does the relationship between Y and X appear to be linear?
(b) Calculate the square root of variable X.
(c) Make an XY-plot of the square root of X against Y. Does this relationship appear to be linear?

Exercise 4.7

Use the data in the example related to costs of production in the electric utility industry (ELECTRIC.XLS), where Y = cost of production and X = output.

(a) Run a regression of Y on X.
(b) Take log transformations of both variables.
(c) Run a regression of $\ln(Y)$ on $\ln(X)$ and interpret your results verbally.

Chapter Summary

1. Simple regression quantifies the effect of an explanatory variable, X, on a dependent variable, Y. Hence, it measures the relationship between two variables.
2. The relationship between Y and X is assumed to take the form, $Y = \alpha + \beta X$, where α is the intercept and β the slope of a straight line. This is called the regression line.
3. The regression line is the best fitting line through an XY graph.
4. No line will ever fit perfectly through all the points in an XY graph. The distance between each point and the line is called a residual.
5. The ordinary least squares, OLS, estimator is the one which minimizes the sum of squared residuals.
6. OLS provides estimates of α and β, which are labeled $\hat{\alpha}$ and $\hat{\beta}$.
7. Regression coefficients should be interpreted as marginal effects (as measures of the effect on Y of a small change in X).

8. R^2 is a measure of how well the regression line fits through the XY graph.
9. OLS estimates and the R^2 are calculated in computer software packages such as Excel.
10. Regression lines do not have to be linear. To carry out nonlinear regression, merely replace Y and/or X in the regression model by a suitable nonlinear transformation (for example, $\ln(Y)$ or X^2).

Appendix 4.1: Mathematical Details

The OLS estimator defines the best fitting line through the points on an XY-plot. Mathematically, we are interested in choosing $\hat{\alpha}$ and $\hat{\beta}$ so as to minimize the sum of squared residuals. The SSR can be written as:

$$SSR = \sum_{i=1}^{N}\left(Y_i - \hat{\alpha} - \hat{\beta}X_i\right)^2.$$

Optional exercise

Take first and second derivatives with respect to $\hat{\alpha}$ and $\hat{\beta}$ of the above expression for SSR. Use these to find values of $\hat{\alpha}$ and $\hat{\beta}$ that minimize SSR. Verify that the solution you have found does indeed minimize (rather than maximize) SSR.

If you have done the previous exercise correctly, you should have obtained the following:[3]

$$\hat{\beta} = \frac{\sum_{i=1}^{N}\left(Y_i - \bar{Y}\right)\left(X_i - \bar{X}\right)}{\sum_{i=1}^{N}\left(X_i - \bar{X}\right)^2}$$

and

$$\hat{\alpha} = \bar{Y} - \hat{\beta}\bar{X},$$

where $\bar{Y}$ and $\bar{X}$ are the means of Y and X (see Chapter 2). These are the OLS estimators for α and β.

These equations can be used to demonstrate the consequences of taking *deviations from means*. By way of explanation, note that we have assumed above that the dependent and explanatory variables, X and Y, are based on the raw data. However, in some cases researchers do not work with just X and Y, but rather with X and Y minus their respective means:

$$y_i = Y_i - \bar{Y}$$

and

$$x_i = X_i - \bar{X}.$$

Consider using OLS to estimate the regression:

$$y = a + bx + e,$$

where we have used the symbols a and b to distinguish them from the coefficients α and β in the regression involving Y and X.

It turns out that the relationship between OLS estimates from the original regression and the one where deviations from means have been taken is a simple one. The OLS estimate of b is always exactly the same as $\hat{\beta}$ and the OLS estimate of a is always zero. In other words, taking deviations from means simplifies the regression model by getting rid of the intercept (there is no point in including an intercept since its coefficient is always zero). This simplification does not have any effect on the slope coefficient in the regression model. It is unchanged by taking deviations from means and still has the same interpretation as a marginal effect.

It is not too hard to prove the statements in the previous paragraph and, if you are mathematically inclined, you might be interested in doing so. As a hint, note that the means of y and x are zero.

In Chapter 6, we will consider the case where there are several explanatory variables. In this case, if you take deviations from means of the dependent *and all of the explanatory variables*, you obtain the same result—the intercept disappears from the regression but all other coefficient estimates are unaffected.

Endnotes

1. Some statistics books draw a dividing line between correlation and regression. They argue that correlation should only be interpreted as a measure of the *association* between two variables, not the *causality*. In contrast, regression should be based on causality in the manner of such statements as: "Economic theory tells us that X causes Y." Of course, this division simplifies the interpretation of empirical results. After all, it is conceptually easier to think of your dependent variable—isolated on one side of the regression equation—as being "caused" by the explanatory variables on the other. However, it can be argued that this division is in actuality an artificial one. As we saw in Chapter 3, there are many cases for which correlation does indeed reflect causality. Furthermore, in future chapters we will encounter some cases in which the regressions are based on causality, some in which they are not, and others about which we are unsure. The general message here is that you need to exercise care when interpreting regression results as reflecting causality. The same holds

for correlation results. Common sense and economic theory will help you in your interpretation of either.

2. If you cannot see this, construct your own numerical example. That is, choose any values for α, β and X, then use the equation $Y = \alpha + \beta X$ to calculate Y (call this "original Y"). Now increase X by one, leaving α and β unchanged and calculate a new Y. No matter what values you originally chose for α, β and X, you will find new Y minus original Y is precisely β. In other words, β is a measure of the effect on Y of increasing X by one unit.

3. There are several equivalent ways of writing the formula for $\hat{\beta}$. If you consult other textbooks you will find alternative expressions for the OLS estimator.

CHAPTER 5

Statistical Aspects of Regression

Statistics is a field of study based on mathematics and probability theory. However, since this book assumes you have no knowledge of these topics, a complete understanding of statistical issues in the regression model will have to await further study.[1] What we will do instead in this chapter is to:

- Discuss what statistical methods in the regression model are designed to do.
- Show how to carry out a regression analysis using these statistical methods and interpret the results obtained.
- Provide some graphical intuition in order to gain a little insight into where statistical results come from and why these results are interpreted in the manner that they are.

We will begin by stressing a distinction which arose in the previous chapter between the regression coefficients, α and β, and the OLS estimates of the regression coefficients, $\hat{\alpha}$ and $\hat{\beta}$. Remember that we began Chapter 4 with a regression model of the form:

$$Y_i = \alpha + \beta X_i + e_i,$$

for $i = 1, \ldots, N$ observations. As noted previously, α and β measure the relationship between Y and X. We pointed out that we do not know what this relationship is—we do not know what precisely α and β are. We derived so-called ordinary least squares or OLS estimates, which we then labeled $\hat{\alpha}$ and $\hat{\beta}$. We emphasized that α *and* β *are* *the unknown true coefficients whereas $\hat{\alpha}$ and $\hat{\beta}$ are merely estimates* (and almost certainly not precisely the same as α and β).

These considerations lead us to ask whether we can gauge how accurate these estimates are. Fortunately we can, using statistical techniques. In particular, these techniques enable us to provide *confidence intervals* for, and to enable us to carry out, *hypothesis tests* on, our regression coefficients.

We say that OLS provides *point estimates* for β (for example $\hat{\beta} = 0.000842$ is the point estimate of β in the regression of deforestation on population density in the previous chapter). You can think of a point estimate as your best guess at what β is. Confidence intervals provide *interval estimates*, allowing us to make statements that reflect the uncertainty we may have about the true value of β (for example, "We are confident that β is greater than 0.0006 and less than 0.0010.") We can obtain different confidence intervals corresponding to different levels of confidence. For instance, in the case of a 95% confidence interval we can say that "we are 95% confident that β lies in the interval"; in the case of a 90% confidence interval we can say that "we are 90% confident that β lies in the interval"; and so on. The degree of confidence we have in a chosen interval (for example, 95%) is referred to as the *confidence level*.

The other major activity of the empirical researcher is *hypothesis testing*. An example of a hypothesis that a researcher may want to test is $\beta = 0$. If the latter hypothesis is true, then this means that the explanatory variable has no explanatory power. Hypothesis testing procedures allow us to carry out such tests.

Both confidence intervals and hypothesis testing procedures will be explained further in the rest of this chapter. For expository purposes, we will focus on β, since it is usually more important than α in economic problems. However, all the procedures we will discuss for β apply equally well for α.

Which Factors Affect the Accuracy of the Estimate $\hat{\beta}$?

We have artificially simulated four different data sets for X and Y from regression models with $\alpha = 0$ and $\beta = 1$. XY-plots for these four different data sets are presented in Figures 5.1, 5.2, 5.3 and 5.4.

All of these data sets have the same true coefficient values of $\alpha = 0$ and $\beta = 1$, and we hope to obtain $\hat{\alpha}$ and $\hat{\beta}$ values that are roughly equal to 0 and 1, respectively, when we run a regression using any of these four data sets. However, if you imagine trying to fit a straight line (as does OLS) through these XY-plots, you would not expect all four of these lines to be equally accurate.

How confident would you feel about the accuracy of the straight line that you have just fitted? It is intuitively straightforward to see that the line fitted for Figure 5.3 would be the most accurate. That is, the straight-line relationship between X and Y "leaps out"

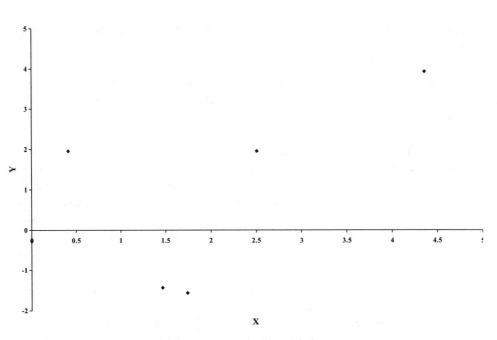

Figure 5.1   Very Small Sample Size.

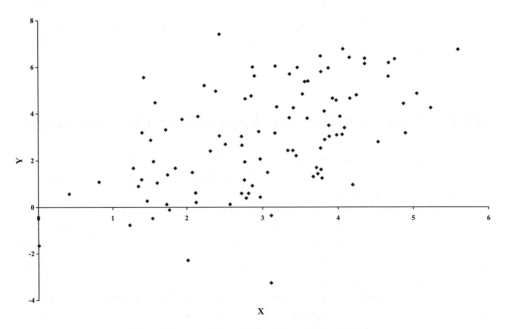

Figure 5.2   Large Sample Size, Large Error Variance.

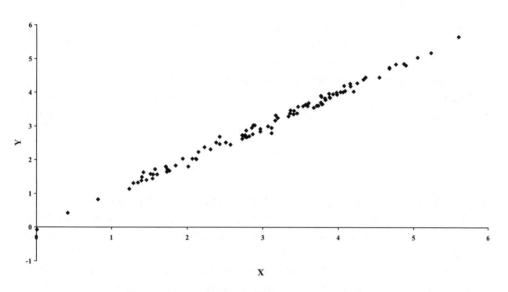

Figure 5.3 Large Sample Size, Small Error Variance.

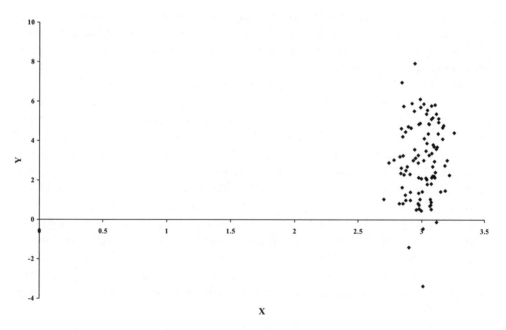

Figure 5.4 Limited Range of X Values.

in Figure 5.3. Even if you were to draw a best fitting line by hand through this XY-plot you would find that the intercept (α) was very close to zero and the slope (β) close to 1. In contrast, you would probably be much less confident about the accuracy of a best-fitting straight line that you drew for Figures 5.1, 5.2 and 5.4.

These figures illustrate three main factors that affect the accuracy of OLS estimates and the uncertainty that surrounds our knowledge of what the true value of β really is:

1. Having more data points improves accuracy of estimation. This can be seen by comparing Figure 5.1 ($N = 5$) and Figure 5.3 ($N = 100$).
2. Having smaller errors improves accuracy of estimation. Equivalently, if the SSR is small or the variance of the errors is small, the accuracy of the estimation will be improved. This can be seen by comparing Figure 5.2 (large variance of errors) with Figure 5.3 (small variance of errors).[2]
3. Having a larger spread of values (a larger variance) of the explanatory variable (X) improves accuracy of estimation. This can be seen by comparing Figure 5.3 (values of the explanatory variable spread all the way from 0 to 6) with Figure 5.4 (values of the explanatory variable all clustered around 3).

The influence of these three factors is intuitively reasonable. With regards to the first two factors, it is plausible that having either more data or smaller errors should increase accuracy of estimation. The third factor is perhaps less intuitive, but a simple example should help you to understand it.

Suppose you are interested in investigating the influence of education levels (X = years of schooling) on the income people receive (Y = income). To understand the nature of this relationship, you will want to go out and interview all types of people (for example, people with no qualifications, people with secondary school education, people with some post-secondary vocational training, people with a university degree or people with Ph.D.s, etc.). In other words, you will want to interview a broad spectrum of the population in order to capture as many of these different education levels as possible. In statistical jargon, this means that you will want X to have a high variance. If you do not follow this strategy—for example, were you to interview only those people possessing Ph.D.s—you would get a very unreliable picture of the effect of education on income. If you only interviewed Ph.D.s, you would not know whether the relationship between education and income was positive. For instance, without collecting data on people who quit school at age 16 you would not know for sure that they are making less income than the Ph.D.s.

In summary, having a large spread of values (i.e. a larger variance) for the explanatory variable, X, is a desirable property in an analysis, whereas having a large spread of values (i.e. a larger variance) for the error, e, is not.

Calculating a Confidence Interval for β

The above three factors are reflected in a commonly used interval estimate for β: the confidence interval. This interval reflects the uncertainty surrounding the accuracy of the estimate $\hat{\beta}$. If the confidence interval is small, it indicates accuracy. Conversely, a large confidence interval indicates great uncertainty over β's true value. In many cases researchers choose to present the confidence interval in addition to the OLS point estimate.

The mathematical formula for the confidence interval for β is:[3]

$$\left[\hat{\beta} - t_b s_b, \hat{\beta} + t_b s_b \right].$$

An equivalent way of expressing the equation above is to say that there is a high level of confidence that the true value of β obeys the following inequality:

$$\hat{\beta} - t_b s_b \leq \beta \leq \hat{\beta} + t_b s_b.$$

The equations above use three numbers that must be calculated: $\hat{\beta}$, t_b and s_b. The first of these, $\hat{\beta}$, is the OLS estimate, which we have already discussed in detail; you may not have seen the latter two before. The confidence interval can be calculated automatically in computer packages such as Excel. Thus, you can calculate confidence intervals without knowing either the above formula or the precise definitions of t_b and s_b. At the most basic level, you can just think of $\hat{\beta}$, t_b and s_b as three numbers calculated by the computer. However, it is worthwhile to have at least some intuition about where the confidence interval comes from as this will aid in your understanding of results.

Below, we discuss each of the three numbers required to calculate a confidence interval, relating them to the issues raised in the material above on the factors affecting the accuracy of estimation of $\hat{\beta}$.

Firstly, $\hat{\beta}$ is always included in the confidence interval (in fact, it will be right in the middle of it).

Secondly, s_b is the standard deviation of $\hat{\beta}$. Somewhat confusingly, s_b is often referred to as the *standard error* as opposed to the standard deviation. In Chapter 2, we introduced the standard deviation as a measure of dispersion (spread, or variability) of a variable. For instance, Figure 2.2 plots a histogram for the variable GDP per capita using the cross-country data set GDPPC.XLS. In Chapter 2, we argued that the standard deviation of GDP per capita was a measure of how much GDP per capita varied across countries. We can treat $\hat{\beta}$ as a variable in the same way as GDP per capita is a variable. In other words, we can calculate its standard deviation and use it as a measure of our uncertainty about the accuracy of the estimate.

Large values of s_b will imply large uncertainty. In this case, $\hat{\beta}$ may be a very inaccurate estimate of β. In contrast, small values of s_b will imply small uncertainty. If the latter, then $\hat{\beta}$ will be an accurate estimate of β.

In other chapters, we have put mathematical formulae in appendices. However, a small amount of mathematics is required to draw out the connections between the formula for the confidence interval and the graphical intuition provided in Figures 5.1–5.4 properly. We present (but do not derive) the following formula for the standard deviation of $\hat{\beta}$:

$$s_b = \sqrt{\frac{SSR}{(N-2)\sum(X_i - \bar{X})^2}}.$$

This expression, which measures the variability or uncertainty in $\hat{\beta}$, reflects all of the issues raised in the context of our discussion of Figures 5.1, 5.2, 5.3 and 5.4.

Looking at the formula for the confidence interval, we can see that the larger s_b is, the wider the confidence interval is. If we combine this consideration with a careful analysis of the components of the formula for s_b, we can say that:

- s_b and hence the width of the confidence interval vary *directly* with SSR (more variable errors/residuals imply less accurate estimation)
- s_b and, hence, the width of the confidence interval, vary *inversely* with N (i.e. more data points imply more accurate estimation)
- s_b and, hence, the width of the confidence interval, vary *inversely* with $\Sigma(X_i - \bar{X})^2$ (i.e. more variability in X implies more accurate estimation).[4]

We stress that these three factors (N, SSR and the standard deviation of X), which affect the width of the confidence interval, are the same as those discussed above as affecting the accuracy of the OLS estimate $\hat{\beta}$.

The third number in the formula for the confidence interval is t_b. It is hard to provide much intuition about this number without some knowledge of statistics.[5] Some informal intuition for what it means, however, can be obtained from the following example.

Example: Election Polls

You may have encountered point estimates and something akin to a confidence interval in political polls, which are regularly taken in the weeks and months before an election. These are usually carried out by staffers telephoning a few hundred potential voters and asking them which party they intend to support on election day. Suppose Party A is running in the election. The newspaper reports that 43% of those surveyed will support Party A. This is the newspaper's point estimate of what voters will do on election day. Of course, in reality the actual result on election day will rarely, if ever, be *exactly* that indicated by the pre-election poll. This discrepancy illustrates a point we stressed earlier in this chapter in the context of the regression model: a point estimate (for example, $\hat{\beta}$) will rarely, if ever, be identical to the true value (for example, β).

Newspapers typically recognize that their surveys will not be precisely accurate and often add statements to their coverage such as: "This result is accurate to within $+/- 2$ percentage points." Although they do not explicitly say it, they are getting this result from a confidence interval (usually a 95% confidence interval).[6] An equivalent statement would be: "We are 95% confident that Party A will receive between 41% and 45% of the vote on election day."

This example provides some additional intuition about what confidence intervals are. If you understand this example, you can also see that different confidence levels imply different confidence intervals. As a trivial example, consider the 100% confidence level. We can be certain that Party A is going to receive between 0% and 100% of the vote on election day. A 100% confidence interval for Party A's percentage of the vote would thus be [0, 100].

Now consider the other extreme: how confident can we be that Party A is going to receive almost precisely 43% of the vote? Probably not very confident for, as noted, in reality we rarely find that opinion polls and election day results will match identically. For this reason, a confidence interval right around 43% (for example, [42.9, 43.1]) will have a very low confidence level (perhaps 10%).

Note that the more confident you wish to be about your interval, the wider it becomes. For instance, 99% confidence intervals will always be wider than 95% confidence intervals. *The number t_b controls the confidence level.* If the level of confidence is high (for example, 99%) t_b will be large, while if the level of confidence is low (for example, 50%) it will be small.

To return to the general statistical theory of regression, we should stress (without explanation beyond that given in the previous example) the following:

- t_b decreases with N (i.e. the more data points you have the smaller the confidence interval will be)
- t_b increases with the level of confidence you choose.

Researchers usually present 95% confidence intervals, although other intervals are possible (for example, 99% or 90% confidence intervals are sometimes presented). A useful (but formally incorrect) intuition for 95% confidence intervals is conveyed by the following statement: "There is a 95% probability that the true value of β lies in the 95% confidence interval." A correct (but somewhat awkward) interpretation of this statement is: "If you repeatedly used (in different data sets) the above formula for calculating confidence intervals, 95% of the confidence intervals constructed would contain the true value for β." Similar statements can be made for 99% or 90% confidence intervals, simply by replacing "95%" with the desired confidence level. Clearly, the interpretation of confidence intervals is relatively straightforward (and will be further illustrated in subsequent examples in this chapter).

The preceding material is intended to provide some intuition and motivation for the statistical theory underlying confidence intervals. Even if you do not fully understand this material, confidence intervals can be calculated quite easily in most standard computer software packages.

Example: Confidence Intervals for the Data sets in Figures 5.1–5.4

Figures 5.1 through 5.4 contained four different data sets, all of which have $\alpha = 0$ and $\beta = 1$. Remember that the data set used in Figure 5.3 has some very desirable properties, i.e. large sample size, spread-out values for the explanatory variables, and small errors. These properties are missing to varying degrees in the other three data sets. Table 5.1 contains OLS point estimates, $\hat{\beta}$, and 90%, 95% and 99% confidence intervals for these four data sets.

Table 5.1 OLS point estimates and confidence intervals for four data sets.

Data set	$\hat{\beta}$	90% confidence interval	95% confidence interval	99% confidence interval
Figure 5.1	0.91	[−0.92, 2.75]	[−1.57, 3.39]	[−3.64, 5.47]
Figure 5.2	1.04	[0.75, 1.32]	[0.70, 1.38]	[0.59, 1.49]
Figure 5.3	1.00	[0.99, 1.01]	[0.99, 1.02]	[0.98, 1.03]
Figure 5.4	1.52	[−1.33, 4.36]	[−1.88, 4.91]	[−2.98, 6.02]

The following points are worth emphasizing:

- Reading across any row, we can see that as the confidence level gets higher the confidence interval gets wider. The widest interval is the 99% confidence interval for the data set in Figure 5.4. In this case, if you want to be 99% confident, you have to say β could be anywhere between −2.98 and 6.02!
- The data set in Figure 5.3—the one with the most desirable properties of all the data sets—yields an OLS estimate of 1.00 which is equal to the true value to two decimal places (more precisely, $\hat{\beta} = 1.002577$ for this data set).

- The data set in Figure 5.3 yields confidence intervals that are much narrower than those for Figures 5.1, 5.2 and 5.4. This makes sense since we would expect the OLS estimate using the data set in Figure 5.3 to be more accurate than the other data sets.
- The data sets in Figures 5.1, 5.2 and 5.4 yield a variety of results. Figure 5.2 contains a data set of the sort usually found in a well-designed empirical project (rarely does one get a data set as good as Figure 5.3). This data set has mostly desirable properties but the errors are moderately large, reflecting the measurement error and imperfections in the underlying economic theory that so often occur in practice. For this representative data set, $\hat{\beta} = 1.04$, which is not too far off the true value of $\beta = 1$. With respect to this data set, we can make statements of the form: "the value of β lies in the interval [0.70, 1.38] with a 95% confidence level" or "we are 99% confident that β lies between 0.59 and 1.49."

Exercise 5.1

The data sets used to calculate Figures 5.1, 5.2, 5.3 and 5.4 are in FIG51.XLS, FIG52.XLS, FIG53.XLS and FIG54.XLS.

(a) Calculate the OLS estimates $\hat{\alpha}$ and $\hat{\beta}$ for these four data sets. How close are they to 0 and 1 (the values we used to artificially simulate the data)?
(b) Calculate confidence intervals for α for the four data sets. Examine how the width of the confidence interval relates to N and the variability of the errors.
(c) Calculate 99% and 90% confidence intervals for the data sets. How do these differ from the 95% confidence intervals in (b)?

Example: The Regression of Deforestation on Population Density

Let us go back to our deforestation (Y) and population density (X) data set (FOREST.XLS). We saw in the last chapter that $\hat{\beta} = 0.000842$. In other words, the marginal effect of population density on deforestation was 0.000842. A 95% confidence interval for this effect is [0.00061, 0.001075], indicating (with a great deal of certitude) that the marginal effect of population on deforestation is greater than 0.00061 and less than 0.001075.

Example: The Regression of Lot Size on House Price

In the previous chapter we investigated the effect of $X =$ lot size on $Y =$ the sales price of a house, using data on 546 houses sold in Windsor, Canada (see data set HPRICE.XLS). Running a regression of Y on X we obtain the following estimated relationship:

$$Y = 34,136 + 6.59X,$$

or, equivalently, $\hat{\alpha} = 34,136$ and $\hat{\beta} = 6.59$. We can say that the OLS estimate of the marginal effect of X on Y is 6.59. This means that our best guess would be that increasing lot size by an extra square foot of lot is associated with a $6.59 increase in house price.

The 95% confidence interval for β is [5.72, 7.47]. This means that, although the effect of lot size on house price is estimated at $6.59, we are not certain that this figure is exactly correct. However, we are extremely confident (95% confident) that the effect of lot size on house price is at least $5.72 and at most $7.47. This interval would be enough for a potential buyer or seller to have a good idea of the value of lot size.

Exercise 5.2

The file ADVERT.XLS contains data on $Y =$ annual sales and $X =$ advertising expenditures (both measured in millions of dollars) for 84 companies in the US.

(a) Run a regression of Y on X and obtain 95% confidence intervals for α and β.
(b) Write a sentence explaining verbally what the 95% confidence interval for β means in terms of the possible range of values that the effect of the explanatory variable on the dependent variable may take.

Exercise 5.3

The file ELECTRIC.XLS contains data on $Y =$ the costs of production (measured in millions of dollars) and $X =$ output (measured in thousands of kilowatt hours) for 123 electric utility companies in the US. Repeat Exercise 5.2 for this data set.

Testing whether $\beta = 0$

Hypothesis testing is another exercise commonly carried out by the empirical economist. As with confidence intervals, we will not go into the statistical theory that underlies hypothesis testing. Instead we will focus on the practical details of how to carry out hypothesis tests and interpret the results. Classical hypothesis testing involves specifying a hypothesis to test. This is referred to as the *null hypothesis,* and is labeled as H_0. It is compared to an *alternative hypothesis,* labeled H_1. A common hypothesis test is whether $\beta = 0$. Formally, we say that this is a test of H_0: $\beta = 0$ against H_1: $\beta \neq 0$.

Note that if $\beta = 0$ then X does not appear in the regression model; that is, the explanatory variable fails to provide any explanatory power whatsoever for the dependent variable. If you think of the kinds of questions of interest to economists (such as "Does education increase an individual's earning potential?" "Will a certain advertising strategy increase sales?" "Will a new government training scheme lower unemployment?") you will see that many are of the form "Does the explanatory variable have an effect on the dependent variable?" or "Does $\beta = 0$ in the regression of Y on X?" The purpose of the hypothesis test of $\beta = 0$ is to answer this question.

The first point worth stressing is that hypothesis testing and confidence intervals are closely related. In fact, one way of testing whether $\beta = 0$ is to look at the confidence interval for β and see whether it contains zero. If it does not then we can, to introduce some statistical jargon, "reject the hypothesis that $\beta = 0$" or conclude "X has significant explanatory power for Y" or "β is significantly different from zero" or "β is statistically significant." If the confidence interval does include zero then we change the word "reject" to "accept" and "has significant explanatory power" with "does not have significant explanatory power" and so on. This confidence interval approach to hypothesis testing is exactly equivalent to the formal approach to hypothesis testing discussed below.

Just as confidence intervals came with various levels of confidence (e.g. 95% is the usual choice), hypothesis tests come with various *levels of significance.* If you use the confidence interval approach to hypothesis testing, then the level of significance is 100% minus the confidence level. That is, if a 95% confidence interval does not include zero, then you may say "I reject the hypothesis that $\beta = 0$ at the 5% level of significance" ($100\% - 95\% = 5\%$). If you had used a 90% confidence interval (and found it did not contain zero) then you would say: "I reject the hypothesis that $\beta = 0$ at the 10% level of significance."

The alternative way of carrying out hypothesis testing is to calculate a *test statistic.* In the case of testing whether $\beta = 0$, the test statistic is known as a t-statistic (or t-ratio or t-stat). It is calculated as:

$$t = \frac{\hat{\beta}}{s_b}.$$

"Large" values[7] of t indicate that $\beta \neq 0$, while "small" values indicate that $\beta = 0$. Mathematical intuition for the preceding sentence is given as: if $\hat{\beta}$ is large relative to its standard deviation, s_b, then we can conclude that β is significantly different from zero. The question arises as to what we mean by "large" and "small." In a formal statistical sense, the test statistic is large or small relative to a "critical value" taken from statistical tables of the "Student-t distribution." A discussion of how to do this is given in the appendix to this chapter. Fortunately, we do not have to trouble ourselves with statistical tables because most common computer software packages print out something called a P-value automatically. The P-value provides a direct measure of whether the t is "large" or "small". A useful (but formally incorrect) intuition would be to interpret the P-value as measuring the probability that $\beta = 0$. If the P-value is small, $\beta = 0$ is unlikely to be true. Accordingly:

- If the P-value is less than 5% (usually written as 0.05 by the computer) then t is "large" and we conclude that $\beta \neq 0$.
- If the P-value is greater than 5% then t is "small" and we conclude that $\beta = 0$.

The preceding test used the 5% level of significance. However, if we were to replace the figure 5% in the above expressions with 1% (i.e. reject $\beta = 0$ if the P-value is less than 1%) our hypothesis test would be carried out at the 1% level of significance.

As an aside, it is worth noting that we are focusing on the test of $\beta = 0$ partly because it is an important one but also because it is the test that is usually printed out by computer packages. You can use it without fully understanding the underlying statistics. However, in order to test other hypotheses (for example, H_0: $\beta = 1$ or hypotheses involving many coefficients in the multiple regression case in the next chapter) you would need more statistical knowledge than is covered here (see the appendix to this chapter for more details). The general structure of a hypothesis test is always of the form outlined above:

1. Specify the hypothesis being tested.
2. Calculate a test statistic.
3. Compare the test statistic to a critical value.

The first of these three steps is typically easy, but the second and third can be much harder. In particular, to obtain the test statistic for more complicated hypothesis tests will typically require some extra calculations beyond merely running the regression. Obtaining the critical value will involve the use of statistical tables. Hence, if you wish to do more complicated hypothesis tests you will have to resort to a basic statistics or econometrics textbook (see endnote 1 of this chapter for some suggestions).

As a practical summary, note that regression techniques provide the following information about β:

- $\hat{\beta}$, the OLS point estimate, or best guess, of what β is.
- The 95% confidence interval, which gives an interval where we are 95% confident β will lie.
- The standard deviation (or standard error) of $\hat{\beta}$, s_b, which is a measure of how accurate $\hat{\beta}$ is. s_b is also a key component in the mathematical formula for the confidence interval and the test statistic for testing $\beta = 0$.
- The test statistic, t, for testing $\beta = 0$.
- The P-value for testing $\beta = 0$.

These five components, ($\hat{\beta}$, confidence interval, s_b, t and the P-value) are usually printed out in a row in computer packages like Excel. In practice, the most important are $\hat{\beta}$, the confidence interval, and the P-value. You can usually interpret your empirical findings without explicit reference to t and s_b. The following examples will serve to illustrate how regression results are presented and can be interpreted.

Example: The Regression of Deforestation on Population Density (Continued)

If we regress $Y =$ deforestation on $X =$ population density, the output in Table 5.2 is produced.

The row labeled "Intercept" contains results for α and the row labeled "X variable" results for β. We will focus discussion on this latter row. The column labeled "Coefficient" presents the OLS estimate and, as we have seen before, $\hat{\beta} = 0.000842$, indicating that increasing population density by one person per hectare is associated with an increase in deforestation rates of 0.000842%. The columns labeled "Lower 95%" and "Upper 95%" give the lower and upper bounds of the 95% confidence interval. For this data set, and as discussed previously, the 95% confidence interval for β is [0.00061, 0.001075]. Thus, we are 95% confident that the marginal effect of population density on deforestation is between 0.00061% and 0.001075%.

Table 5.2 Regression of deforestation on population density.

	Coefficient	Standard error	t-stat	P-value	Lower 95%	Upper 95%
Intercept	0.599965	0.112318	5.341646	1.15E-06	0.375837	0.824093
X variable	0.000842	0.000117	7.227937	5.5E-10	0.00061	0.001075

The columns labeled "Standard error" and "t-stat" indicate that $s_b = 0.000117$ and $t = 7.227937$. These numbers are not essential to carrying out a hypothesis test of $\beta = 0$ when the P-value is given. For most purposes we can ignore these two columns.[8]

The hypothesis test of $\beta = 0$ can be done in two equivalent ways. First, we can find a 95% confidence interval for β of [0.00061, 0.001075]. Since this interval does not contain 0, we can reject the hypothesis that $\beta = 0$ at the 5% level of significance. In other words, there is strong evidence for the hypothesis that $\beta \neq 0$ and that population density has significant power in explaining deforestation. Second, we can look at the P-value, which is 5.5×10^{-10},[9] and much less than 0.05. This means that we can reject the hypothesis that population density has no effect on deforestation at the 5% level of significance. In other words, we have strong evidence that population density does indeed affect deforestation rates.

Exercise 5.4

Using the table above (or running a regression yourself using data set FOREST. XLS) test the hypothesis that $\alpha = 0$.

Exercise 5.5

In addition to Y = deforestation rate, data set FOREST.XLS also contains data on W = the percentage increase in cropland (labeled "Crop ch") and Z = percentage change in pasture land (labeled "Pasture Ch").

(a) Run a regression of Y on W and interpret your results. Can you reject the hypothesis that expansion of cropland has an effect on deforestation rates?

(b) Run a regression of Y on Z and interpret your results. Can you reject the hypothesis that expansion of pastureland has an effect on deforestation rates?

Exercise 5.6

Use data sets FIG51.XLS, FIG52.XLS, FIG53.XLS and FIG54.XLS.

(a) Test whether $\beta = 0$ using the confidence interval approach for each of the four data sets.
(b) Test whether $\beta = 0$ using the P-value approach and the four data sets. Use the 5% level of significance.
(c) Redo (a) and (b) for α.
(d) Redo parts (a), (b) and (c) using the 1% level of significance.
(e) Are your results sensible in light of the discussion in this chapter of the factors affecting the accuracy of OLS estimates?

Example: The Regression of Lot Size on House Price (Continued)

Previously, we found a 95% confidence interval in the regression of $Y =$ house price on $X =$ lot size to be [5.27, 7.47]. Since this interval does not contain zero, we can reject the hypothesis that $\beta = 0$ at the 5% level of significance. Lot size does indeed seem to have a statistically significant effect on house prices.

Alternatively, the P-value is 6.77×10^{-42}, which is much less than 0.05. As before, we can reject the hypothesis that $\beta = 0$ at the 5% level of significance. Note also that, since, 6.77×10^{-42} is less than 0.01 we can also reject the hypothesis that $\beta = 0$ at the 1% level of significance. This is strong evidence indeed that lot size affects house prices.

Exercise 5.7

We have used the file ADVERT.XLS before. Remember that it contains data on the sales and advertising expenditures of 84 companies. Set up and run a regression using this data and discuss your results verbally as you would in a report. Include a discussion of the marginal effect of advertising on sales and a discussion of whether this marginal effect is statistically significant.

Hypothesis Testing Involving R^2: The F Statistic

Most computer packages which include regression, such as Excel, also print out results for the test of the hypothesis H_0: $R^2 = 0$. The definition and interpretation of R^2 was given in the previous chapter. Recall that R^2 is a measure of how well the regression line fits the data or, equivalently, of the proportion of the variability in Y that can be explained by X. If $R^2 = 0$ then X does not have any explanatory power for Y. The test of the hypothesis $R^2 = 0$ can therefore be interpreted as a test of whether the regression explains anything at all. For the case of simple regression, this test is equivalent to a test of $\beta = 0$.

In the next chapter, we will discuss the case of multiple regression (where there are many explanatory variables), in which case this test will be different. To preview our discussion of the next chapter, note that the test of $R^2 = 0$ will be used as a test of whether *all of the explanatory variables* jointly have any explanatory power for the dependent variable. In contrast, the t-statistic test of $\beta = 0$ will be used to investigate whether *a single individual explanatory variable* has explanatory power.

The strategy and intuition involved in testing $R^2 = 0$ proceed along the same lines as above. That is, the computer software calculates a test statistic that you must then compare to a critical value. Alternatively, a P-value can be calculated which directly gives a measure of the plausibility of the null hypothesis $R^2 = 0$ against the alternative hypothesis, $R^2 \neq 0$. Most statistical software packages will automatically calculate the P-value and, if so, you don't need to know the precise form of the test statistic or how to use statistical tables to obtain a critical value. For completeness, though, we present the test statistic, the F statistic,[10] which is calculated as:

$$F = \frac{(N-2)R^2}{(1-R^2)}.$$

As before, "large" values of the test statistic indicate $R^2 \neq 0$ while "small" values indicate $R^2 = 0$. As for the test of $\beta = 0$, we use the P-value to decide what is "large" and what is "small" (whether R^2 is significantly different from zero or not). The test is performed according to the following strategy:

- if the P-value for the F statistic is less than 5% (0.05), we conclude $R^2 \neq 0$
- if it is greater than 5% (0.05), we conclude $R^2 = 0$.

The previous strategy provides a statistical test with a 5% level of significance. To carry out a test at the 1% level of significance, merely replace 5% (0.05) with 1% (0.01) in the preceding sentences. Other levels of significance (such as 10%) can be calculated in an analogous manner.

Example: The Regression of Deforestation on Population Density (Continued)

In the case of the deforestation and population density data set, $F = 52.24308$. Is this "large"? If you said yes you are right, since the P-value for the F-statistics is 5.5×10^{-10}, which is less than 0.05. We can conclude in light of this finding that population density does have explanatory power for Y. Formally, we can say that "R^2 is significantly different from zero at the 5% level", or that "X has statistically significant explanatory power for Y" or that "The regression is significant." Note that the P-value for the F-statistic is equal to the P-value in the test of $\beta = 0$, stressing the equivalence of these two tests in the case of simple regression.

Exercise 5.8

Use data sets FIG51.XLS, FIG52.XLS, FIG53.XLS and FIG54.XLS. Test whether $R^2 = 0$ for each of the four data sets. Compare your results with those of Exercise 5.6.

Example: Cost of Production in the Electric Utility Industry

We used the file ELECTRIC.XLS in Chapter 4. Recall that it contains data on $Y =$ the costs of production and $X =$ output in 123 electric utility companies. If we run the regression of Y on X we obtain the results in Table 5.3.

Furthermore, $R^2 = 0.916218$. The P-value for testing $R^2 = 0$ is 5.36E-67.

It is worthwhile, by way of summary of the material in Chapters 4 and 5, to illustrate how the results presented above might be written up in a formal report. A typical report would include the presentation of the statistical material in a table

Table 5.3   Regression of Y on X.

	Coefficient	Standard error	t-stat	P-value	Lower 95%	Upper 95%
Intercept	2.186583	1.879484	1.163395	0.246958	−1.534354	5.90752
X variable	0.004789	0.000132	36.37623	5.36E-67	0.004528	0.005049

as above, followed by a verbal summary discussing the *economic* intuition behind the analysis and the *statistical* findings in light of this intuition. The report might go as follows:

The above table presents results from an OLS regression using the electric industry data set for the US.[11] We are interested in investigating how different output choices by firms influence their costs of production, so we select costs of production as our dependent variable and output as the explanatory variable. This table reveals that the estimated coefficient on output is 0.004789, and suggests that electric utility firms with higher levels of output tend to have higher costs of production. In particular, increasing output by 1,000 kWh tends to increase costs by $4,789.

It can be observed that the marginal effect of output on costs is strongly statistically significant because the P-value is very small (much smaller, say, than 1%). An examination of the 95% confidence interval shows that we can be quite confident that increasing output by 1,000 kWh is associated with an increase of costs of at least $4,528 and at most $5,049. An examination of the R^2 reinforces the view that output provides a large part of the explanation for why costs vary across utilities. In particular, 92% of the variability in costs of production across firms can be explained by different output levels. The P-value for the F statistic is much smaller than 1%, indicating significance of the R^2 at the 1% level.

Chapter Summary

1. The accuracy of OLS estimates depends on the number of data points, the variability of the explanatory variable and the variability of the errors.
2. The confidence interval provides an interval estimate of β (an interval in which you can be confident β lies). It is calculated in most computer software packages.
3. The width of the confidence interval depends on the same factors as affect the accuracy of OLS estimates. In addition, the width of the confidence interval depends on the confidence level (the degree of confidence you want to have in your interval estimate).
4. A hypothesis test of whether $\beta = 0$ can be used to find out whether the explanatory variable belongs in the regression. The P-value, which is calculated automatically in most spreadsheet or statistical computer packages, is a measure of how plausible the hypothesis is.

5. If the P-value for the hypothesis test of whether $\beta = 0$ is less than 0.05 then you can reject the hypothesis at the 5% level of significance. Hence, you can conclude that X does belong in the regression.
6. If the P-value for the hypothesis test of whether $\beta = 0$ is greater than 0.05 then you cannot reject the hypothesis at the 5% level of significance. Hence, you cannot conclude that X belongs in the regression.
7. A hypothesis test of whether $R^2 = 0$ can be used to investigate whether the regression helps explain the dependent variable. A P-value for this test is calculated automatically in most spreadsheet and statistical computer packages and can be used in a similar manner to that outlined in points 5 and 6.

Appendix 5.1: Using Statistical Tables for Testing whether $\beta = 0$

The P-value is all that you will need to know in order to test the hypothesis that $\beta = 0$. Most computer software packages (for example, Excel, Stata, E-views, MicroFit or SHAZAM) will automatically provide P-values. However, if you do not have such a computer package or are reading a paper that presents the t-statistic, not the P-value, then it is useful to know how to carry out hypothesis testing using statistical tables. Virtually any statistics or econometrics textbook will describe the method in detail and will also provide the necessary statistical table for you to do so. Here we offer only a brief discussion along with a rough rule of thumb which is applicable to the case when the sample size, N, is large.

Remember that hypothesis testing involves the comparison of a test statistic to a number called a critical value. If the test statistic is larger (in absolute value) than the critical value, the hypothesis is rejected. Here, the test statistic is the t-stat given in the body of the chapter. This must be compared to a critical value taken from the Student-t statistical table. It turns out that this critical value is precisely what we have called t_b in our discussion of confidence intervals. If N is large and you are using the 5% level of significance, then $t_b = 1.96$. This suggests the following rule of thumb: if the t-statistic is greater than 1.96 in absolute value (i.e. $|t| > 1.96$), then reject the hypothesis that $\beta = 0$ at the 5% level of significance. If the t-statistic is less than 1.96 in absolute value then accept the hypothesis that $\beta = 0$ at the 5% level of significance.

If the hypothesis that $\beta = 0$ is rejected, then we say that "X is significant" or that "X provides statistically significant explanatory power for Y."

This rule of thumb is likely to be quite accurate if sample size is large. Formally, the critical value equals 1.96 if sample size is infinity. However, even moderately large sample sizes will yield similar critical values. For instance, if $N = 120$, the critical value is 1.98. If $N = 40$, it is 2.02. Even the quite small sample size of $N = 20$ yields a critical value of 2.09, which is not that different from 1.96. However, you should be careful when using this rule of thumb if N is very small or the t-statistic is very close to 2.00. If you look back at the examples included in the body of this chapter you can see that the strategy outlined here works quite well. For instance, in our example entitled "Cost of Production in the Electric Utility Industry," the t-statistic for testing whether $\beta = 0$ was 36.4, which is much larger than 1.96. Hence we concluded that output is a statistically significant explanatory variable for cost of production. In this example (and all others) both the P-value and confidence interval approaches lead to the same conclusion as the strategy described in this appendix.

The previous discussion related to the 5% level of significance. The large sample critical value for the 10% level of significance is 1.65. For the 1% level of significance, it is 2.58.

By far the most common hypothesis to test for is H_0: $\beta = 0$. Using the techniques outlined in this appendix we can generalize this hypothesis slightly to that of: H_0: $\beta = c$, where c is some number that may not be zero (for example, $c = 1$). In this case, the test statistic changes slightly, but the critical value is exactly the same as for the test of $\beta = 0$. In particular, the test statistic becomes:

$$t = \frac{\hat{\beta} - c}{s_b}.$$

This will not be produced automatically by a computer package, but it can be calculated quite easily in a spreadsheet or on a calculator. That is, $\hat{\beta}$ and s_b are calculated by the computer, and you have to provide c, depending on the hypothesis that you are interested in testing. These three numbers can be combined using the equation above to give you a value for your test statistic. If this value is greater than 1.96 in absolute value, you will conclude that $\beta \neq c$ at the 5% level of significance. The caveats about using this rule of thumb if your sample size is very small apply here.

Endnotes

1. As mentioned previously, a good basic statistics book is Wonnacott and Wonnacott (1990). A good introductory econometrics textbook is Hill, Griffiths and Judge (1997).
2. If you are having trouble grasping this point, draw a straight line with intercept = 0 and slope = 1 through Figures 5.2 and 5.3 and then look at some of the resulting residuals (constructed as in Figure 4.1). You should see that most of the residuals in Figure 5.2 will be much bigger (in absolute value) than those in Figure 5.3. This will result in a larger *SSR* (see the formula in Chapter 4) and, since residuals and errors are very similar things, a bigger

variance of the errors (see the formula for the standard deviation of a variable in the descriptive statistics section of Chapter 2 and remember that the variance is just the standard deviation squared).

3. The notation that "the variable W lies between a and b" or "W is greater than or equal to a and less than or equal to b" is expressed mathematically as "W lies in the interval $[a,b]$." We will use this mathematical notation occasionally in this book.

4. Note that, as described in Chapter 2, $\Sigma(X_i - \bar{X})^2$ is a key component of the standard deviation of X. In particular, large values of this expression are associated with large standard deviations of X.

5. For those with some knowledge of statistics, note that t_b is a value taken from statistical tables for the Student-t distribution. The appendix to this chapter provides some additional discussion about t_b.

6. The choice of a 95% confidence interval is by far the most common one, and whenever a confidence interval is not specified you can assume it is 95%.

7. We mean large in an absolute value sense.

8. In the examples in this book we never use s_b and rarely use t. For future reference, the only places we use t are in the Dickey–Fuller and Engle–Granger tests, which will be discussed in Chapters 9 and 10, respectively.

9. Note that 5.5E–10 is the way most computer packages write 5.5×10^{-10}, which can also be written as 0.00000000055.

10. Formally, the F statistic is only one in an entire class of test statistics that take their critical values from the so-called "F distribution." The appendix to Chapter 11 offers some additional discussion of this topic.

11. In a report, the data used would likely be discussed in detail in a separate section of the paper. See Appendix A at the back of this book for a more substantial discussion of the organization of a typical report.

References

Hill, C., Griffiths, W. and Judge, G. (1997) *Undergraduate Econometrics*, John Wiley & Sons, Ltd, Chichester.

Wonnacott, T. and Wonnacott, R. (1990) *Introductory Statistics for Business and Economics*, 4th edn, John Wiley & Sons, Ltd, Chichester.

CHAPTER 6

Multiple Regression

The discussion of simple regression in Chapter 5 involved two variables: the dependent variable, Y, and the explanatory variable, X. As we discussed at the beginning of Chapter 4, most analyses in economics involve many variables. Multiple regression extends simple regression to the case where there are many explanatory variables. Since it is the most common tool used in applied economics, the present chapter is very important. Fortunately, most of the intuition and statistical techniques of multiple regression are very similar to those of simple regression.

The key elements of Chapters 4 and 5 were:

- The development of graphical intuition for regression techniques as the fitting of a straight line through an XY-plot.
- The introduction of the regression coefficient as measuring a marginal effect.
- The description of the OLS estimate as a best fitting line (in terms of minimizing the sum of squared residuals) through an XY-plot.
- The introduction of R^2 as a measure of fit of a regression model.
- The introduction of statistical techniques such as confidence intervals and hypothesis tests.

With some exceptions (highlighted below) these five elements do not differ for the multiple regression model. You should look back on Chapters 4 and 5 if you are having difficulty remembering the underlying intuition or statistical aspects of regression. This chapter covers these five elements for the multiple regression case very briefly, summarizing similarities with and differences from the simple regression model. Much of the chapter will involve the discussion of an example that illustrates how to interpret multiple regression results.

Example: Explaining House Prices

Much research in applied microeconomics and marketing focuses on the pricing of goods. One common approach involves building a model in which the price of a good depends on the characteristics of that good. Data set HPRICE.XLS contains data on an application of this so-called hedonic pricing approach to the housing market. We worked with part of this data set in previous chapters. Recall that it contains data on $N = 546$ houses sold in Windsor, Canada. Our dependent variable, Y, was the selling price of the house in Canadian dollars, and lot size was our explanatory variable.

Of course, the price of a house is affected by more than just lot size. Any serious attempt to explain the determinants of house prices must include more explanatory variables than lot size. In this chapter we focus on the following four explanatory variables:

- $X_1 =$ the lot size of the property (in square feet)
- $X_2 =$ the number of bedrooms
- $X_3 =$ the number of bathrooms
- $X_4 =$ the number of storeys (excluding the basement).

The data set HPRICE.XLS also contains other explanatory variables that we will use in later chapters and in exercises.

Exercise 6.1

(a) Create XY-plots using the four explanatory variables in the house pricing example one at a time (plot Y and X_1, then plot Y and X_2, and so forth).
(b) Perform simple regressions using the explanatory variables one at a time (regress Y on X_1, then regress Y on X_2 and so forth).
(c) Comment on the relationships you find in (a) and (b).

Regression as a Best Fitting Line

As we saw in Chapter 4, the simple regression model can be thought of as a technique aimed at fitting a line through an XY-plot. Multiple regression implies the existence of more than two variables (for example, X_1, X_2, X_3, X_4 and Y) so we cannot draw an XY-plot on a two-dimensional graph, in which one variable is plotted on the vertical axis and the other on the horizontal axis. Nevertheless, the same line-fitting intuition holds (although this could only be illustrated if we could somehow create high-dimensional graphs). For instance, if we had three explanatory variables, we could show how multiple regression involves fitting a line through a four-dimensional graph, in which Y is plotted on one axis, X_1 on the second, X_2 on the third, and X_3 on the fourth. The graph would be impossible to create. (What does a four-dimensional graph look like?)

Ordinary Least Squares Estimation of the Multiple Regression Model

The multiple regression model with k explanatory variables is written as:[1]

$$Y = \alpha + \beta_1 X_1 + \beta_2 X_2 + \ldots + \beta_k X_k + e.$$

Instead of estimating just α and β, we now have α and β_1, β_2 ..., β_k. However, the strategy for finding estimates for all these coefficients is exactly the same as for the simple regression model. That is, we define the sum of squared residuals:

$$SSR = \sum \left(Y_i - \hat{\alpha} - \hat{\beta}_1 X_{1i} - \ldots - \hat{\beta}_k X_{ki} \right)^2,$$

where X_{1i} is the ith observation on the first explanatory variable (for $i = 1, \ldots, N$ observations; for example, lot size of house i for houses $i = 1, \ldots, 546$). The other explanatory variables are defined in an analogous way. The OLS estimates (which can be interpreted as providing the best fitting line) are found by choosing the values of $\hat{\alpha}$ and $\hat{\beta}_1, \hat{\beta}_2, \ldots, \hat{\beta}_k$ that minimize the SSR. Conceptually, this is a straightforward mathematical problem.[2] The resulting formulae are complicated and are not listed here.[3] But computer software packages will calculate these OLS estimates $\left(\hat{\alpha}, \hat{\beta}_1, \ldots, \hat{\beta}_k \right)$ automatically.

Statistical Aspects of Multiple Regression

As noted, the statistical aspects of multiple regression are essentially identical to the simple regression case (see Chapter 5). In particular, the R^2 is still a measure of fit and is calculated in the same way. Note, however, that it should be interpreted as a measure of the explanatory power of all the explanatory variables together rather than as just the one explanatory variable in the simple regression model. Similarly, the F-statistic for testing if $R^2 = 0$ has a slightly different formula (the $N - 2$ in the formula is replaced by $N - k - 1$) but is essentially the same and P-values for this test are produced by relevant computer software packages. If we find that $R^2 \neq 0$, then we can say that "The explanatory variables in the regression, taken together, help explain the dependent variable," whereas if we find $R^2 = 0$, we can say that "The explanatory variables are not significant and do not provide any explanatory power for the dependent variable."

The general formulae for calculating confidence intervals for the regression coefficients and for testing whether they are equal to zero are the same as in the previous chapter. However, the actual numbers that comprise the formulae (for example, s_b) are calculated in a slightly more complicated way. Nevertheless, the practical intuition remains unchanged. In other words, a 95% confidence interval will provide an interval estimate such that you can say that "I am 95% confident that my coefficient lies in the 95% confidence interval." Similarly, most computer software packages will produce P-values for testing the hypothesis that each coefficient in the regression equals zero. If the P-value is less than 0.05 we can conclude that the relevant explanatory variable is significant at the 5% level. It is worth stressing that there is now a P-value and a confidence interval associated with each of the coefficients, $\beta_1, \dots, \beta_k$ rather than just the one β in the simple regression model. However, from the point of view of a researcher wishing to interpret computer output for use in a report, the statistical aspects of multiple regression are essentially the same as for simple regression.[4]

Interpreting OLS Estimates

It is in the interpretation of OLS estimates that some subtle (and important) distinctions exist between the simple and multiple regression case. This section will provide a few ways of thinking about or interpreting coefficients in the multiple regression model. Before we begin, it is important to be clear about the notation we will use.

When we speak of a property that holds generally for any of the coefficients we will denote the coefficient by β_j, (the coefficient on the jth explanatory variable where j could be any number between 1 and k). When we wish to talk about a specific coefficient we will give an exact number for j (for example, β_1 has $j = 1$ and is the coefficient on the first explanatory variable).

In the simple regression case we saw how β could be interpreted as a marginal effect (as a measure of the effect that a change in X has on Y or as a measure of the influence of X on Y). In multiple regression, β_j can still be interpreted as a marginal effect but in a slightly different way. In particular, β_j is the marginal effect of X_j on Y, *holding all other explanatory variables constant*.[5] The preceding sentence is of critical importance to the correct interpretation of regression results. For this reason, we will spend some time illustrating precisely what we mean by it, by way of consideration of our house price example.

Example: Explaining House Prices (Continued)

Table 6.1 contains results from the regression of Y = sale price on X_1 = lot size, X_2 = number of bedrooms, X_3 = number of bathrooms and X_4 = number of storeys. The table is in the form that many computer packages produce regression output.[6]

The first column lists the explanatory variables. In this example there are four of them (plus the intercept). Each row contains the same information as in the table for the simple regression model (the OLS estimate of the relevant coefficient followed by its standard deviation, t-statistic, P-value for testing whether $\beta_j = 0$ and the lower and upper bounds of the 95% confidence interval for the coefficient). As stressed above, each of these statistical results is now available for each coefficient and they will all be different (for instance, the P-value for testing $\beta_1 = 0$ will be different from the P-value for testing $\beta_3 = 0$).

Using the information in the table, we can write the fitted regression equation as:

$$\hat{Y} = -4009.55 + 5.43X_1 + 2824.61X_2 + 17105.17X_3 + 7634.90X_4.$$

Table 6.1 Regression of sale price on lot size, number of bedrooms, number of bathrooms and number of storeys.

	Coefficient	Standard error	t-stat	P-value	Lower 95%	Upper 95%
Intercept	−4009.5500	3603.109	−1.1128	0.266287	−11087.3	3068.248
X1	5.4291737	0.369250	14.70325	2.05E-41	4.703835	6.154513
X2	2824.61379	1214.808	2.325153	0.020433	438.2961	5210.931
X3	17105.1745	1734.434	9.862107	3.29E-21	13698.12	20512.22
X4	7634.897	1007.974	7.574494	1.57E-13	5654.874	9614.92

Furthermore, $R^2 = 0.54$ and the P-value for testing $R^2 = 0$ is 1.18E–88.

As an example, consider the coefficient for the first explanatory variable, lot size. It can be seen that $\hat{\beta}_1 = 5.43$. Below are some (very similar) ways of verbally stating what this value means.

- "An extra square foot of lot size will tend to add another $5.43 on to the price of a house, *ceteris paribus*."
- "If we consider houses with the same number of bedrooms, bathrooms and storeys, an extra square foot of lot size will tend to add another $5.43 onto the price of the house."
- "If we compare houses with the same number of bedrooms, bathrooms and storeys, those with larger lots tend to be worth more. In particular, an extra square foot of lot size is associated with an increased price of $5.43."

It is worth expanding on the motivation for the latter two expressions. We cannot simply say that "houses with bigger lots are worth more" because this is not the case (for example, some nice houses on small lots will be worth more than poor houses on large lots). However, we can say that "if we consider houses that vary in lot size, *but are comparable in other respects*, those with larger lots tend to be worth more." The two expressions above explicitly incorporate the qualification "but are comparable in other respects." We did not have to include this qualification in Chapter 4.

Alternatively, let us consider $\hat{\beta}_2$ (the coefficient on the number of bedrooms), which is 2842.61. This might be expressed as:

- "Houses with an extra bedroom tend to be worth $2,842.61 more than those without the extra bedroom, *ceteris paribus*."
- "If we consider comparable houses (for example, those with 5,000 square foot lots, two bathrooms and two storeys), those with three bedrooms tend to be worth $2,842.61 more than those with two bedrooms."

There are many different ways to express the interpretation of these coefficients. However, the general point we wish to make is as follows: In the case of simple regression we can say that "β measures the influence of X on Y"; in the case of multiple regression we say that "β_j measures the influence of X_j on Y all other explanatory variables being equal." The expressions above are just different ways of verbally saying "all other explanatory variables being equal."

The coefficients on the other explanatory variables can be interpreted in analogous ways. For instance, $\hat{\beta}_3 = 17105.174$. In words, we might say that "Houses with an extra bathroom tend to be worth $17,105.17 more, *ceteris paribus*." Since $\hat{\beta}_4 = 7634.897$, we might say "If we compare houses that are similar in all other respects, those with an extra storey tend to be worth $7,634.90 more."

Remember that in a discussion of the statistical properties of the regression coefficients, the confidence interval and the P-value are the most important numbers. These can be interpreted in the same way as for the simple regression. For instance, since the P-values for all of the explanatory variables (except the intercept) are less than 0.05 we can say that "The coefficients β_1, β_2, β_3 and β_4 are statistically significant at the 5% level," or equivalently, that "We can reject the four separate hypotheses that any of the coefficients is zero at the 5% level of significance."

By way of another example, let us consider the 95% confidence interval for β_2, which is [438.2761,5210.931]. This information might be presented verbally as: "Although our point estimate indicates that the marginal effect of number of bedrooms on house prices (holding other explanatory variables constant) is $2,842.61, this estimate is imprecise. The 95% confidence interval indicates that we can only be confident that this marginal effect lies somewhere between $438.28 and $5,210.93." Alternatively, the confidence interval for β_4 is [5654.874,9614.92] and we can say: "We are 95% confident that the marginal effect of the number of storeys on house price (holding other explanatory variables constant) lies between $5,654.87 and $9,614.92."

The hypothesis test of whether $R^2 = 0$ yields a P-value of much less than 5%, indicating that X_1, X_2, X_3 and X_4 have statistically significant explanatory power for the dependent variable. In fact, the value R^2 implies that variations in lot size and the number of bedrooms, bathrooms and storeys account for 54% of the variability in house prices.

Pitfalls of Using Simple Regression in a Multiple Regression Context

To emphasize the difference between simple and multiple regression, we will run a simple regression of Y = sales price on X_2 = number of bedrooms. Table 6.2 contains the results from this regression.

As $\hat{\beta} = 13,269.98$ in this simple regression, we are able to make statements of the kind: "The marginal effect of number of bedrooms on house prices is $13,269.98" or "Houses with an extra bedroom tend to cost $13,269.98 more." You should contrast this statement with the one above. For the simple regression we have left out the *ceteris paribus* conditions that are implicit in the part of the sentence: "If we consider comparable houses (for example, those with 5,000 square foot lots, two bathrooms and two storeys) ..."

Table 6.2 Regression of sales price on number of bedrooms.

	Coefficient	Standard error	*t*-stat	P-value	Lower 95%	Upper 95%
Intercept	28773.4327	4413.753	6.519	1.6E-10	20103.34	37443.53
X2	13269.9801	1444.598	9.186	8.5E-19	10432.30	16107.66

Note also that the coefficient on number of bedrooms in the simple regression is much higher than for the multiple regression. Why is this the case? To answer this question, first imagine that a friend in Windsor wanted to build an extra bedroom in her house and asked you, the economist, how much that extra bedroom would add to the value of the house. How would you answer?

The simple regression here contains data only on house price and number of bedrooms. You can think of it as observing all the houses in the sample and concluding that those with more bedrooms tend to be more expensive (for example, those with three bedrooms tend to be worth $13,269.98 more than those with two bedrooms).

However, this does not necessarily mean that adding an extra bedroom to the house will raise its price by $13,269.98. The reason is that there are many factors other than the number of bedrooms that potentially influence house prices. Furthermore, these factors may be highly correlated (in practice, big houses tend to have more bedrooms, more bathrooms, more storeys and larger lot size). To investigate the possibility, let us first examine the correlation matrix (see Chapter 3) of all the variables in Table 6.3:

Table 6.3 Correlation matrix of all the variables in the example.

	Sale price	Lot size	No. bedrooms	No. bathrooms	No. storeys
Sale price	1				
Lot size	0.535795	1			
No. bedrooms	0.366447	0.151851	1		
No. bathrooms	0.516719	0.193833	0.373768	1	
No. storeys	0.421190	0.083674	0.407973	0.324065	1

All the elements of the correlation matrix are positive so it follows that each pair of variables is positively correlated with each other (for example, the correlation between the number of bathrooms and the number of bedrooms is 0.37, indicating that houses with more bathrooms also tend to have more bedrooms). In cases like this, simple regression cannot disentangle the influences of the individual variables on house prices. So when the simple regression method examines all the houses and notes that those with more bedrooms cost more, this does not necessarily mean than bedrooms are adding value to the house. Buyers may really be valuing bathrooms or lot size over bedrooms. In other words, houses with more bathrooms may be worth more. But houses with more bathrooms also have more bedrooms. The simple regression model simply looks at house price and number of bedrooms and sees that those with more bedrooms tend to be worth more. What it does not take into account is that it is really *the number of bathrooms that people value.* Thus, if you advise your friend that an extra bedroom is worth \$13,269.98, you may be seriously misleading her. In essence, in the simple regression model we leave out important explanatory variables such as lot size, the number of bathrooms and the number of storeys. The regression combines the contribution of all these factors together and allocates it to the only explanatory variable it can: bedrooms. Hence $\hat{\beta}$ is very big.[7]

In contrast, multiple regression allows us to disentangle the individual contributions of the four explanatory variables assumed to affect house prices. The figure of $\hat{\beta}_2 = \$2,842.61$ comes closer to being a genuine measure of the effect of adding an extra bedroom.[8] By presenting this figure to your friend, you can be confident that you are not making the error above. That is, you can be sure that it is more likely to be the bedroom that is adding the value—and that you are not confounding the contributions of the various explanatory variables.

Omitted Variables Bias

The problems discussed in the previous section relate to a statistical issue called *omitted variables bias.* We will not develop the statistical theory necessary to formally explain what this means. Informally, however, we can say that *if we omit explanatory variables that should be present in the regression and if these omitted variables are correlated with explanatory variables that are included, then the coefficients on the included variables will be wrong.* In the previous example, the simple regression of Y = sales price on X = number of bedrooms, omitted many variables that were important for explaining house prices (for example, lot size or number of bathrooms). These omitted variables were also correlated with number of bedrooms. Hence the simple regression estimate $\hat{\beta} = 13,269.98$ is unreliable due to omitted variables bias.

The intuition behind why the omission of variables causes bias is provided in the previous section. For instance, lot size is an important explanatory variable for house prices, and thus "wants to" enter into the regression. If we omit it from the regression, it will try to enter in the only way it can—through its positive correlation with the explanatory variable: number of bedrooms. In other words, the coefficient on number of bedrooms will confound the effect of bedrooms and lot size on house prices.

One practical consequence of omitted variables bias is that you should always try to include all those explanatory variables that could affect the dependent variable. Unfortunately, in practice, this is rarely possible. House prices, for instance, depend on many other explanatory variables than those found in the data set HPRICE.XLS (for example, the state of repair of the house, how pleasant the neighbors are, closet and storage space, whether the house has hardwood floors and the quality of the garden). In practice, there are too many variables on which to collect data, and many will be subjective (how do you measure "pleasantness of the neighbors?"). You will virtually always have omitted variables and there is little that can be done about it—other than to hope that the omitted variables do not have much explanatory power and that they are not correlated with the explanatory variables included in the analysis.

The previous paragraphs provide a justification for working with as many explanatory variables as possible. However, there is a counter argument to be made for using as *few* explanatory variables as possible. It can be shown that the inclusion of irrelevant variables decreases the accuracy of the estimation of all the coefficients (even the ones that are not irrelevant). This decrease in accuracy will be reflected in overly large confidence intervals and P-values.

How should we trade off the benefits of including many variables (reducing the risk of omitted variables bias) with the costs of possibly including irrelevant variables (reducing the accuracy of estimation)? A common practice is to begin with as many explanatory variables as possible,[9] then discard those that are not statistically significant (and then rerun the regression with the new set of explanatory variables). Statistical significance of an individual explanatory variable can, of course, be assessed using the P-values produced by computer packages. Once you have discarded the insignificant explanatory variables, you can run a new regression involving fewer explanatory variables, in which the risk of including irrelevant variables is greatly reduced.

Exercise 6.2

Use data set HPRICE.XLS and let Y = house price be the dependent variable and consider the following potential explanatory variables:

- X_1 = the lot size of the property (in square feet)
- X_2 = the number of bedrooms
- X_3 = the number of bathrooms
- X_4 = the number of storeys (excluding the basement).

(a) Regress Y on X_1, X_2, X_3 and X_4 (recreate the example above) and discuss your results.
(b) Regress Y on various subsets of X_1, X_2, X_3 and X_4 and discuss your results.
(c) Comparing your results for a) and b), examine the effect of omitting explanatory variables.

Multicollinearity

Multicollinearity is a statistical issue that relates to the previous discussion. It is a problem that arises if some or all of the explanatory variables are highly correlated with one another. If it is present, the regression model has difficulty telling which explanatory variable(s) is influencing the dependent variables. A multicollinearity problem reveals itself through low t-statistics and therefore high P-values. In these cases, you may conclude that coefficients are insignificant and hence should be dropped from the regression. In an extreme case, it is possible for you to find all the coefficients are insignificant using t-statistics, while the R^2 is quite large and significant. Intuitively, this means that the explanatory variables together provide a great deal of explanatory power but that multicollinearity makes it impossible for the regression to decide which particular explanatory variable(s) is providing the explanation.

There is not much that can be done to correct this problem other than to drop out some of the highly correlated variables from the regression. However, there are many cases when you would not want to do so. For instance, in our house price example, multicollinearity would be a problem if number of bedrooms and number of bathrooms had been found to be highly correlated. But you may hesitate to throw out one of these variables because common sense indicates that both of them influence housing prices. The following example illustrates a case where a multicollinearity problem exists and how to correct for it by omitting an explanatory variable.

Example: The Effect of Interest Rates on the Exchange Rate

Suppose you want to examine the effect of interest rate policy on the exchange rate. One way to would be to select an exchange rate (for example, the £/$ rate) as the dependent variable and run a regression of it on the interest rate. But there are many possible interest rates that could be used as explanatory variables (for example, the bank prime rate or the Treasury bill rate). These interest rates are very similar to one another and will be highly correlated. If you include more than one of them you will probably run into a multicollinearity problem. The solution to this problem is clear: include only one of the interest rates. Since the various interest rates are essentially measures of the same phenomenon, common sense says that throwing out all but one of the interest rate variables will not cause any loss in explanatory power and will address the multicollinearity problem.[10]

Example: Multicollinearity Illustrated using Artificial Data

To illustrate the multicollinearity problem and how to address it, we first artificially generate $N = 50$ data points from the regression model:

$$Y = 0.5X_1 + 2X_2 + e.$$

We expect OLS estimates to be roughly $\hat{\alpha} = 0$, $\hat{\beta}_1 = 0.5$ and $\hat{\beta}_2 = 2$ since these values were used to create the data. However, the data generated have a correlation between X_1 and X_2 that is extremely high. In fact, it equals 0.98, indicating that multicollinearity could be a problem. Table 6.4 gives regression results using these data.

These results are very different from those we had hoped to get. The OLS point estimates are very different from those used to generate the data. For instance, $\hat{\beta}_1 = 2.08$ even though $\beta_1 = 0.5$ was used to generate the data. In fact, the OLS estimate for β_1 is almost exactly the same as the true value for β_2! This result illustrates how OLS can become "confused" about the role played by individual explanatory variables when they are highly correlated. Note also that one of the explanatory variables is not statistically significant at the 5% level and that the other is only marginally significant. Furthermore, 95% confidence intervals for all coefficients are very large. These results suggest that the explanatory variables have only weak explanatory power. In contrast, the R^2 is very large and strongly statistically significant, suggesting that the explanatory variables have excellent explanatory power.

Given the problem of multicollinearity, many econometricians would advocate omitting X_2 from the regression. If we follow their advice and rerun the regression we obtain the results in Table 6.5.

Table 6.4   Regression results.

	Coefficient	Standard error	t-stat	P-value	Lower 95%	Upper 95%
Intercept	0.166191	0.1025278	1.57859	0.121137	−0.045601	0.377983
X1	2.083733	0.952938	2.18664	0.033782	0.16667	4.00080
X2	0.147775	0.965767	0.153013	0.879043	−1.7951	2.09065

Furthermore, $R^2 = 0.76$ and the P-value for testing if $R^2 = 0$ is 1.87E–15.

Table 6.5 Results for rerun regression.

	Coefficient	Standard error	t-stat	P-value	Lower 95%	Upper 95%
Intercept	0.166715	0.104146	1.60078	0.115989	−0.042685	0.376115
$X1$	2.22690	0.178806	12.4543	1.2E–16	1.86739	2.58641

$R^2 = 0.76$ and the P-value for testing whether it equals zero is 1.2E–16.

Note that these results look much better from a statistical point of view. β_1 is strongly statistically significant and the confidence interval indicates it is estimated quite precisely. So, in one sense, omitting X_2 has solved the multicollinearity problem. The only problem is that $\hat{\beta}_1$ is nowhere near its true value of 0.5 (and the confidence interval does not contain 0.5). What is happening is that, since X_2 is omitted from the model, X_1 attempts to take its place. Since X_1 is so highly correlated with X_2, the former can proxy for the latter quite well. Hence $\hat{\beta}_1$ combines the effects of both explanatory variables. In other words, just as omitting important explanatory variables in the house price example gave us a biased view of the effect of bedrooms on house prices, omitting X_2 here gives us a biased view of the effect of X_1 on Y. There is nothing you can really do about this other than to note that it may occur if multicollinearity is present and interpret your results with caution.

Note that multicollinearity involves correlations between explanatory variables, not between explanatory variables and the dependent variable. Indeed having a high correlation between an explanatory variable and a dependent variable is a good thing indicating that the explanatory variable will have a lot of explanatory power for the dependent variable.

For multicollinearity to be a problem, the correlations between explanatory variables must be extremely high. If we return to the house pricing example, we can see that the explanatory variables are moderately correlated with one another (for example, some correlations are around 0.3 or 0.4). But this moderate correlation does not lead to a multicollinearity problem since all the coefficients are significantly different from zero (see the P-values in the table).

Exercise 6.3

For this question, use data set FOREST.XLS with Y = deforestation, X_1 = population density, X_2 = percentage change in cropland and X_3 = percentage change in pasture land. Carry out a multiple regression analysis of this data set addressing the issues raised in this chapter. For instance, you may want to:

(a) Regress Y on X_1, X_2 and X_3 and verbally interpret the coefficient estimates you obtain.
(b) Discuss the statistical significance of the coefficients? Are there explanatory variables that can be dropped?
(c) Discuss the fit of the regression.
(d) Calculate a correlation matrix. Through consideration of this and regression results, discuss the issue of multicollinearity.

Example: The Cost of Production in the Electric Utility Industry

The ability to interpret multiple regression results is probably the most important skill that the applied economist can develop. Below we offer another example, with results written as they might be in a brief report.

Microeconomic theory tells us that the cost of production of a firm depends on the prices of the inputs used in the production process as well as the amount of output produced. Thus, in an investigation of the costs of productions, costs should be the dependent variable, and output and input prices should be explanatory variables. We use data on these variables for 123 electric utility companies in the US in 1970.[11] Specifically, the data measure:

- Y = costs of production (measured in millions of dollars per year)
- X_1 = output (measured in thousands of kWh per year)
- X_2 = price of labor (measured in dollars per worker per year)
- X_3 = price of capital (measured in dollars per unit of capital per year)
- X_4 = price of fuel (measured in dollars per million BTUs).

Results from the regression involving these variables are given in Table 6.6:

Table 6.6   Results for regression of variables X_1 to X_4.

	Coefficient	Standard error	t-stat	P-value	Lower 95%	Upper 95%
Intercept	−70.49511	12.69501	−5.55298	1.76E–07	−95.6347	−45.3556
X1	0.00474	0.00011	43.22597	3.41E–74	0.004514	0.004948
X2	0.00363	0.00106	3.43660	0.000814	0.001537	0.005717
X3	0.28008	0.12949	2.16301	0.032557	0.023663	0.536503
X4	0.78346	0.16579	4.72566	6.39E–06	0.455154	1.11177

Furthermore, $R^2 = 0.94$ and the P-value for testing $R^2 = 0$ is 9.73E–73.

Note that coefficients all have the expected sign: Increasing output or prices of any of the inputs tends to increase costs. The magnitudes of the coefficients are also reasonable. Hence:

- Increasing output by one thousand kWh tends to increase costs by $4,740, *ceteris paribus*. We are 95% confident that this marginal effect is at least $4,514 and at most $4,948.
- Increasing the annual salary of an average worker by $1 tends to increase costs by $3,630 per year, *ceteris paribus*. We are 95% confident that this marginal effect is at least $1,537 and at most $5,717. This indicates a fair degree of uncertainty, despite the fact that this coefficient is strongly significant (P-value < 0.01).
- Increasing the price of capital by $1 per unit tends to increase costs by $280,080 per year, *ceteris paribus*. The 95% confidence interval for this coefficient is also quite wide.
- Increasing the price of fuel by $1 per million BTUs tends to increase costs by $783,460 per year, *ceteris paribus*.

As $R^2 = 0.94$, the explanatory variables jointly account for 94% of the variability in costs. This is a very high number and is strongly statistically significant. The fact that we are explaining the dependent variable almost perfectly indicates that it is unlikely that any important explanatory variables have been omitted. If we look at the coefficients individually, we can see that the P-values are all statistically significant at the 5% level. The correlation matrix in Table 6.7 shows that the explanatory variables are not strongly correlated with one another. The maximum correlation is the one between the price of labor and the price of fuel and it is only 0.32. Other correlations are much smaller, indicating that multicollinearity is not a problem.

Table 6.7 Correlation matrix showing lack of correlation between explanatory variables.

	Output	Price—labor	Price—capital	Price—fuel
Output	1			
Price—labor	0.056399	1		
Price—capital	0.021481	−0.078686	1	
Price—fuel	0.053507	0.318349	0.155224	1

A possible exception to the generally strong statistically significant results involves X_3, the price of capital. The coefficient on this variable has a slightly broader confidence interval and the P-value for testing the hypothesis that $\beta_3 = 0$ is a little over 3%. This means that we cannot reject the hypothesis that $\beta_3 = 0$ at the 1% level of significance. In practice, you would probably not use the 1% level of significance (5% is more common). However, for the sake of the present illustration, let us assume that you did. In this case, you would conclude that β_3 was not statistically significant and omit the price of capital as an explanatory variable. If you were to do so and then reran the regression excluding X_3, you would obtain the results shown in Table 6.8.[12]

Table 6.8 is presented merely to illustrate a common statistical strategy (drop out explanatory variables that are insignificant and rerun the regression). Omitting X_3 does not change the results very much, so we will not repeat the discussion above on the interpretation of results.

Table 6.8 Results from regression that has been rerun without insignificant explanatory variables.

	Coefficient	Standard error	t-stat	P-value	Lower 99%	Upper 99%
Intercept	−49.75804	8.449311	−5.88900	3.68E–08	−71.8765	−27.6396
X1	0.004736	0.000111	42.6218	6.4E–74	0.004445	0.005027
X2	0.003313	0.0001061	3.12145	0.002259	0.000535	0.006091
X4	0.851586	0.165266	5.15282	1.03E–06	0.418956	1.284216

Furthermore, $R^2 = 0.94$ and the P-value for testing $R^2 = 0$ is 3.5E–73.

Chapter Summary

1. The multiple regression model is very similar to the simple regression model. This chapter emphasized only differences between the two.
2. The interpretation of regression coefficients is subject to *ceteris paribus* conditions. For instance, β_j measures the marginal effect of X_j on Y, *holding the other explanatory variables constant.*
3. If important explanatory variables are omitted from the regression the estimated coefficients can be misleading, a condition known as "omitted variables bias." The problem is worse if the omitted variables are strongly correlated with the included explanatory variables.
4. If the explanatory variables are highly correlated with one another, coefficient estimates and statistical tests may be misleading. This is referred to as the multicollinearity problem.

Appendix 6.1: Mathematical Interpretation of Regression Coefficients

Readers who know some calculus can use this knowledge to obtain some mathematical intuition of the difference between simple and multiple regression. In the case of the simple regression model, basic calculus can be used to derive the relationship:

$$\frac{dY}{dX} = \beta.$$

That is, the regression coefficient, β, can be interpreted as a measure of how much Y changes when X is changed a small amount. This is a *total derivative*.

In the case of the multiple regression model, we can say:

$$\frac{\partial Y}{\partial X_j} = \beta_j.$$

In other words, the coefficients are *partial derivatives* rather than total derivatives. This partial derivative can be interpreted as measuring the effect of a small change in X_j on Y, *treating all the other explanatory variables as though they are constant.*

Endnotes

1. Formally, we should put an "i" subscript on all the variables to indicate each observation. In other words, we should have written: $Y_i = \alpha + \beta_1 X_{1i} + \beta_2 X_{2i} + \ldots + \beta_k X_{ki} + e_i$. However, adding so many subscripts is messy and makes the equation hard to read. So here and throughout this book we will often drop the "i" subscript (or "t" subscript with time series data) unless it is important to specify the individual observation.

2. Readers familiar with calculus should note that we can find OLS estimates in the multiple regression model using standard methods for finding the minimum of a function. That is, we can take first derivatives with respect to α and $\hat{\beta}_1, \hat{\beta}_2, \ldots, \hat{\beta}_k$, set these derivatives to zero, and then solve.

3. Matrix algebra is essential for theoretical derivations or proofs involving the multiple regression model because the formulae can be extremely complex without it. Matrix algebra is beyond the scope of this book but if you do further study in econometrics you will come to see the value of its use.

4. With regards to hypothesis testing, the methods described for one explanatory variable in the appendix to Chapter 5 also apply to the case of many explanatory variables. That is, each coefficient will have a t-statistic that can be compared to the critical value of 1.96 if the sample size is large. In cases where there are many explanatory variables you might also want to test complicated hypotheses involving several coefficients (for example, H_0: $\beta_1 + \beta_2 = \beta_3$). These tests are more difficult to carry out than those covered here. However, you may wish to consult the appendix to Chapter 11, which has some discussion of hypothesis testing in such cases.

5. The Latin phrase for this concept is *ceteris paribus*, a commonly used phrase in economics.

6. Note that in this table, as elsewhere, we write numbers as the computer produces them. That is, we include as many decimal places as possible and use the "E" notation for exponents. In a report you probably would want to use only a few decimal places and replace, say, 1.57E–13 with 1.57×10^{-13}.

7. If you find this reasoning confusing, think back to the chapter on correlation. There we considered an example involving the variables cigarette smoking, alcohol drinking and lung cancer. We pointed out there that scientific studies indicate that it is smoking that causes lung cancer. However, smokers also tend to drink more alcohol than nonsmokers. Hence, the correlation between drinking and lung cancer is positive even though drinking does not cause lung cancer. This is exactly the type of issue we are addressing in this example. That is, a simple regression involving only the lung cancer and drinking variables would indicate that the effect of drinking on lung cancer is large, even though drinking does not cause lung cancer. Why does this occur? Because we have left out the smoking variable, which is an important explanatory variable for lung cancer. This left-out explanatory variable is correlated with the explanatory variable being used in the simple regression (drinking).

8. Although, even this multiple regression is likely omitting some important explanatory variables.

9. But, if you put in too many irrelevant explanatory variables to begin with, you could find virtually all explanatory variables to be insignificant. Hence, some common sense is required about what a good initial regression might be.

10. We will not give a numerical example here since interest rates and exchange rates are time series data. As we shall see in future chapters, a naive use of multiple regression techniques with time series data can yield misleading results.
11. This data is in Excel file ELECTRIC.XLS.
12. Note that, since we are using the 1% level of significance, the table now has a 99% confidence interval.

7

Regression with Dummy Variables

Previous chapters used quantitative data to demonstrate important statistical concepts. However, many of the data economists use are qualitative.[1] Dummy variables, briefly described in Chapter 2, are a way of turning qualitative variables into quantitative variables. Once the variables are quantitative, then the correlation and regression techniques described in previous chapters can be used. Formally, a dummy variable is a variable that can take on only two values, 0 or 1.

Example: Explaining House Prices

In the previous chapter we worked through an extended example that investigated the factors influencing housing prices in Windsor, Canada. Recall that the explanatory variables we used in that chapter were all quantitative (for example, lot size of property measured in square feet, the number of bathrooms). However, other factors that might influence housing prices are not directly quantitative. Examples include the presence of: a driveway, air conditioning, a recreation room, a basement and gas central heating. All these variables are yes/no qualitative variables (for example, "yes" = the house has a driveway/"no" = the house does not have a driveway).

In order to carry out a regression analysis using these explanatory variables, we first need to transform them into dummy variables by changing the yes/no into 1/0. Using the letter D to indicate dummy explanatory variables, we can define:

- $D_1 = 1$ if the house has a driveway (=0 if it does not)
- $D_2 = 1$ if the house has a recreation room (=0 if not)
- $D_3 = 1$ if the house has a basement (=0 if not)
- $D_4 = 1$ if the house has gas central heating (=0 if not)
- $D_5 = 1$ if the house has air conditioning (=0 if not).

For instance, a house with a driveway, basement and gas central heating, but no air conditioning and no recreation room would have values for these variables of $D_1 = 1, D_2 = 0, D_3 = 1, D_4 = 1$ and $D_5 = 0$. These variables (and many others) are in data set HPRICE.XLS.

Once qualitative explanatory variables have been transformed into dummy variables, regression can be carried out in the standard way and all the theory and intuition developed in previous chapters can be used.

Why, then, are we allocating an entire chapter to this topic? There are two answers to this question: First, regression with dummy explanatory variables is extremely common and the interpretation of coefficient estimates is somewhat different. For this reason it is worthwhile to discuss the interpretation in detail. Second, regression with dummy explanatory variables is closely related to another set of techniques called Analysis of Variance (or ANOVA for short). ANOVA is rarely used in economics, but it is an extremely common tool in other social and physical sciences such as sociology, education, medical statistics, and epidemiology.

Most computer software packages such as Excel have ANOVA capabilities but the terminology of ANOVA is quite different from that used by economists, so ANOVA may seem confusing and unfamiliar to you. What we should note here, however, is that *regression with dummy explanatory variables can do anything ANOVA can.* In fact, regression with dummy variables is a more general and more powerful tool than ANOVA. For instance, the terms "single-factor ANOVA" or "two-factor ANOVA" refer to the number of dummy explanatory variables. Excel (and most common computer packages that perform ANOVA) can handle no more than two. However, Excel allows for up to 16 explanatory variables in its multiple regression facilities and thus can handle very complicated ANOVA models. In short, if you know how to use and understand regression, then you have no need to learn about ANOVA.

Exercise 7.1

Using the data set HPRICE.XLS, calculate and interpret descriptive statistics and a correlation matrix for the five dummy variables listed in the example above. How can you interpret the mean of a dummy variable?

Simple Regression with a Dummy Variable

We begin by considering a regression model with one dummy explanatory variable, D:

$$Y = \alpha + \beta D + e.$$

If we carry out OLS estimation of the above regression model, we obtain $\hat{\alpha}$ and $\hat{\beta}$. We can look at confidence intervals for α or β; examine P-values to test whether the coefficients are statistically significant; calculate R^2; perform an F-test for the significance of the regression and so forth, exactly as before. Refer back to Chapters 4, 5 and 6 if you are still unfamiliar with any of this material. An important topic at this stage for discussion, however, is the interpretation of the coefficients.

The straight-line relationship between Y and D gives a fitted value for the ith observation of:

$$\hat{Y}_i = \hat{\alpha} + \hat{\beta} D_i.$$

Note, since D_i is either 0 or 1, $\hat{Y}_i = \hat{\alpha}$ or $\hat{Y}_i = \hat{\alpha} + \hat{\beta}$. An example will serve to illustrate how this fact can be used to interpret regression results.

Example: Explaining House Prices (Continued)

Table 7.1 gives computer output from a regression of Y = house prices on D = air conditioning dummy using data from HPRICE.XLS.

Note that an examination of the P-value or the confidence interval (upper 95%, lower 95%) shows us that β is strongly significant. Furthermore, $\hat{\alpha} = 59,885$ and $\hat{\beta} = 25,996$. How can we interpret these numbers? We can, of course, use the same marginal effect intuition as we used in Chapter 4. That is, we can say that β is a measure of how much Y tends to change when X is changed by one unit. But, with the present dummy explanatory variable a "one unit" change implies a change from "no air conditioner" to "having an air conditioner." That is, we can say

Table 7.1 Regression of house prices on air conditioning dummy variable.

	Coefficient	Standard error	t-stat	P-value	Lower 95%	Upper 95%
Intercept	59884.85	1233.50	48.55	7.1E–200	57461.84	62307.86
D	25995.74	2191.36	11.86	4.9E-29	21691.18	30300.32

"houses with an air conditioner tend to be worth $25,996 more than houses without an air conditioner."

However, there is another, closely related, way of thinking about regression results when the explanatory variable is a dummy. In the case of houses without air conditioning $D_i = 0$ and hence $\hat{Y}_i = 59{,}885$. In other words, our regression model finds that houses without air conditioning are worth on average $59,885. In the case of houses with air conditioning, $D_i = 1$ and the regression model finds that $\hat{Y}_i = \hat{\alpha} + \hat{\beta} = 85{,}881$. Thus, houses with air conditioning are worth on average $85,881. This is one attractive way of presenting the information provided by the regression.

To provide more intuition, note that if we had not carried out a regression, but simply calculated the average price for houses with air conditioning, we would have found this figure to be $85,881. If we had then calculated the average price for houses without air conditioning, we would have found them to be worth $59,885. That is, we would have found exactly the same results as in the regression analysis.

Remember, however, the discussion of the omitted variables bias in Chapter 6. The simple regression in this example is omitting many important explanatory variables. We definitely cannot use the results of this simple regression to make statements like "adding an air conditioner to your house will raise its value by $25,996." Since air conditioners cost a few hundred (or at most a few thousand) dollars, the previous statement is clearly ridiculous.

Multiple Regression with Dummy Variables

Now, consider the multiple regression model with several dummy explanatory variables:

$$Y = \alpha + \beta_1 D_1 + \ldots + \beta_k D_k + e.$$

OLS estimation of this regression model and statistical analysis of the results can be carried out in the standard way. To aid in interpretation, we return to the house-pricing example.

Example: Explaining House Prices (Continued)

Consider the case where we have two dummy explanatory variables, $D_1 = 1$ if the house has a driveway (=0 if not) and $D_2 = 1$ if the house has a recreation room (=0 if not). These dummy variables implicitly classify the houses in the data set into four different groups:

1. Houses with a driveway and recreation room ($D_1 = 1$ and $D_2 = 1$).
2. Houses with a driveway, but no recreation room ($D_1 = 1$ and $D_2 = 0$).
3. Houses with no driveway, but with a recreation room ($D_1 = 0$ and $D_2 = 1$).
4. Houses with no driveway and no recreation room ($D_1 = 0$ and $D_2 = 0$).

Keep this classification in mind as we interpret Table 7.2, which contains results from a regression of house price (Y) on D_1 and D_2.

Putting in either 0 or 1 values for the dummy variables, we obtain the fitted values for Y for the four categories of houses:

1. If $D_1 = 1$ and $D_2 = 1$, then $\hat{Y} = \hat{\alpha} + \hat{\beta}_1 + \hat{\beta}_2 = 47,099 + 21,160 + 16,024 = 84,283$. In other words, the average price of houses with a driveway and recreation room is \$84,283.
2. If $D_1 = 1$ and $D_2 = 0$, then $\hat{Y} = \hat{\alpha} + \hat{\beta}_1 = 47,099 + 21,160 = 68,259$. In other words, the average price of houses with a driveway but no recreation room is \$68,259.
3. If $D_1 = 0$ and $D_2 = 1$, then $\hat{Y} = \hat{\alpha} + \hat{\beta}_2 = 47,099 + 16,024 = 63,123$. In words, the average price of houses with a recreation room but no driveway is \$63,123.
4. If $D_1 = 0$ and $D_2 = 0$, then $\hat{Y} = \hat{\alpha} = 47,099$. In words, the average price of houses with no driveway and no recreation room is \$47,099.

In short, multiple regression with dummy variables may be used to classify the houses into different groups and to find average house prices for each group. Alternatively, results may be presented directly as coefficient estimates. For instance, $\hat{\beta}_1$ is a measure of the extra value of a house with a driveway relative to a house with no driveway holding the other features of the house (in this case the presence or absence of a recreation room) constant.

Table 7.2 Regression of house price (Y) on D_1 and D_2.

	Coefficient	Standard error	t-stat	P-value	Lower 95%	Upper 95%
Intercept	47099.08	2837.62	16.60	2.42E–50	41525.02	52673.14
D1	21159.91	3062.44	6.91	1.37E–11	15144.22	27175.60
D2	16023.69	2788.63	5.75	1.52E–08	10545.86	21501.51

Exercise 7.2

Interpret the statistical information in the above example. Are all of the explanatory variables statistically significant?

Exercise 7.3

For this question use Y = the price of a house and the dummy variables $D_1 = 1$ if the house has a driveway (=0 otherwise) and $D_2 = 1$ if the house has a rec. room (=0 otherwise) from the house price example (it can be obtained from HPRICE. XLS). Without using regression techniques, calculate the average price of the four types of houses listed in the previous example (for instance a house with a driveway and a rec. room and so forth). Hint: what do you obtain if you multiply a dummy variable by Y? How do these average price numbers relate to the regression coefficients and results in the previous example?

Exercise 7.4

For this question use data set HPRICE.XLS and the five dummy variables, D_1 to D_5, listed at the beginning of the chapter (the dummy variables for whether a house has a driveway, recreation room, basement, gas central heating and air conditioning).

(a) With five dummy variables, how many classes of houses are possible? (For example, houses with a driveway, rec. room, basement and gas central heating but no air conditioning comprise one class.) What implications does this have for interpreting regression results as in the previous example?
(b) How would you calculate the number of houses in each group? For instance, of the 546 houses in the data set, how many have a driveway, gas central heating and air conditioning, but no recreation room and no basement?
(c) Run a regression of Y = house price on the five dummies.
(d) Discuss the statistical significance of the explanatory variables.
(e) Calculate the average price for a few chosen types of housing (for example, those with a driveway, recreation room and basement but no gas central heating and no air conditioning).
(f) Which house characteristic tends to raise the price of a house the most?

Multiple Regression with Dummy and Nondummy Explanatory Variables

In the previous discussion, we have assumed that all the explanatory variables are dummies, but in practice, you may often have a mix of different types of explanatory variables. The simplest such case is one where there is one dummy variable (D) and one quantitative explanatory variable (X) in a regression:

$$Y = \alpha + \beta_1 D + \beta_2 X + e.$$

The interpretation of results from such a regression can be illustrated in the context of an example.

Example: Explaining House Prices (Continued)

If we regress Y = house price on D = air conditioner dummy and X = lot size, we obtain $\hat{\alpha} = 32,693$, $\hat{\beta}_1 = 20,175$ and $\hat{\beta}_2 = 5.638$. Above we noted that the dummy can take on only the values 0 or 1, and demonstrated that the fitted value for Y can take on a different value for each group of houses. Hence regression results could be interpreted as revealing the average price of a house in each possible group.

Here things are not quite so simple since we obtain $\hat{Y}_i = 52,868 + 5.638X_i$ if $D_i = 1$ (the ith house has an air conditioner) and $\hat{Y}_i = 32,693 + 5.638X_i$ if $D_i = 0$ (the house does not have an air conditioner). In other words, there are two different regression lines depending on whether the house has an air conditioner or not. Contrast this point with the discussion in example above where we had only one dummy explanatory variable. In that case, the regression implied that the average price of the house differed between houses with and without air conditioners. Here we are saying a wholly different regression line exists. In other words, we cannot simply state (as we did in examples in previous examples in this chapter) what the average value of different groups of houses will be.

We can, however, say that $\hat{\beta}_1 = 20,175$ is a measure of the extra value that an air conditioner will add to the value of a house, *ceteris paribus*. In other words, if we compare two houses with the same value of X (in this case, lot size), $\hat{Y}_i$ will always be $20,175 higher for the house with an air conditioner relative to a house with no air conditioner.

It is worthwhile to examine more closely the two different regression lines that exist for houses with and without air conditioners. Note that they both have the same slope, $\hat{\beta}_2 = 5.638$ and differ only in the intercept (if $D_i = 1$ the intercept is 52,868, if $D_i = 0$ the intercept is 32,693). As they have the same slope (and the slope is the marginal effect), the marginal effect of lot size on house price is the same for houses with and without air conditioning. For instance, we can say "An extra square foot of lot size is associated with adding an extra $5.63 on the price of a house."

We can extend the previous discussion to the case of many dummy and nondummy explanatory variables. An example having two dummy and two nondummy explanatory variables is the following regression model:

$$Y = \alpha + \beta_1 D_1 + \beta_2 D_2 + \beta_3 X_1 + \beta_4 X_2 + e.$$

The interpretation of results from this regression model combines elements from all the previous examples in this chapter.

Example: Explaining House Prices (Continued)

If we regress $Y =$ house price on $D_1 =$ dummy variable for driveway, $D_2 =$ dummy variable for recreation room, $X_1 =$ lot size and $X_2 =$ number of bedrooms we obtain: $\hat{\alpha} = -2736$, $\hat{\beta}_1 = 12,598$, $\hat{\beta}_2 = 10,969$, $\hat{\beta}_3 = 5.197$ and $\hat{\beta}_4 = 10,562$. We can interpret these results by working out what the fitted regression lines ($\hat{Y}$) are for the different possible values of the dummy variables.

1. If $D_1=1$ and $D_2=1$, then $\hat{Y}=\hat{\alpha}+\hat{\beta}_1+\hat{\beta}_2+\hat{\beta}_3 X_1+\hat{\beta}_4 X_2=20,831+5.197X_1+10,562X_2$.

This is the regression line for houses with a driveway and recreation room.

2. If $D_1 = 1$ and $D_2 = 0$, then

$$\hat{Y} = 9,862 + 5.197X_1 + 10,562X_2.$$

This is the regression line for houses with a driveway but no recreation room.

3. If $D_1 = 0$ and $D_2 = 1$, then $\hat{Y} = 8,233 + 5.197X_1 + 10,562X_2$.

This is the regression line for houses with a recreation room but no driveway.

4. If $D_1 = 0$ and $D_2 = 0$, then $\hat{Y} = -2{,}736 + 5.197X_1 + 10{,}562X_2$.

This is the regression line for houses with no driveway and no recreation room.

That is, with two dummy variables we have four different regression lines. All of these lines have the same slopes but different intercepts. The coefficients on the dummy variables, $\hat{\beta}_1$ and $\hat{\beta}_2$, measure the additional value associated with having a driveway and a recreation room, respectively. The coefficients on the nondummy variables, $\hat{\beta}_3$ and $\hat{\beta}_4$, can be interpreted as the marginal effects of lot size and of number of bedrooms respectively.

The following are a few of the types of verbal statements that we can make about the regression results:

- "Houses with driveways tend to be worth $12,598 more than similar houses with no driveway."
- "If we consider houses with the same number of bedrooms, then adding an extra square foot of lot size will tend to increase the price of a house by $5,197."
- "An extra bedroom will tend to add $10,562 to the value of a house, *ceteris paribus*."

We should stress, however, that all such statements assume that omitted variables bias is not a problem in the regression. Furthermore, statements which imply causality (for example "adding an extra square foot of lot size will *tend to increase* the price of the house by $5,197") are only valid if it is truly the case that the explanatory variable causes the dependent variable (see Chapters 4 and 6 for further discussion of causality in regression).

Exercise 7.5

For this question use data set HPRICE.XLS, the five dummy variables, D_1 to D_5, listed in Exercise 7.4 and the following four nondummy explanatory variables:

- X_1 = the lot size of the property (in square feet)
- X_2 = the number of bedrooms
- X_3 = the number of bathrooms
- X_4 = the number of storeys (excluding the basement).

(a) Run a regression of Y on D_1, ..., D_5, X_1, ..., X_4.

(b) Discuss which variables are statistically significant.

(c) Which of the characteristics measured by the dummies has the largest effect on housing prices?

(d) Choose particular configurations of the dummy variables (for example, one indicating a house with: a driveway, no recreation room, a basement, no gas central heating and no air conditioner) and write out the formula for the regression line.

(e) Discuss results relating to the nondummy explanatory variables, paying particular reference to the *ceteris paribus* conditions.

Interacting Dummy and Nondummy Variables

We used the dummy variables above in a way that allowed for different intercepts in the regression line, but the slope of the regression line was always the same. We can, however, allow for different slopes by interacting dummy and nondummy variables. To understand this consider the following regression model:

$$Y = \alpha + \beta_1 D + \beta_2 X + \beta_3 Z + e.$$

D and X are dummy and nondummy explanatory variables, as above. However, here we have added a new variable Z into the regression and we define $Z = DX$.

How do we interpret results from a regression of Y on D, X and Z? This question can be answered by noting that Z is either 0 (for observations with $D = 0$) or X (for observations with $D = 1$). If, as before, we consider the fitted regression lines with $D = 0$ and $D = 1$ we obtain:

- If $D = 1$ then $\hat{Y} = \left(\hat{\alpha} + \hat{\beta}_1\right) + \left(\hat{\beta}_2 + \hat{\beta}_3\right)X$.
- If $D = 0$, then $\hat{Y} = \hat{\alpha} + \hat{\beta}_2 X$.

In other words, two different regression lines corresponding to $D = 0$ and $D = 1$ exist and have different intercepts and slopes. One implication is that the marginal effect of X on Y is different for $D = 0$ and $D = 1$. In a written report, you could write up each of the regression lines separately using the terminology and interpretation of Chapters 4 and 6.

Example: Explaining House Prices (Continued)

If we regress Y = house price on three explanatory variables: D = air conditioner dummy, X = lot size and $Z = DX$, we obtain $\hat{\alpha} = 35{,}684$, $\hat{\beta}_1 = 7{,}613$, $\hat{\beta}_2 = 5.02$ and $\hat{\beta}_3 = 2.25$. This implies that the marginal effect of lot size on housing is 7.27 (adding an extra square foot of lot size is associated with a \$7.27 increase in house prices) for houses with air conditioners and only \$5.02 for houses without. Furthermore, the P-value corresponding to $\hat{\beta}_3$ is 0.02, so the difference in marginal effects is statistically significant. This finding indicates that increasing lot size will tend to add more to the value of a house if it has an air conditioner than if it does not.

Exercise 7.6

For this question use data set HPRICE.XLS, the five dummy variables, D_1 to D_5 and the four nondummies X_1, ..., X_4 discussed in Exercise 7.5. Experiment with different configurations of these explanatory variables with some interaction terms (for instance, try including ten explanatory variables, D_1 to D_5, and the four nondummies X_1, ..., X_4 plus an interaction term, such as D_1X_2). Can you find any interaction terms (Zs) that are statistically significant? Explain in words what your findings are.

What if the Dependent Variable is a Dummy?

Thus far, we have focused on the case where the explanatory variables can be dummies. However, in some cases the dependent variable may be a dummy. For instance, a transportation economist might be interested in investigating individual choice between public transport and the private automobile. An empirical analysis might involve collecting data from many different individuals about their transport habits. Potential explanatory variables would include: commuting time, individual income, and so on. The dependent variable, however, would be qualitative (for instance, each individual may say "yes, I take my car to work" or "no, I do not take my car to work") and the economist would have to create a dummy dependent variable.

Exercise 7.7

Excel file, WAGEDISC.XLS contains data on $N = 100$ employees in a particular occupation. Suppose interest centers on investigating the factors that explain salary differences in this occupation with a view to addressing the issue of sex discrimination in this occupation. The data set contains the following variables:

- Y = salary (measured in thousands of dollars)
- X_1 = education level (measured in years of schooling)
- X_2 = experience level (measured in years of employment)
- D = dummy for sex (=1 for male, =0 for female).

(a) Calculate and discuss descriptive statistics for this data set. For instance, what is the mean salary?
(b) Calculate the mean salary for female employees and male employees separately. Compare.
(c) Run a simple regression of Y on D. Is the slope coefficient in this regression statistically significant? Compare your regression result with your finding in (b). Can you use these findings to conclude that women are discriminated against in this occupation?
(d) Run a multiple regression of Y on X_1, X_2 and D. Write a short report outlining your findings and addressing the issue of wage discrimination in this occupation. Are your results statistically significant?
(e) Compare your results in part (d) to part (c). Why do they differ? Hint: calculate a correlation matrix for all the explanatory variables and think intuitively about what the correlations mean.
(f) Construct a new variable $Z = DX_2$ and run a regression of Y on X_1, X_2, D and Z. Is Z statistically significant? How would the short report you wrote in part (d) change? Explain verbally what the coefficient on Z measures.

The techniques for working with dummy dependent variables[2] are beyond the scope of this book. However, there are two facts worth noting:

- There are some problems with using OLS estimation in this case. However, these problems are not enormous, so that OLS estimation might be adequate in many circumstances.
- Nevertheless, there are better estimation methods than OLS. The two main alternatives are termed Logit and Probit. Computer software packages with only basic

statistical capabilities (such as Excel) do not have the capability to perform these estimation methods. But more sophisticated econometric software packages will allow you to work with Logit and Probit.

Chapter Summary

1. Dummy variables can take on a value of either 0 or 1. They are often used with qualitative data.
2. The statistical techniques associated with the use of dummy explanatory variables are exactly the same as with nondummy explanatory variables.
3. A regression involving *only* dummy explanatory variables implicitly classifies the observations into various groups (for example, houses with air conditioning and those without). Interpretation of results is aided by careful consideration of what the groups are.
4. A regression involving dummy and nondummy explanatory variables implicitly classifies the observations into groups and says that each group will have a regression line with a different intercept. All these regression lines have the same slope.
5. A regression involving dummy, nondummy and interaction (dummy times nondummy variables) explanatory variables implicitly classifies the observations into groups and says that each group will have a different regression line with a different intercept and slope.
6. If the dependent variable is a dummy, then other techniques that are not covered in this book should be used.

Endnotes

1. See Chapter 2 for a discussion of the distinction between qualitative and quantitative data.
2. To introduce some jargon, such models are types of "limited dependent variable" models. That is, the dependent variable can take on a limited range of values.

CHAPTER 8

Regression with Time Lags: Distributed Lag Models

Many fields of economics (such as macroeconomics and finance) are concerned with the analysis of time series data. However, you may have noticed that all the examples in Chapters 3–7 use cross-sectional data. So far we have intentionally avoided discussing time series data since they involve issues that do not arise with cross-sectional data. The purpose of this chapter is to offer an introduction to these issues and to explain why we devote nearly half the book to the topic of time series as separate from multiple regression. After this introductory material, we consider the simplest tool for working with time series data: the *distributed lag model*.

The goal of the economist working with time series data does not differ too much from that of the economist working with cross-sectional data: Both aim to develop a regression relating a dependent variable to some explanatory variables. However, the economist using time series data will face two problems that the economist using cross-sectional data will not encounter:

- one time series variable can influence another with a time lag
- if the variables are *nonstationary*, a problem known as *spurious regression* may arise.

At this stage, you are not expected to understand the second of these problems. The terms *nonstationary, stationary* and *spurious regression* will be discussed in detail in subsequent chapters of this book. But keep in mind this general rule: *if you have nonstationary time series variables then you should not include them in a regression model.* The appropriate route is to transform the variables before running a regression in order to make them stationary. There is one exception to this general rule, which we shall discuss later, and which occurs where the variables in a regression model are *cointegrated*. We will elaborate on what we mean by these terms later. If you find it confusing for them to be introduced now without definitions, just think in the following terms: *Some problems arise with time series data that do not arise with cross-sectional data. These problems make it risky to use multiple regression naively in the manner of Chapters 4–7.* The purpose of the next four chapters is to show you how to correctly use multiple regression with time series data.

In this chapter, we will assume all variables in the regression are *stationary*. The next chapter explains what this means. At this point, note only that the second of the problems noted above will not occur and that we can therefore focus on the first problem.

The first problem can be understood intuitively with some simple examples. When we estimate a regression model we are interested in measuring the effect of one or more explanatory variables on the dependent variable. In the case of time series data we have to be very careful in our choice of explanatory variables since their effect on the dependent variable may take time to manifest.

For instance, if a central bank is worried that inflation is rising it might raise interest rates. The impact of such interest rate changes would likely take more than a year to feed through the economy and to affect other important variables (for example, the unemployment rate). In general, all of the basic tools of monetary and fiscal policy the government has as its disposal will have impacts that will be felt only in some future period. This problem is most common in macroeconomics but can also occur in microeconomics. To give an example: a firm's decision to carry out a new investment (for example, to purchase new computers) will not immediately affect production. It takes time to purchase the computers, install them and train workers in their use. Investment will only influence production some time in the future.

To put this concept in the language of regression, we say that the value of the dependent variable at a given point in time should depend not only on the value of the explanatory variable at that time period, but also on values of the explanatory variable in the past. The simplest model to incorporate such *dynamic* effects is known as the *distributed lag model*. It is a regression model with the form:[1]

$$Y_t = \alpha + \beta_0 X_t + \beta_1 X_{t-1} + \ldots + \beta_q X_{t-q} + e_t.$$

This is precisely the same as the multiple regression model in Chapter 6, with the exception that the "explanatory variables" are not entirely different variables (such as lot size, number of bathrooms and number of bedrooms) but are just one explanatory variable that is observed at different time periods. In this model, the right-hand side variables are referred to as *lagged variables* and q, the *lag order* or *lag length*. We will focus on the case where the dependent variable depends on one explanatory variable and its lags.

However, everything we say can be generalized in a straightforward fashion to several explanatory variables, all having time lags.

The distributed lag model is a regression model so everything we said in Chapters 4–6 about regression is relevant here. For instance, computer packages can provide OLS estimates of coefficients, confidence intervals and P-values for testing whether coefficients are equal to zero. Coefficients can be interpreted as measures of the influence of the explanatory variable on the dependent variable. In this case, we have to be careful with timing. For instance, we interpret results as: "β_2 measures the effect of the explanatory variable *two periods ago* on the dependent variable, *ceteris paribus*." Other than these minor differences, both the statistical methods and interpretation are very similar to the tools we described previously. Nevertheless, it is worth discussing this class of models separately as it will help us to develop some time series terminology and introduce ideas that we will build on in subsequent chapters.

Before turning to an illustrative example of how to work with distributed lag models, we will make two brief detours. One of these describes what lagged variables are and how to calculate them in a spreadsheet software package. Even if you are not using a spreadsheet, you may find this material useful to clearly see what lagged variables are and how the computer calculates them. The other clarifies the notation that will be used in this and subsequent chapters.

Aside on Lagged Variables

The concept of a lagged variable is fundamental to time series data, so we will describe in some detail what it means and how to construct and work with lagged variables on the computer.

Suppose we have time series data for $t = 1, ..., T$ periods on a variable X. As before, we denote individual observations by X_t for $t = 1, ..., T$. Consider creating a new variable W, which has observations $W_t = X_t$ for $t = 2, ..., T$ and a new variable Z, which has observations $Z_t = X_{t-1}$ for $t = 2, ..., T$. Why do we write $t = 2, ..., T$ instead of $t = 1, ..., T$? If we had written $t = 1, ..., T$ then the first observation of the variable Z, Z_1, would be set equal to X_0. But we do not know what X_0 is because variable X is observed only from $t = 1, ..., T$. So we instead work with $t = 2, ..., T$ and, thus, W and Z have only $T-1$ observations. Note also that if we had written $Z_t = X_{t-2}$ then the new variable Z would have had observations from $t = 3, ..., T$ and only $T-2$ observations.

The new variables W and Z both have $T-1$ observations. If we imagine W and Z as two columns containing $T-1$ numbers each (as in a spreadsheet), we can see that the first element of W will be X_2 and the first element of Z will be X_1. The second element of W and Z will be X_3 and X_2, etc. In words, we say that W contains X and Z contains X one period ago or *lagged one period*. In general, we can create variables "X

lagged one period"—or "lagged X" for short—"X lagged two periods"—or, in general, "X lagged j periods."

You can think of "X," "X lagged one period," "X lagged two periods" and so forth as different explanatory variables in the same way as you can of "house price," "lot size," or "number of bedrooms" as different explanatory variables.

Note, however, that if you want to include several explanatory variables in a multiple regression model, all variables must have the same number of observations. Let us consider the implication of this statement in the present context. Suppose a regression includes $X =$ the interest rate lagged j periods as an explanatory variable. If you began with $t = 1, \ldots, T$ observations on the interest rate, then X lagged j periods will contain only $T-j$ observations. This variable contains only $T-j$ observations so you must make sure that all the other variables in the model also contain exactly $T-j$ observations. In words, each variable in a time series regression must contain the number of observations equal to T minus the maximum number of lags that any variable has.

Many of the more sophisticated econometric software packages will create lagged variables automatically with a simple command but not most spreadsheet packages like Excel. This is a key reason why, when working with time series data, you might want to learn an econometric software package and not work with a spreadsheet such as Excel. When working with a spreadsheet you will have to create lagged variables yourself before running a regression involving them. A brief explanation of how to do this will be useful when you work with spreadsheets and will provide a practical way to illustrate the material above.

As an example, suppose we have ten observations on variables Y and X ($t = 1, \ldots, 10$) and we wish to run a regression model that includes X, lagged X, X lagged two periods and X lagged three periods. That is, we wish to estimate the regression model:

$$Y_t = \alpha + \beta_0 X_t + \beta_1 X_{t-1} + \beta_2 X_{t-2} + \beta_3 X_{t-3} + e_t.$$

Table 8.1 shows how the data would look in a spreadsheet format.

Note that spreadsheets label each observation by row and column as in the example. Each column contains a variable (for example, Column C contains the variable X lagged one period) and each row contains observations. Note that each of the variables contains seven observations, which is T minus maximum number of lags ($10 - 3 = 7$). Looking across any row (for example, Row 4) you can see that: (a) Y and X contain data at a particular point in time (for example, Y_7 and X_7 or $t = 7$); (b) X lagged one period will contain the observation from one period previously (for example, X_6); (c) X lagged two periods will contain the observation from two periods previously (for example, X_5); and (d) X lagged three periods will contain the observation from three periods previously (for example, X_4).

Table 8.1 Data in spreadsheet format.

	Col. A	Col. B	Col. C	Col. D	Col. E
	Y	X	X lagged 1 period	X lagged 2 periods	X lagged 3 periods
Row 1	Y_4	X_4	X_3	X_2	X_1
Row 2	Y_5	X_5	X_4	X_3	X_2
Row 3	Y_6	X_6	X_5	X_4	X_3
Row 4	Y_7	X_7	X_6	X_5	X_4
Row 5	Y_8	X_8	X_7	X_6	X_5
Row 6	Y_9	X_9	X_8	X_7	X_6
Row 7	Y_{10}	X_{10}	X_9	X_8	X_7

Aside on Notation

It is also important to make sure that our notation is clear. Consider a variable, X (for instance, population density). After collecting data on X we will have observations X_i for $i = 1, \ldots, N$ for cross-sectional data and X_t for $t = 1, \ldots, T$ for time series data (see Chapter 2).

In other words, X is a generic notation for the variable and X_i or X_t indicates a particular observation of the variable (for example, X_i = population density in the ith country or X_t = population density in the tth time period). In our discussion of regression in Chapters 4–7 we often wrote equations of the form:

$$Y = \alpha + \beta X + e.$$

Expressed in words, the above implied that "the dependent variable Y depends on the explanatory variable X." When we have actual data we can write:

$$Y_i = \alpha + \beta X_i + e_i.$$

Expressed in words, "observation i of Y depends on observation i of X." For instance, "deforestation *in country i* depends on population density *in country i*." Both of these equations are perfectly correct. But, as the subscript i in the latter equation is a little obvious (it is obvious that deforestation in Jamaica depends on population density in Jamaica—it certainly will not depend on population density in Uganda), you often see the i subscript dropped out from the latter equation for simplicitys sake.

We complicated our notation even more in Chapter 6 in our discussion of multiple regression, in which $X_1, X_2, \ldots, X_k$ were k different explanatory variables. Here the subscript on X indicated which explanatory variable we were referring to, not which observation. In the rare cases when we wanted to be more explicit we wrote, for example, X_{2i}, to indicate the ith observation of the second explanatory variable. However, as it is usually obvious in the multiple regression case that Y_i (for example, deforestation *in country i*) depends on X_{1i} (for example, population density *in country i*) and on X_{2i} (for example, change in pastureland *in country i*), the *i* subscript was often dropped from the equation.

In short, throughout this book our subscript notation, which distinguishes between a variable and a particular observation of a variable, has been a little loose. This is okay (and common in textbooks), because the meaning is fairly obvious from the context and the alternative is to clutter up equations with numerous subscripts. In the time series chapters of this book, we will show similar informality, using the notation X_{t-j} to indicate both a particular observation (for example, if $t = 1968$ and $j = 3$, then X_{t-j} is the value of variable X in 1965) and the variable X lagged j periods. The context will clarify which is which.

Example: The Effect of Safety Training on Accidents

Losses due to industrial accidents can be quite substantial in large companies. Accordingly, many companies provide safety training to their workers in an effort to reduce accidents. They are often interested in learning how effective their safety training programs are. Excel file SAFETY.XLS contains safety data from a particular company collected on a monthly basis over five years (60 months) on the following variables:

- Y = losses due to accidents (£s per month)
- X = hours of safety training provided to each worker per month.

These are time series data and it is likely that previous months' safety training affect current accident rates, so it is necessary to include lags of X in the regression. Table 8.2 contains OLS estimates of the coefficients in a distributed lag model in which losses are allowed to depend on present safety training and safety training up to four months ago. That is:

$$Y_t = \alpha + \beta_0 X_t + \beta_1 X_{t-1} + \beta_2 X_{t-2} + \beta_3 X_{t-3} + \beta_4 X_{t-4} + e_t.$$

What can the company conclude about the effectiveness of its safety training programs? Increasing the safety training of each worker by one hour per month in a given month is associated with:

Table 8.2   OLS estimates of the coefficients in a distributed lag model.

	Coefficient	Standard error	t-stat	P-value	Lower 95%	Upper 95%
Intercept	92001.51	2001.71	45.96	5.86E–42	87978.91	96024.11
X_t	−145.00	47.62	−3.04	0.0037	−240.70	−49.30
X_{t-1}	−462.14	47.66	−9.70	5.52E–13	−557.91	−366.38
X_{t-2}	−424.47	46.21	−9.19	3.12E–12	−517.33	−331.62
X_{t-3}	−199.55	47.76	−4.18	0.00012	−295.52	−103.58
X_{t-4}	−36.90	47.45	−0.78	0.44	−132.25	58.45

- an immediate reduction of losses due to accidents of £145.00, *ceteris paribus*
- a reduction of losses of £462.14 one month later, *ceteris paribus*
- a reduction of losses of £424.47 two months later, *ceteris paribus*
- a reduction of losses of £199.55 three months later, *ceteris paribus*
- a reduction of losses of £36.90 four months later, *ceteris paribus*.

Confidence intervals can be interpreted in the standard way. For instance, we are 95% confident that the immediate reduction of losses due to accidents is at least £49.30 and at most £240.70, *ceteris paribus*.

To provide some intuition about what the *ceteris paribus* condition implies in this context note that, for example, we can also express the second of these statements as: "Increasing safety training in a given month will tend to reduce losses due to accidents in the following month by £462.12, *assuming that no other changes in the company's safety training policy are made*."

If we examine the statistical results in the preceding table, we can see that all of the coefficients are statistically significant, except for β_4. The P-value for this last coefficient is 0.44, which is *not* less than 0.05. Also we note that the confidence interval for β_4 includes zero. Hence we cannot reject the hypothesis that $\beta_4 = 0$. In words, we cannot reject the hypothesis that safety training four months ago has no effect on current losses due to accidents. Perhaps workers forget their safety training after four months. This is probably useful information for the company because it may suggest that it should hold safety-training sessions every four months.

In general the effect of safety training on accidents exhibits a hump-shaped pattern over time: The immediate effect of training on accidents is fairly small (£145). The effect then increases to over £400 for each of the two subsequent months, falls to roughly £200 three months later and then drops to about zero four months later. Note that increasing safety training in a given period will tend to reduce losses not only immediately but also for the next few periods. If we add up the benefit of increasing one hour of safety training in each period ($£145.00 + £462.14 + £424.47 + £199.55 + £36.90 = £1,268.06)^2$ we receive a measure of the total benefit of the safety training program. In other words, we can say that: "Adding one hour of safety training tends to yield a benefit that totals £1,268.06 over the month in which the training is carried out and in the subsequent four months."

By calculating this total benefit and examining the pattern of the coefficients over time, the company gains important information, which it can then use to redesign its safety training programs. Such results, however, assume that the distributed lag model is not missing any explanatory variables. For instance, we are implicitly assuming that X_{t-5} (safety training five months ago) has no effect on current accident losses. If this assumption is incorrect, our estimates of the benefit of safety training may be incorrect. This issue relates closely to the problem of omitted variables bias discussed in Chapter 6, and emphasizes the importance of correct choice of lag length (q in the distributed lag model), a topic to which we now turn.

Exercise 8.1

Use the data set, SAFETY.XLS, discussed in the previous example for this question. This data set contains $T = 60$ observations on $Y =$ accident losses and $X =$ hours spent in safety training.

(a) Create the explanatory variables you would use in a distributed lag model with lag length equal to 4. (If you are having trouble, look in the file SAFETY1. XLS, which contains the answer to this question.) How many observations do the explanatory variables have?

(b) Using your answer to (a), recreate the table in the example above.

(c) Create the explanatory variables you would use in a distributed lag model with lag length equal to 2. How many observations do the explanatory variables have?

(d) Using your answer to (c), estimate the distributed lag model with $q = 2$.

(e) Compare your answers to part (d) and part (b). Discuss why they differ, paying particular attention to the question of omitted variables bias (see Chapter 6 if you have forgotten what this is).

Selection of Lag Order

When working with distributed lag models we rarely know beforehand exactly how many lags we should include. In the previous example, why did we assume that losses depend on safety training up to 4 months ago? Why not 3 or 6 or even 8? That is, we don't know which explanatory variables in a distributed lag model belong in the regression before we actually sit down at the computer and start working with the data. Appropriately, the issue of lag length selection becomes a data-based one where we use statistical means to decide how many lags to include.

There are many different approaches to lag length selection in the econometrics literature. Here we outline a common one that does not require any new statistical techniques beyond those developed in Chapter 5. This method uses t-tests for whether $\beta_q = 0$ to decide lag length. A common strategy is to: (a) Begin with a fairly large lag length,[3] $q\max$, and test whether the coefficient on the maximum lag is equal to zero (i.e. test whether $\beta_{q\max} = 0$). (b) If it is, drop the highest lag and re-estimate the model with maximum lag equal to $q\max - 1$. (c) If you find $\beta_{q\max-1} = 0$ in this new regression, then lower the lag order by one and re-estimate the model. (d) Keep on dropping the lag order by one and re-estimating the model until you reject the hypothesis that the coefficient on the longest lag is equal to zero.

This informal description of lag length selection can be formalized in the following series of steps:

- Step 1. Choose the maximum possible lag length, $q\max$, that seems reasonable to you.
- Step 2. Estimate the distributed lag model:

$$Y_t = \alpha + \beta_0 X_t + \beta_1 X_{t-1} + \ldots + \beta_{q\max} X_{t-q\max} + e_t.$$

If the P-value for testing $\beta_{q\max} = 0$ is less than the significance level you choose (e.g. 0.05) then go no further. Use qmax as lag length. Otherwise go on to the next step.

- Step 3. Estimate the distributed lag model:

$$Y_t = \alpha + \beta_0 X_t + \beta_1 X_{t-1} + \ldots + \beta_{q\max-1} X_{t-q\max+1} + e_t.$$

If the P-value for testing $\beta_{q\max-1} = 0$ is less than the significance level you choose (for example 0.05) then go no further. Use $q\max - 1$ as lag length. Otherwise go on to the next step.

- Step 4. Estimate the distributed lag model:

$$Y_t = \alpha + \beta_0 X_t + \beta_1 X_{t-1} + \ldots + \beta_{q\max-2} X_{t-q\max+2} + e_t.$$

If the P-value for testing $\beta_{q\,max-2} = 0$ is less than the significance level you choose (e.g. 0.05) then go no further. Use $q\,max - 2$ as lag length. Otherwise go on to the next step, etc.

As an aside of practical relevance to note when you are working with a spreadsheet, the number of observations used in a distributed lag model is equal to the original number of observations, T, minus the lag length. This means that, in Step 2, we are working with T-$q\,max$ observations; in Step 3, with T-$q\,max + 1$ observations; in Step 4 with T-$q\,max + 2$, observations; etc. Each step will require some cutting and pasting in the spreadsheet to create variables with the appropriate number of observations.[4]

Example: The Effect of Safety Training on Accidents (Continued)

Suppose we have selected $q\,max = 4$ in the distributed lag regression of accident losses on safety training. In other words, we believe that 4 months is the maximum time period that we can reasonably expect safety training to impact on losses due to accidents. The strategy outlined above says we should begin by estimating a distributed lag model with lag length equal to 4. Results are given in the previous table. The P-value corresponding to the explanatory variable X_{t-4} is greater than 0.05 so we cannot reject the hypothesis that $\beta_4 = 0$ at the 5% level of significance. Accordingly, we drop this variable from the model and re-estimate with lag length set equal to 3, yielding the results in Table 8.3.

The P-value for testing $\beta_3 = 0$ is 0.0003, which is much less than 0.05. We therefore conclude that the variable X_{t-3} does indeed belong in the distributed lag model. Hence $q = 3$ is the lag length we select for this model. In a formal report, we would present this table of results. Since these results are similar to those discussed above, we will not repeat the interpretation of them.

Table 8.3 Re-estimation with lag length set equal to 3.

	Coefficient	Standard error	t-stat	P-value	Lower 95%	Upper 95%
Intercept	90402.22	1643.18	55.02	9.19E–48	87104.94	93699.51
X_t	−125.90	46.24	−2.72	0.0088	−218.69	−33.11
X_{t-1}	−443.49	45.88	−9.67	3.32E–13	−535.56	−351.42
X_{t-2}	−417.61	45.73	−9.13	2.18E–12	−509.38	−325.84
X_{t-3}	−179.90	46.25	−3.89	0.0003	−272.72	−87.09

Exercise 8.2

Use the data set, SAFETY.XLS, which contains $T = 60$ observations on $Y =$ accident losses and $X =$ hours spent in safety training. Suppose you believe that six months is the maximum time that safety training might affect accident losses and accordingly, you set $q_{max} = 6$. Using the strategy described above, select the lag length of the distributed lag model.

Exercise 8.3

Development economists are often interested in the effect of education spending on economic growth. However, they suspect that the positive effects of raising education levels may take five or as many as ten years to manifest themselves in higher growth rates. In light of these considerations, use the following data set to estimate a model and write a brief report on the effect of primary education spending on economic growth.

Data set EDUC.XLS contains annual data for a country from 1910 to 1995 on the variables:

• $Y =$ GDP growth (measured as percentage change per year)
• $X =$ education spending (measured as dollars per child under age 16).

Chapter Summary

1. Regressions with time series variables involve two issues that we have not addressed in the past. First, one variable can influence another with a time lag. Second, if the variables are nonstationary, the spurious regressions problem can result. The latter issue will be dealt with in Chapter 10.
2. Distributed lag models have the dependent variable depending on an explanatory variable and time lags of the explanatory variable.
3. If the variables in the distributed lag model are stationary, then OLS estimates are reliable and the statistical techniques of multiple regression (for example, looking at P-values or confidence intervals) can be used in a straightforward manner.
4. The lag length in a distributed lag model can be selected by sequentially using t-tests beginning with a reasonably large lag length.

Appendix 8.1: Other Distributed Lag Models

The distributed lag model considered in this chapter is very general. There are no restrictions on what values the coefficients $\beta_0, \beta_1, \ldots, \beta_q$, can take. There are, however, many other models in the literature that are distributed lag models but which place restrictions on the coefficients. Working with these models is somewhat more difficult (at least in a spreadsheet) so we will only briefly discuss them in appendix form.

There are many models that place restrictions on distributed lag models (for example, the arithmetic lag model, geometric lag model and the Koyck model) but we will not discuss them in any detail. A *polynomial distributed lag* (or *Almon lag*) model can be taken as representative of these types of models and used to illustrate the main issues involved. A polynomial distributed lag model is the same as the distributed lag model with the added restriction that:

$$\beta_i = \gamma_0 + \gamma_1 i + \gamma_i i^2.$$

That is, the distributed lag coefficients are restricted to be a quadratic function of lag length.[5] This quadratic function depends on three unknown coefficients, γ_0, γ_1 and γ_2, which have to be estimated. Note that, once we obtain estimates of γ_0, γ_1 and γ_2 we can use them and the above equation to obtain estimates of β_i for $i = 0,1, \ldots, q$. Once we have estimates for the latter coefficients we can interpret them in the same way as before.

How do we obtain estimates of γ_0, γ_1 and γ_2? We can run an OLS regression but one with rather unusual explanatory variables. We illustrate this for the case $q = 3$. The distributed lag model can be written as:

$$Y_t = \alpha + \beta_0 X_t + \beta_1 X_{t-1} + \beta_2 X_{t-2} + \beta_3 X_{t-3} + e_t.$$

If we replace the β_s using the quadratic equation above we can write the polynomial distributed lag model as:

$$Y_t = \alpha + \gamma_0 V_t + \gamma_1 W_t + \gamma_2 Z_t + e_t,$$

where $V_t = X_t + X_{t-1} + X_{t-2} + X_{t-3}$, $W_t = X_{t-1} + 2X_{t-2} + 3X_{t-3}$ and $Z_t = X_{t-1} + 4X_{t-2} + 9X_{t-3}$. In other words, we can obtain OLS estimates of γ_0, γ_1 and γ_2 by running a regression of Y on V, W and Z. The explanatory variables, V, W and Z, in this regression have to be created.

We have now seen what a polynomial distributed lag model is and how to estimate it. However, it is probably unclear why you should use such an estimate. There are two related reasons for considering putting these polynomial restrictions on a distributed lag model:

- The polynomial distributed lag model will have fewer coefficients to estimate. In the quadratic case above, it will always have three coefficients, γ_0, γ_1 and γ_2. The distributed lag model will have $q + 1$ coefficients. In practice, q might be quite large (for example, you might want $q = 12$ if you have monthly data and want a time lag of up to a year). It can be difficult to make reliable estimates for a large number of coefficients unless the number of observations is large.

- Distributed lag models can sometimes suffer from multicollinearity (see Chapter 6). For instance, X_t and X_{t-1} can be highly correlated with one another. By way of example, suppose X is an interest rate. Since interest rates usually change very slowly over time X_t and X_{t-1} will often be very similar (or even identical) to one another. This causes them to be highly correlated and leads to multicollinearity problems. Polynomial distributed lag models usually do not suffer from multicollinearity (for example, V, W and Z in the example above typically are not highly correlated).

In many cases, however, the latter reason is not a problem for the analysis. When it is, it is often due to the explanatory variable being nonstationary. We will discuss nonstationary explanatory variables in Chapter 10 and show you a way for solving the multicollinearity problem in this case without having to place restrictions on the coefficients.

The first justification for the use of polynomial distributed lag models can be compelling if you have very few observations. But with the sort of moderately large data sets available to macroeconomists today, the justification loses its force. Furthermore, placing restrictions on the coefficients can lead to misleading results if the restrictions are wrong. Remember that β_i measures the influence of a change in the explanatory variable i periods ago on the current value of the dependent variable. In the distributed lag model this influence can be of any magnitude. The polynomial distributed lag model states that the β_is must bear a quadratic relationship to one another. If they do not, results from the polynomial distributed lag model can be very misleading.

Overall, we would argue that there is rarely a compelling case for placing restrictions on distributed lag models and, for this reason, we do not emphasize them here.

Endnotes

1. We can, of course, label our coefficients using any convention we want. The convention chosen here relates the subscript on β to the number of periods ago to which the explanatory variables refers. For instance, β_1 is the coefficient on X_{t-1}, which is the value of the explanatory variable one period ago.
2. The value £1,268.06 is the estimate of the total benefit. It is possible to calculate a confidence interval as well but this would require a more complicated formula and is beyond the scope of this book.

3. Although not too large! Remember that each variable in a distributed lag model will have number of observations equal to T minus the maximum number of lags. If you set the maximum number of lags too large, you will be left with very few observations.
4. Alternatively, some researchers simply use $T-q$max observations for all regressions. This has the advantage that, at each step, the researcher uses the same observations. However, this strategy uses a smaller data set than necessary. Remember from Chapter 5 that having more observations increases the accuracy of OLS estimates.
5. The quadratic is the most popular choice for the polynomial in this distributed lag model. However, others, such as the cubic, are possible.

Univariate Time Series Analysis

In the previous chapter we discussed distributed lag models, which are a simple type of regression model for use with time series data. Remember that they assume that the dependent variable, Y_t, depends on an explanatory variable, X_t, *and lags of the explanatory variable, X_{t-1} ... , X_{t-q}.* Such models are a useful first step in understanding important concepts in time series analysis.

In many cases, distributed lag models can be used without any problems; however, they can be misleading in cases where either:

- the dependent variable Y_t depends on *lags of the dependent variable* as well, possibly, as $X_t, X_{t-1}, \ldots , X_{t-q}$, or
- the variables are nonstationary.

Accordingly, in this chapter and the next, we develop tools for dealing with both issues and define what we mean by "nonstationary." To simplify the analysis, in this chapter we ignore X, and focus solely on Y. In statistical jargon, we will concentrate on *univariate time series* methods. As the name suggests, these relate to one variable or, in the jargon of statistics, one *series* (for example, Y = real GDP). As we shall see, it is important to understand the properties of each individual series before proceeding to regression modeling involving several series.

Example: US Personal Income

Figure 9.1 is a time series plot of one series, the natural logarithm of personal income in the US from the first quarter of 1954 through to the last quarter of 1994.[1] In other words, Y_t is personal income for $t = 1954Q1, \ldots , 1994Q4$. The data are available in Excel file INCOME.XLS. The original personal income variable is measured in millions of dollars.

Note that personal income seems to be increasing over time at a roughly constant rate. You can see some variation (for example, the brief falls in personal income corresponding to the recessions of the mid-1970s and early 1980s) but, overall, the time series plot is roughly a straight line with a positive slope. This sustained (in this case upward) movement is referred to as a *trend*. Many macroeconomic variables (for example, GDP, the price level, industrial production, consumption and government spending) exhibit trends of this sort.

It is convenient at this point to introduce the concept of *differencing*. Formally, if Y_t ($t = 1, \ldots , T$) is a time series variable, then $\Delta Y_t = Y_t - Y_{t-1}$ is the first difference of Y_t.[2] ΔY_t measures the change or growth in a variable over time. If we take natural logarithms of the original series, Y_t, then ΔY_t measures the percentage change in the original variable between time $t - 1$ and t. ΔY_t is often called "ΔY," "delta Y" or "the change in Y." Moreover, it is common to refer to Y_{t-1} as "Y_t lagged one period" or "personal income lagged one period" or "lagged Y" and so on. Figure 9.2 plots the change in personal income using the data in INCOME.XLS.

Note that Figure 9.2 looks very different from Figure 9.1. The trend behavior noted in Figure 9.1 has disappeared completely (we will return to this point later). The figure indicates that personal income tends to be growing around 1% per quarter, although there is considerable variability to this growth rate over time. In some recessionary periods personal income is falling, while in some expansionary periods, it is growing by as much as 3% or 4% per quarter.

Exercise 9.1

The file INCOME.XLS contains data on the logs of personal income and personal consumption.

(a) Calculate and interpret descriptive statistics for both personal income and change in personal income data. Do the same for personal consumption and its change.

(b) Plot and interpret figures analogous to Figures 9.1 and 9.2 using the personal consumption variable and its change.

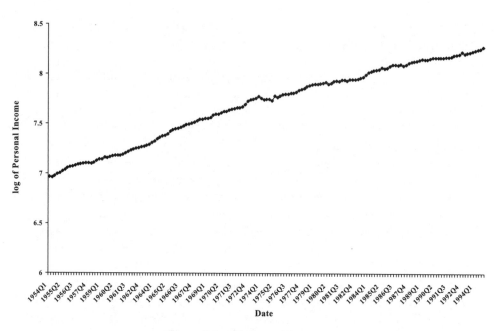

Figure 9.1   US Personal Income.

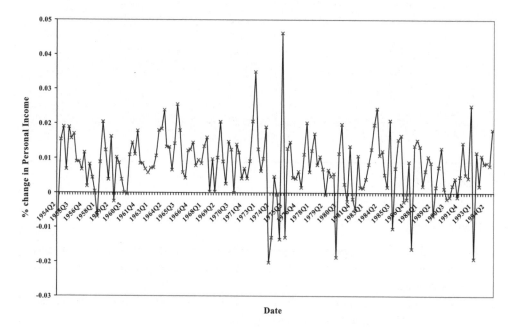

Figure 9.2   Change in US Personal Income.

Another property of time series data, not usually present in cross-sectional data, is the existence of correlation across observations. Personal income today, for example, is highly correlated with personal income last quarter.[3] In the jargon of Chapter 8, the variable "personal income" is correlated with the variable "personal income lagged one period." In fact, if we calculate the correlation between personal income and lagged personal income we obtain 0.999716. Yet, if we calculate the correlation between the *change* in personal income and the *change* in personal income lagged once, we obtain −0.00235. These findings make intuitive sense. Macroeconomic time series such as income, GDP and consumption change only slowly over time; even in deep recessions they rarely fall by more than 1% or 2% per quarter. Consequently, this quarter's income tends to be quite similar to last quarter's and both are highly correlated. Yet, the change or growth of macroeconomic time series is more erratic. This quarter's and last quarter's change in personal income can be quite different, as reflected in the near-zero correlation between them.

Figures 9.1 and 9.2 and the correlation results discussed in the previous paragraph were calculated using US personal income. But other macroeconomic time series in many other countries exhibit very similar types of behavior. Y, in other words, tends to exhibit trend behavior and to be highly correlated over time, but ΔY tends to the opposite, i.e. exhibits no trend behavior and is not highly correlated over time. These properties are quite important to regression modeling with time series variables as they relate closely to the issue of nonstationarity. Appropriately, we will spend the rest of this chapter developing formal tools and models for dealing with them.

The Autocorrelation Function

The correlations discussed above are simple examples of *autocorrelations* (correlations involving a variable and a lag of itself). The *autocorrelation function* is a common tool used by researchers to understand the properties of a time series. We will use expressions like "the correlation between Y and lagged Y." We denote this as r_1. If you need a review of lagged variables, you might wish to go back and look at the sections "Aside on Lagged Variables" and "Aside on Notation" from Chapter 8.

In general, we may be interested in the correlation between Y and Y lagged p periods. For instance, our personal income data are observed quarterly, so the correlation between Y and Y lagged $p = 4$ periods is the correlation between income now and income a year ago (a year is four quarters). We will denote this correlation by r_p and refer to it as "the autocorrelation at lag p." The *autocorrelation function* treats r_p as a function of p (it calculates r_p for $p = 1, \ldots , P$). P is the maximum lag length considered and is typically chosen to be quite large (for example, $P = 12$ for monthly data). The autocorrelation function is a commonly used tool in univariate time series analysis, precisely because it reveals quite a bit of information about the series.

Exercise 9.2

The file INCOME.XLS contains data on personal income and consumption in the US.

(a) For each of these two series individually create an XY-plot between the variable and the variable lagged one period.

(b) For each of these variables, calculate r_1.

(c) First difference each of these variables and repeat (a) and (b). How would you interpret the data you have constructed and the correlations and XY-plots?

Asides

1. The correlation between a variable (say, Y) and Y lagged p periods is r_p. In our discussion of r_1 we noted Y_1 lagged one period was Y_0, which did not exist. For this reason, we used data from $t = 2, \ldots, T$ to define lagged Y and calculate r_1. An even more extreme form of the problem occurs in the calculation of r_p. Consider creating a new variable W, which has observations $W_t = Y_t$ for $t = p + 1, \ldots, T$ and a new variable Z which has observations $Z_t = Y_{t-p}$ for $t = p + 1, \ldots, T$. The correlation between W (Y) and Z (Y lagged p periods) is r_p. Note that each of the new variables contains $T - p$ observations. So when we calculate r_p we are implicitly "throwing away" the first p observations. If we considered extremely long lags, we would be calculating autocorrelations with very few observations. In the extreme case, if we set $p = T$ we have no observations left to use. This is a justification for not letting p become too big. The issues raised in this paragraph are very similar to those raised in distributed lag models (see Chapter 8, under "aside on lagged variables").

2. The autocorrelation function involves autocorrelations with different lag lengths. In theory, we can use data from $t = 2, \ldots, T$ to calculate r_1; data from $t = 3, \ldots, T$ to calculate r_2, and so forth, ending with data from $t = P + 1, \ldots, T$ to calculate r_P. But, note that this means that each autocorrelation is calculated with a different number of data points. For this reason, it is standard practice to select a maximum lag (P) and use data from $t = P + 1, \ldots, T$ for calculating *all* of the autocorrelations.

Example: US Personal Income (Continued)

The Table 9.1 presents the autocorrelation functions for $Y =$ US personal income and $\Delta Y =$ the change in personal income (using data from INCOME.XLS) using a maximum lag of 12 ($P = 12$).

This information can also be presented graphically by making a bar chart with the lag length on the X-axis and the autocorrelation on the Y-axis, as in Figures 9.3 and 9.4.

A striking feature of the table and figures is that autocorrelations tend to be virtually 1 for personal income, even in the case of high lag lengths. In contrast, the autocorrelations for the change in personal income are very small and exhibit a pattern that looks more or less random; the autocorrelations, in other words, are essentially zero. This pattern is common to many or most macroeconomic time series: The series itself has autocorrelations near one, but the change in the series has autocorrelations that are much smaller (often near zero). Below are a few ways of thinking about these autocorrelations:

- Y is highly correlated over time. Even personal income three years ago ($p = 12$) is highly correlated with income today. ΔY does not exhibit this property. The growth in personal income this quarter is essentially uncorrelated with the growth in previous quarters.

Table 9.1 Autocorrelation functions.

Lag length (p)	Personal income	Change in personal income
1	0.9997	−0.0100
2	0.9993	0.0121
3	0.9990	0.1341
4	0.9986	0.0082
5	0.9983	−0.1562
6	0.9980	0.0611
7	0.9978	−0.0350
8	0.9975	−0.0655
9	0.9974	0.0745
10	0.9972	0.1488
11	0.9969	0.0330
12	0.9966	0.0363

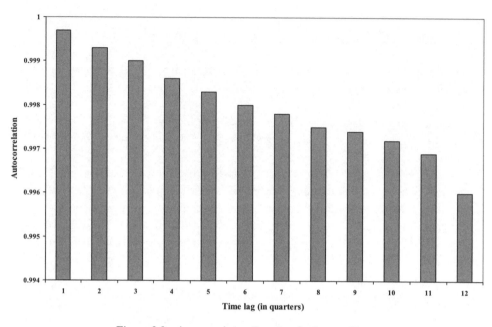

Figure 9.3   Autocorrelation Function for Income Data.

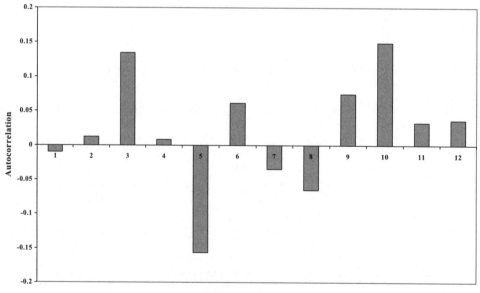

Figure 9.4   Autocorrelation Function for Change in Income.

- If you knew past values of personal income, you could make a very good estimate of what personal income was this quarter. However, knowing past values of the change in personal income will not help you predict the change in personal income this quarter.
- Generally, Y "remembers the past" (it is highly correlated with past values of itself). This is an example of *long memory* behavior. ΔY does not have this property.
- Y is a *nonstationary* series while ΔY is *stationary*. We have not formally defined the words "nonstationary" and "stationary" but they are quite important in time series econometrics. We will have more to say about them later but note for now that the properties of the autocorrelation function for Y are characteristic of nonstationary series.

Exercise 9.3

Use the data on Y = personal consumption given in INCOME.XLS.

(a) Calculate the autocorrelation function for Y and ΔY with a maximum lag of 4 ($P = 4$).
(b) Plot these autocorrelation functions in a bar chart.
(c) Interpret the results you have obtained in (a) and (b).

The Autoregressive Model for Univariate Time Series

The autocorrelation function is a useful tool for summarizing the properties of a time series. Yet, in Chapters 3 and 4 we argued that correlations have their limitations and that regression was therefore a preferable tool. The same reasoning holds here. Autocorrelations, in other words, are just correlations, and for this reason it may be desirable to develop more sophisticated models to analyze the relationships between a variable and lags of itself. Many such models have been developed in the statistical literature on univariate time series analysis but the most common model, which can also be interpreted as a regression model, is the so-called *autoregressive model*. As the name suggests, it is a regression model where the explanatory variables are lags of the dependent variable ("auto" means "self" and hence an autoregression is a regression of a variable on lags of itself). The word "autoregressive" is usually shortened to "AR".

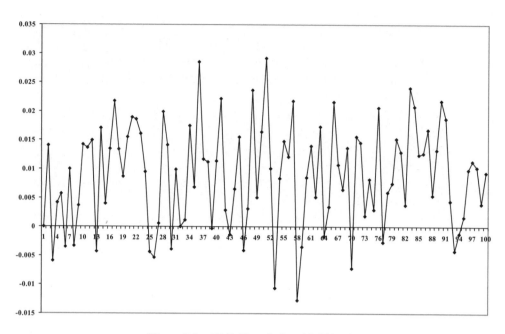

Figure 9.5 AR(1) Time Series with Phi = 0.

We begin by discussing the autoregressive model with the explanatory variable being the dependent variable lagged one period. This is called the AR(1) model:

$$Y_t = \alpha + \phi Y_{t-1} + e_t$$

for $t = 2, \dots , T$. It looks exactly like the regression model discussed in previous chapters,[4] except that the dependent variable is Y_{t-1}. The value of ϕ in the AR(1) model is closely related to the behavior of the autocorrelation function and to the concept of nonstationarity.

In order to understand the types of behavior characteristic of the AR(1) series, let us artificially simulate three different time series using three different choices for ϕ: $\phi = 0, 0.8$ and 1. All three series have the same values for α (i.e. $\alpha = 0.01$) and the same errors. Figures 9.5 above and 9.6 and 9.7 below provide time series plots of the three data sets.

Note that Figure 9.5 (with $\phi = 0$) exhibits random fluctuations around an average of about 0.01 (the value of α). In fact, it is very similar to Figure 9.2, which contains a time series plot of the change in personal income. Figure 9.7 (with $\phi = 1$) exhibits trend behavior and looks very similar to Figure 9.1, which plots personal income. Figure 9.6 (with $\phi = 0.8$) exhibits behavior that is somewhere in between the random fluctuations of Figure 9.5 and the strong trend of Figure 9.7.

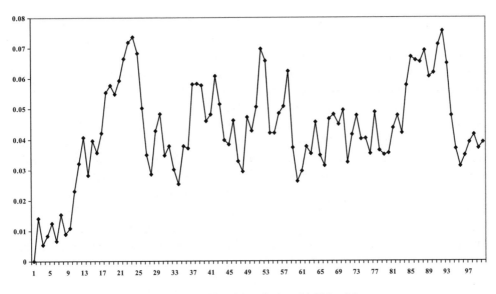

Figure 9.6 AR(1) Time Series with Phi = 0.8.

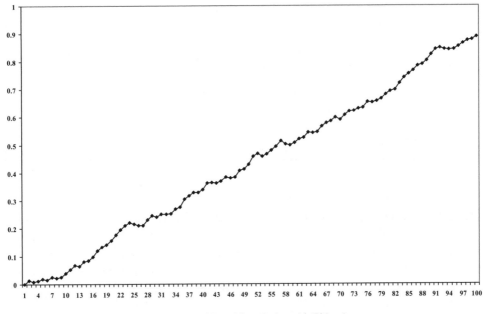

Figure 9.7 AR(1) Time Series with Phi = 1.

Figures 9.5–9.7 illustrate the types of behavior that AR(1) models can capture and show why they are commonly used in macroeconomics. For different values of ϕ, these models can allow for the randomly fluctuating behavior typical of growth rates of many macroeconomic time series, for the trend behavior typical of the macroeconomic series themselves, or for intermediate cases between these extremes.

Note also that $\phi = 1$ implies the type of trend behavior we have referred to above as nonstationary, while the other values of ϕ imply stationary behavior. This allows us to provide a formal definition of the concepts of *stationarity* and *nonstationarity*, at least for the AR(1) model: *For the AR(1) model, we can say that* Y *is stationary if* $|\phi| < 1$ *and is nonstationary if* $\phi = 1$. The other possibility, $|\phi| > 1$, is rarely considered in economics. The latter possibility implies that the time series is exhibiting explosive behavior over time. Since such explosive behavior is only observed in unusual cases (for example, hyperinflation), it is of little empirical relevance and we shall not discuss it here. Mathematical intuition for the properties of the AR(1) model and how it relates to the issue of nonstationarity is given in the appendix to this chapter.

Exercise 9.4

Use the data in files FIG95.XLS, FIG96.XLS and FIG97.XLS, which were used to create Figures 9.5–9.7, respectively.

(a) Calculate the autocorrelation function for each time series using a maximum lag of 4.
(b) Relate your findings in (a) to your answers to Exercise 9.3. Focus in particular on the question of whether the AR(1) model is capable of generating the types of behavior observed in the macroeconomic time series on personal consumption.

Nonstationary versus Stationary Time Series

Above we introduced the terms "nonstationary" and "stationary" without providing any formal definition (except for the AR(1) model). As we shall see, the distinction between stationary and nonstationary time series is extremely important. To formally define these concepts requires that we get into statistical issues that are beyond the scope of this book. But we provide some general intuition for these concepts below.

Formally, "nonstationary" merely means "anything that is not stationary." Economists usually focus on the one particular type of nonstationarity that seems to be present in many macroeconomic time series: *unit root* nonstationarity. We will generalize this concept later but at this stage it is useful to think of a unit root as implying $\phi = 1$ in the AR(1) model. Different ways of thinking about whether a time series variable, Y, is stationary or has a unit root include:

- In the AR(1) model, if $\phi = 1$, then Y has a unit root. If $|\phi| < 1$ then Y is stationary.
- If Y has a unit root then its autocorrelations will be near 1 and will not drop much as lag length increases.
- If Y has a unit root, then it will have a long memory. Stationary time series do not have long memory.
- If Y has a unit root then the series will exhibit trend behavior (especially if α is nonzero).
- If Y has a unit root, then ΔY will be stationary. For this reason, series with unit roots are often referred to as *difference stationary* series.

The final point can be seen most clearly by subtracting Y_{t-1} from both sides of the equation in the AR(1) model, yielding:

$$\Delta Y_t = \alpha + \rho Y_{t-1} + e_t$$

where $\rho = \phi - 1$. Note that, if $\phi = 1$, then $\rho = 0$ and the previous equation can be written solely in terms of ΔY_t, implying that ΔY_t fluctuates randomly around α. For future reference, note that we can test for $\rho = 0$ to see if a series has a unit root. Furthermore, a time series will be stationary if $-1 < \phi < 1$ which is equivalent to $-2 < \rho < 0$. We will refer to this as the *stationarity condition*.

By way of providing more intuition (and jargon!) for the AR(1) model, let us consider the case where $\phi = 1$ (or, equivalently, $\rho = 0$). In this case we can write the AR(1) model as:

$$Y_t = \alpha + Y_{t-1} + e_t.$$

This is referred to as the *random walk* model. More precisely, the random walk model has no intercept ($\alpha = 0$), whereas the preceding equation is referred to as a *random walk with drift*. The presence of the intercept allows for changes in variables to be, on average, nonzero. So, for instance, if Y is (the log of) a stock price of a particular company then the random walk with drift model can be written as:

$$Y_t - Y_{t-1} = \alpha + e_t.$$

The left hand of this equation is the percentage change in the stock price, which is the stock return (exclusive of dividends), so the model says stock returns are equal to α (a benchmark return relevant for this company taking into account its risk and so forth) plus a random error. This model is commonly thought to hold for phenomena like stock prices and the prices of other financial assets.

In the random walk model, since $\phi = 1$, Y has a unit root and is nonstationary.

Example: US Personal Income (Continued)

The AR(1) model is a regression model. Accordingly, we can use OLS to regress the variable Y on lagged Y.[5] If we do this, we find $\hat{\alpha} = 0.039$ and $\hat{\phi} = 0.996$. Since the OLS estimate, $\hat{\phi}$, and the true value of the AR(1) coefficient, ϕ, will rarely if ever be identical, it is quite possible that $\phi = 1$ since the OLS estimate is very close to 1.

If we regress ΔY_t on Y_{t-1}, we obtain an OLS estimate of ρ which is -0.004. Note that we are finding $\hat{\rho} = \hat{\phi} - 1$, just as we would expect.

Exercise 9.5

Use the data in files FIG95.XLS, FIG96.XLS and FIG97.XLS, which were used to create Figures 9.5–9.7, respectively.

(a) Calculate OLS estimates of ρ and ϕ in the two variants of the AR(1) model.
(b) Relate your results in (a) to the question of whether any of the series contain a unit root.
(c) Repeat (a) and (b) using the personal consumption data in INCOME.XLS.

Extensions of the AR(1) Model

We have argued above that the AR(1) model can be interpreted as a simple regression model where last period's Y is the explanatory variable. However, it is possible that more lags of Y should be included as explanatory variables. This can be done by extending the AR(1) model to the autoregressive of order p, AR(p), model:

$$Y_t = \alpha + \phi_1 Y_{t-1} + \ldots + \phi_p Y_{t-p} + e_t$$

for $t = p + 1, \ldots, T$. We will not discuss the properties of this model, other than to note that they are similar to the AR(1) model but are more general in nature. That is, this model can generate the trend behavior typical of macroeconomic time series and the randomly fluctuating behavior typical of their growth rates. In discussing unit root behavior it is convenient to subtract Y_{t-1} from both sides of the previous equation. With some rearranging we obtain:

$$\Delta Y_t = \alpha + \rho Y_{t-1} + \gamma_1 \Delta Y_{t-1} + \ldots + \gamma_{p-1} \Delta Y_{t-p+1} + e_t$$

where the coefficients in this regression, ρ, γ_1, ... , γ_{p-1} are simple functions of ϕ_1, ... , ϕ_p. For instance, $\rho = \phi_1 + ... + \phi_p - 1$. Note that this is identical to the AR(p) model, but is just written differently. Hence we refer to both previous equations as AR(p) models. In case you are wondering where the Y_{t-p} term from the first equation went to in the second, note that it appears in the second equation in the ΔY_{t-p+1} term (i.e. $\Delta Y_{t-p+1} = Y_{t-p+1} - Y_{t-p}$). Note also that both variants have the same number of coefficients, $p + 1$ (the first variant has α, ϕ_1, ... , ϕ_p whereas the second variant has α, ρ, γ_1, ... , γ_{p-1}). However, in the second variant the AR(p) model has last coefficient γ_{p-1}. Don't let this confuse you—it is just a consequence of the way we have rearranged the coefficients in the original specification.

The key points to note here are that the above equation is still in the form of a regression model; and $\rho = 0$ *implies that the AR(p) time series Y contains a unit root; if $-2 < \rho < 0$, then the series is stationary.* Looking at the previous equation with $\rho = 0$ clarifies an important way of thinking about unit root series which we have highlighted previously: If a time series contains a unit root then a regression model involving only ΔY is appropriate (i.e. if $\rho = 0$ then the term Y_{t-1} will drop out of the equation and only terms involving ΔY or its lags appear in the regression). It is common jargon to say that "if a unit root is present, then the data can be differenced to induce stationarity."

As we will discuss in the next chapter, with the exception of a case called cointegration, we do not want to include unit root variables in regression models. This suggests that, if a unit root in Y is present, we will want to difference it and use ΔY. In order to do so, we must know first if Y has a unit root. In the past, we have emphasized that unit root series exhibit trend behavior. Does this mean that we can simply examine time series plots of Y for such trending to determine if it indeed has a unit root? The answer is no. To explain why, let us introduce another model.

We showed previously that many macroeconomic time series contain trends and that AR models with unit roots also imply trend behavior. However, there are other models that also imply trend behavior. Imagine that Figure 9.1 (or Figure 9.7) is an XY-plot where the X-axis is labeled time and that we want to build a regression model using this data. You might be tempted to fit the following regression line:

$$Y_t = \alpha + \delta t + e_t,$$

where the coefficient on the explanatory variable, time, is labeled δ to distinguish it from the ϕ in the AR(1) model. Note that you can interpret this regression as involving the variable Y and another variable with observations 1, 2, 3, 4, ... , T. This is another regression model that yields trend behavior. To introduce some jargon, the term δt is referred to as a *deterministic trend* since it is an exact (i.e. deterministic) function of time. In contrast, unit root series contain a so-called *stochastic trend*.[6]

We can even combine this model with the AR(1) model to obtain:

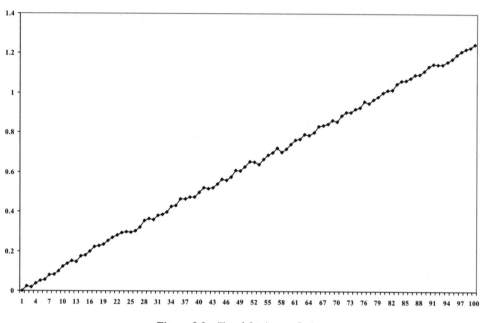

Figure 9.8 Trend Stationary Series.

$$Y_t = \alpha + \phi Y_{t-1} + \delta t + e_t.$$

Figure 9.8 is a time series plot of artificial data generated from the previous model with $\alpha = 0$, $\phi = 0.2$ and $\delta = 0.01$. Note that this series is stationary since $|\phi| < 1$. Yet, Figure 9.8 looks a bit like Figure 9.7 (or Figure 9.1). Stationary models with a deterministic trend can yield time series plots that closely resemble those from nonstationary models having a stochastic trend. Thus, you should remember that *looking at time series plots alone is not enough to tell whether a series has a unit root.*

The discussion in the previous paragraph motivates jargon that we will use and introduce in the context of the following summary:

- The *nonstationary* time series variables on which we focus are those containing a *unit root*. These series contain a *stochastic trend*. But if we difference these time series, the resulting time series will be stationary. For this reason, they are also called *difference stationary*.

- The *stationary* time series on which we focus have $-2 < \rho < 0$ in the AR(p) model. However, these series can exhibit trend behavior through the incorporation of a *deterministic trend*. In this case, they are referred to as *trend stationary*.

Exercise 9.6

The data in FIG98.XLS was used to create Figure 9.8.

(a) Calculate the autocorrelation function for this trend stationary series.
(b) In light of your answer to (a), discuss whether the autocorrelation function is a useful tool for testing for a unit root.

If we add a deterministic trend to the AR(p) model, we obtain a very general model that is commonly used in univariate time series analysis:

$$\Delta Y_t = \alpha + \rho Y_{t-1} + \gamma_1 \Delta Y_{t-1} + \ldots + \gamma_{p-1} \Delta Y_{t-p+1} + \delta t + e_t.$$

We refer to the above as the *AR(p) with deterministic trend model* and use it later. You may wonder why we don't just use the original AR(p) specification introduced at the beginning of this section (the one where the explanatory variables are $Y_{t-1}, \ldots, Y_{t-p}$). There are two reasons. First, we are going to test for a unit root. With the present specification, this is simply a test of $\rho = 0$. Testing for whether regression coefficients are zero is a topic that we have learned previously (refer to Chapter 5). With the original AR(p) model, testing for a unit root is more complicated. Second, $Y_{t-1}, Y_{t-2}, \ldots, Y_{t-p}$ are often highly correlated with each other (see the autocorrelation function in Figure 9.3). If we were to use them as explanatory variables in our regression we would no doubt run into serious multicollinearity problems (see Chapter 6). However, in the present model we use $Y_{t-1}, \Delta Y_{t-1}, \ldots, \Delta Y_{t-p+1}$ as explanatory variables, which tend not to be highly correlated (see Figure 9.4), thereby avoiding the problem.

Example: US Personal Income (Continued)

Table 9.2 contains output from an OLS regression of ΔY_t on $Y_{t-1}, \Delta Y_{t-1}, \Delta Y_{t-2}, \Delta Y_{t-3}$ and a deterministic time trend, created by using the data on personal income from INCOME.XLS. In other words, it provides regression output for the AR(4) with deterministic trend model. We suspect this personal income series may contain a unit root, a supposition supported somewhat by the table. In particular, a unit root is present if ρ (the coefficient on Y_{t-1}) is zero. As we can see, the estimate of ρ is indeed very small ($\hat{\rho} = -0.018$).

Table 9.2   AR(4) with deterministic trend model.

	Coefficient	Standard error	t-stat	P-value	Lower 95%	Upper 95%
Intercept	0.138	0.108	1.279	0.203	−0.075	0.351
Y_{t-1}	−0.018	0.015	−1.190	0.236	−0.049	0.012
ΔY_{t-1}	−0.017	0.081	−0.217	0.829	−0.177	0.142
ΔY_{t-2}	0.014	0.081	0.172	0.863	−0.145	0.173
ΔY_{t-3}	0.130	0.080	1.627	0.106	−0.028	0.288
Time	0.00012	0.00012	0.955	0.341	−0.00013	0.00037

You should note that when time series data exhibit seasonal patterns or *seasonality*, further extensions of the AR(p) with deterministic trend model are required. Examples of time series that contain seasonal patterns can easily be found. For instance, an exceptionally large level of consumer spending takes place in the period around Christmas (in the fourth quarter of the year). Likewise, much construction in the building sector is carried out in the summer (when the weather is best). Unemployment rates also exhibit seasonal variation in that they tend to be lowest in the summer when construction and agricultural employment are at their highest. All of these variables have a predictable seasonal pattern that we might want to incorporate in a regression model.

Note that government statistical agencies typically provide *deseasonalized* data. Such data remove seasonal patterns so that you will not have to worry about them. However, in some cases you may not have such deseasonalized data or you may be interested in the seasonal patterns themselves. In these cases, you will need to know how to work with this particular type of data.

It is beyond the scope of this book to discuss the procedures for dealing with seasonality in any detail, but one such method of which you should be aware involves the use of dummy variables, and can be mentioned briefly here.[7] Remember, at its most basic level, regression analysis seeks to explain the properties of the dependent variable using explanatory variables. Since seasonal patterns can be important properties of the dependent variable, we want explanatory variables to explain them. One set of explanatory variables that can be used are *seasonal dummies*. We can include such dummy variables as additional explanatory variables in the AR(p) with deterministic trend model. For instance, with quarterly data, you can create the dummy variables: (a) $D_1 = 1$ if an observation is from the first quarter (= 0 otherwise); (b) $D_2 = 1$ if an observation is from the second quarter (= 0 otherwise); and (c) $D_3 = 1$ if an observation is from the third quarter (= 0 otherwise). Note that if you include these three dummy variables as explanatory variables in the AR(p) with deterministic trend model, no new statistical issues arise. That is, OLS provides good estimates of all coefficients and you can use P-values to test whether their coefficients are zero, and so forth. In short, you can add seasonal dummies in a straightforward manner to any of the time series models you encounter in this book.

You may be wondering why we included dummies for only three seasons (D_1, D_2 and D_3) in the previous example using quarterly data. The reason is that had we included D_4, the dummy for the fourth quarter, we would have encountered a case of perfect multicollinearity.[8] It is rather hard to show the reason for this in a nontechnical way but, if you want to verify this statement yourself, run a regression with quarterly time series data using an intercept and D_1, D_2, D_3 and D_4 as explanatory variables and see what happens. To understand further how to interpret results when dummy explanatory variables are used, look back at Chapter 7. The section headed "multiple regression with both dummy and nondummy explanatory variables" is particularly relevant.

Testing in the AR(p) with Deterministic Trend Model

In Chapters 5 and 6, we described how to test whether regression coefficients were equal to zero. These techniques can be used in the AR(p) with deterministic trend model (i.e. if you wish to omit explanatory variables whose coefficients are not significantly different from zero). In particular, testing is usually done to help choose lag length (p) and to decide whether the series has a unit root. In fact, it is common to first test to select lag length, and then test for a unit root.

However, one important complication occurs in the AR(p) model that was not present in earlier chapters. To understand it, let us divide the coefficients in the model into two groups: (a) α, γ_1, ... , γ_{p-1}, and δ, and (b) ρ. In other words, *we consider hypothesis tests involving ρ independently of those involving the other coefficients.*

Testing involving α, γ_1, ... , γ_{p-1}, and δ

Many sophisticated statistical criteria and testing methods exist to determine the appropriate lag length in an AR(p) model. Nonetheless, simply looking at the t-statistics or P-values in regression outputs can be quite informative. For instance, an examination of the table above reveals that the P-values associated with the coefficients on the lagged ΔY terms are insignificant, and that they may be deleted from the regression (i.e. the P-values are greater than 0.05). Alternatively, a more common route is to proceed sequentially, as we did in the distributed lag model; that is, to choose a maximum lag length, $p$max and then sequentially drop lag lengths if the relevant coefficients are insignificant.

More specifically, begin with an AR(p max). If the $p$max[th] lag is insignificant, we reduce the model to an AR(p max-1). If the (p max-1)[th] lag is insignificant in the AR(p max-1) then drop it and use an AR($p$max-2)—and so forth. Generally, you should start with a fairly large choice for $p$max.

In the AR(p) with deterministic trend model we also have to worry about testing whether $\delta = 0$. This can be accomplished in the standard way by checking whether its P-value is less than the level of significance (for example, 0.05).[9] This test can be done at any stage, but it is common to carry it out after following the sequential procedure for choosing p.

A short summary of this testing strategy is outlined below:

- Step 1. Choose the maximum lag length, $p$max, that seems reasonable to you.
- Step 2. Estimate using OLS the AR($p$max) with deterministic trend model:

$$\Delta Y_t = \alpha + \rho Y_{t-1} + \gamma_1 \Delta Y_{t-1} + \ldots + \gamma_{p\max-1} \Delta Y_{t-p\max+1} + \delta t + e_t.$$

If the P-value for testing $\gamma_{p\max-1} = 0$ is less than the significance level you choose (for example, 0.05) then go to Step 5, using $p$max as lag length. Otherwise go on to the next step.
- Step 3. Estimate the AR($p$max $- 1$) model:

$$\Delta Y_t = \alpha + \rho Y_{t-1} + \gamma_1 \Delta Y_{t-1} + \ldots + \gamma_{p\max-2} \Delta Y_{t-p\max+2} + \delta t + e_t.$$

If the P-value for testing $\gamma_{p\max-2} = 0$ is less than the significance level you choose (0.05) then go to Step 5, using $p$max $- 2$ as lag length. Otherwise go on to the next step.
- Step 4. Repeatedly estimate lower order AR models until you find an AR(p) model where γ_{p-1} is statistically significant (or you run out of lags).
- Step 5. Now test for whether the deterministic trend should be omitted; that is, if the P-value for testing $\delta = 0$ is greater than the significance level you choose then drop the deterministic trend variable.

Example: US Personal Income (Continued)

If we carry out the preceding strategy on the personal income data, beginning with $p$max = 4, the model reduces to:

$$\Delta Y_t = \alpha + \rho Y_{t-1} + e_t.$$

Table 9.3 AR(1) model.

	Coefficient	Standard error	t-stat	P-value	Lower 95%	Upper 95%
Intercept	0.039	0.014	2.682	0.008	0.010	0.067
Y_{t-1}	−0.004	0.002	−2.130	0.035	−0.0077	−0.0003

That is, we first estimated an AR(4) with deterministic trend (see previous table) and found the coefficient on ΔY_{t-3} to be insignificant. Accordingly, we estimated an AR(3) with deterministic trend and found the coefficient on ΔY_{t-2} to be insignificant. We then dropped the latter variable and ran an AR(2), etc. Eventually, after finding the deterministic trend to be insignificant, we settled on the AR(1) model. OLS estimation results for this model are given in Table 9.3.

This is the table of results you might report in a paper or empirical project, including a brief but coherent explanation of the strategy that you used to arrive at this final specification.

These results lead us to the next, most important, testing question: Does Y contain a unit root? Remember that, if $\rho = 0$, then Y contains a unit root. In this case, the series must be differenced in the regression model (i.e. it is difference stationary). You may think that you can simply test $\rho = 0$ in the same manner as you tested the significance of the other coefficients. For instance, the P-value listed in the preceding table for the coefficient ρ is 0.035. Since this is less than 0.05, you may be tempted to conclude that ρ is not zero and, therefore, that Y does not have a unit root. *This is incorrect!* In hypothesis testing, ρ is different from other coefficients and we must treat it differently.

Testing involving ρ

To understand fully why you cannot carry out a unit root test of $\rho = 0$ in the same manner as we would test other coefficients requires you to have knowledge of statistics beyond that covered in this book. Suffice it to note here that most regression packages like Excel implicitly assume that all of the variables in the model are stationary when they calculate P-values. If the explanatory variable Y_{t-1} is nonstationary, its P-value will be incorrect. A correct way of testing for a unit root has been developed by two statisticians named Dickey and Fuller and is known as the *Dickey–Fuller test*.[10] They recommend using the familiar t-statistic for testing $\rho = 0$, but correcting the P-value.

We can motivate the Dickey–Fuller test in terms of the following: In Chapter 5 we said that testing could be done by comparing a test statistic (here the *t*-stat) with a critical value to determine whether the former was either "small" (in which case the hypothesis was accepted) or "large" (in which case the hypothesis was rejected). In the standard (stationary) case, the critical values are taken from statistical tables of the Student-*t* distribution. Dickey and Fuller demonstrated that in the unit root case, this is incorrect. They calculated the correct statistical tables from which to take critical values.

The previous paragraphs were meant to motivate why the standard testing procedure was incorrect. Admittedly, they are not very helpful in telling you what to do in practice. If you are going to work extensively with time series data, it is worthwhile to either:

- Use a computer software package that is more suitable for time series analysis than a spreadsheet. Many econometric computer packages will automatically provide you with correct critical values or P-values for your unit root test. As before, you will reject the unit root if the P-value is less than 0.05 or if the *t*-stat is greater than the critical value (in an absolute value sense).
- Read further in time series econometrics and learn how to use the Dickey–Fuller statistical tables.[11]

However, a rough rule of a thumb can be used that will not lead you too far wrong if your number of observations is moderately large (for example $T > 50$). This approximate rule is given in the following strategy for testing for a unit root:

1. Use the strategy outlined in Steps 1 to 5 above to estimate the AR(p) with deterministic trend model. Record the *t*-stat corresponding to ρ (the coefficient on Y_{t-1}).
2. If the final version of your model *includes a deterministic trend*, the Dickey–Fuller critical value is approximately −3.45. If the *t*-stat on ρ is more negative than −3.45, reject the unit root hypothesis and conclude that the series is stationary. Otherwise, conclude that the series has a unit root.
3. If the final version of your model *does not include a deterministic trend*, the Dickey–Fuller critical value is approximately −2.89. If the *t*-stat on ρ is more negative than −2.89, reject the unit root hypothesis and conclude that the series is stationary. Otherwise, conclude that the series has a unit root.[12]

In the previous example, the final version of the AR(p) model did not include a deterministic trend. The *t*-stat on ρ is −2.13, which is *not* more negative than −2.89. Hence we can *accept* the hypothesis that personal income does contain a unit root. Be careful using this crude rule of thumb when your *t*-stat is close to the critical values listed here.

Exercise 9.7

In this chapter we have recommended a strategy according to which you begin with an AR(p) with deterministic trend model, choose lag length (p), decide whether the deterministic trend should be included or excluded, and then test for a unit root. Carry out this strategy using the following series:

(a) Those in FIG95.XLS and FIG96.XLS (which you know are stationary).
(b) That in FIG97.XLS (which you know has a unit root).
(c) That in FIG98.XLS (which is trend stationary, but exhibits strong trending behavior).
(d) That in INCOME.XLS labeled "consumption."

Exercise 9.8

In Exercise 9.7, we tested for unit roots in many series. We noted that if a time series has one unit root, then its difference will be stationary. Verify that this is true for the series having unit roots in Exercise 9.7. That is, discuss how you would test to see if the *change* in the series has a unit root. Then carry out this test.

Some words of warning about unit root testing: the Dickey–Fuller test exhibits what statisticians refer to as *low power*. In other words, the test can make the mistake of finding a unit root even when none exists. Intuitively, trend stationary series can look a lot like unit root series (compare Figures 9.7 and 9.8) and it can be quite hard to tell them apart. Furthermore, other kinds of time series models can also appear to exhibit unit root behavior, when in actuality they do not have unit roots. A prime example is the time series model characterized by abrupt changes or breaks. These *structural breaks* can occur in macroeconomic time series models, and can be precipitated by events such as wars or crises in supply (for example, the OPEC oil embargo). Stock prices can exhibit structural breaks due to market crashes; and commodity prices, due to droughts and other natural disasters. All in all, structural breaks are potentially a worry for many types of time series data and some caution needs to be taken when interpreting the results of Dickey–Fuller tests.

Chapter Summary

1. Many time series exhibit trend behavior, while their differences do not exhibit such behavior.
2. The autocorrelation function is a common tool for summarizing the relationship between a variable and lags of itself.
3. Autoregressive models are regression models used for working with time series variables. Such models can be written in two ways: one with Y_t as the dependent variable, the other with ΔY_t as the dependent variable.
4. The distinction between stationary and nonstationary models is a crucial one.
5. Series with unit roots are the most common type of nonstationary series considered in economics.
6. If Y_t has a unit root then the AR(p) model with ΔY_t as the dependent variable can be estimated using OLS. Standard statistical results hold for all coefficients except the coefficient on Y_{t-1}.
7. The Dickey–Fuller test is a test for the presence of a unit root. It involves testing whether the coefficient on Y_{t-1} is equal to zero. Software packages such as Excel do not print out the correct P-value for this test.

Appendix 9.1: Mathematical Intuition for the AR(1) Model

Mathematical insight into the properties of the AR(1) model can be gained by writing it in a different way. For simplicity, we will set $\alpha = 0$ in order to focus on the role that lagged Y plays. Note that the AR(1) model will hold at any point in time so we can lag the whole AR(1) equation given in the body of the chapter and write:

$$Y_{t-1} = \phi Y_{t-2} + e_{t-1}.$$

If we substitute this expression for Y_{t-1} into the original AR(1) model we obtain:

$$Y_t = \phi^2 Y_{t-2} + e_t + \phi e_{t-1}.$$

Note that the previous expression depends on Y_{t-2}, but we can write:

$$Y_{t-2} = \phi Y_{t-3} + e_{t-2}$$

and substitute this expression for Y_{t-2} in the other equation. If this procedure is repeated we end up with an alternative expression for the AR(1) model:

$$Y_t = \phi^{t-1}Y_1 + \sum_{i=0}^{t-2} \phi^i e_{t-i}.$$

This expression looks complicated, but we can consider two special cases as a means of breaking it down. In the first of these we assume $\phi = 1$ and the previous equation reduces to:

$$Y_t = Y_1 + \sum_{i=0}^{t-2} e_{t-i}.$$

The important point to note about the two terms on the right-hand side of the previous equation is that they illustrate a long memory property; the value the time series starts at Y_1, which always enters the expression for Y_t, even if t becomes very large. That is, the time series "never forgets" where it started from. It also "never forgets" past errors (for example, e_2 always enters the above formula for Y_t even if t gets very large). It can be shown that the trending behavior of this model arises as a result of the second term, which says that current Y contains the sum of all past errors. Statisticians view these errors as random or "stochastic" and this model is often referred to as containing a *stochastic trend*. This is a key property of nonstationary series.

A second special case stands in contrast to the properties described above. If we suppose $|\phi| < 1$, we can see that ϕ^{t-1} will be decreasing at t increases (for example, if $\phi = 0.5$, then $\phi^2 = 0.25$, $\phi^{10} = 0.001$ and $\phi^{100} = 7.89 \times 10^{-31}$ and so forth). The influence of Y_1 and past errors on Y_t will gradually lessen as t increases and Y slowly "forgets the past." Y will not exhibit the long memory property we observed for the case where $\phi = 1$. This is a key property of stationary series.

Endnotes

1. Details about logarithms are given in any standard mathematical economics textbook and are also discussed in Chapters 2 and 4 (see especially the discussion on nonlinearity in regression). This footnote is intended to refresh your memory of this material. In macroeconomics, it is common to take the natural logarithm of the time series if it seems to be growing over time. If a series, Y, is growing at a roughly constant rate, then the time series plot of $\ln(Y)$ will approximate a straight line. In this common case, $\ln(Y)$ will generally be well behaved. Note also that in regressions of logged variables, the coefficients can be interpreted as elasticities. It can also be shown that $\ln(Y_t) - \ln(Y_{t-1})$ is approximately equal to the percentage change in Y between periods $t-1$ and t. For all these reasons, it is often convenient to work with logged series. Note that this log transformation is so common that many reports and papers will initially explain that the variables are logged but thereafter drop the explicit mentioning of the log transformation. For instance, an author might refer

to "the natural log of personal income" as "personal income" for brevity. We will follow this tradition in the examples in this book.

2. Since Y_0 is not known, ΔY_t runs from $t = 2, \ldots, T$ rather than from $t = 1, \ldots, T$. We focus on the empirically useful case of first differencing but we can define higher orders of differencing. For instance, the second difference of Y_t is defined as: $\Delta^2 Y_t = \Delta Y_t - \Delta Y_{t-1}$.

3. Put another way, if you knew personal income was today (let's say, $1 trillion), you could make a fairly good guess about roughly what it would be next quarter. That is, it might go up or down a couple of percentage points in an expansion or a recession but it is highly unlikely to be, say, $500 billion or $1.5 trillion. This ability to predict well is evidence of high correlation.

4. It is common practice to use Greek letters to indicate coefficients in regression models. We can, of course, use any Greek symbol we want to denote the slope coefficient in a regression. Here we have called it ϕ rather than β. We will reserve β (perhaps with a subscript) to indicate coefficients relating to the explanatory variable X.

5. Small statistical problems arise with OLS estimation of this model, particularly if the model is nonstationary or nearly so (ρ is close to zero). Nevertheless, OLS is still a very common estimation method for AR models, which suggests that these problems are not that important. If you take courses in econometrics or time series statistics in the future, you will undoubtedly learn about other estimators.

6. Justification for the term "stochastic trend" is given in the appendix to this chapter.

7. Many time series books devote a great deal of space to the topic of seasonality. One introductory text is Franses (1983).

8. This statement assumes that there is an intercept in the model.

9. This way of treating the deterministic term is commonly used in practice. But it is formally correct only if the series is trend stationary. If the series has a unit root then the distribution of the t-statistic no longer has a Student-t distribution and the P-value reported by an OLS regression command will be incorrect. If you are worried by this you can always simply include the deterministic trend (although this could make your unit root test less powerful).

10. Some authors use the term "Dickey–Fuller test" for testing for $\rho = 0$ in the AR(1) model and use the term "augmented Dickey–Fuller test" for testing in the AR(p) model (the basic unit root test is "augmented" with extra lags).

11. Chapter 16 of Hill, Griffiths and Judge (1997) is a good place to start.

12. Formally, -3.45 and -2.89 are the critical values for $T = 100$ using a 5% level of significance. Critical values for values of T between 50 and infinity are within 0.05 of these values.

References

Franses, P. H. (1983) *Time Series Models for Business Economics and Forecasting*, Cambridge University Press, Cambridge.

Hill, C., Griffiths, W. and Judge, G. (1997) *Undergraduate Econometrics*, John Wiley & Sons, Ltd, Chichester.

CHAPTER 10

Regression with Time Series Variables

In regression analysis, researchers are typically interested in measuring the effect of an explanatory variable or variables on a dependent variable. As mentioned in Chapter 8, this goal is complicated when the researcher uses time series data because an explanatory variable may influence a dependent variable with a time lag. This often necessitates the inclusion of lags of the explanatory variable in the regression. Furthermore, as discussed in Chapter 9, the dependent variable may be correlated with lags of itself, suggesting that lags of the dependent variable should also be included in the regression.

These considerations motivate the commonly used autoregressive distributed lag (or ADL) model, which includes lags of both the dependent and the explanatory variables:

$$Y_t = \alpha + \delta t + \phi_1 Y_{t-1} + \ldots + \phi_p Y_{t-p} + \beta_0 X_t + \beta_1 X_{t-1} + \ldots + \beta_q X_{t-q} + e_t.$$

In this model, the dependent variable, Y, depends on p lags of itself, the current value of an explanatory variable, X, as well as q lags of X. The model also allows for a deterministic trend (t). Since the model contains p lags of Y and q lags of X we denote it by ADL(p,q).[1] In this chapter, we focus on the case where there is only one explanatory variable, X. Note, however, that we could equally allow for many explanatory variables in the analysis.

Estimation and interpretation of the ADL(p,q) model depend on whether the series, X and Y, are stationary or not. We consider these two cases separately here. Note though, that we assume throughout that X and Y have the same stationarity properties; that is, that they either must *both* be stationary or *both* have a unit root. Intuitively, regression analysis involves using X to explain Y. If X's properties differ from Y's it becomes difficult for X to explain Y. For instance, it is hard for a stationary series to explain the stochastic trend variation in a unit root series. In practice this means that, before running any time series regression, you should examine the univariate properties of the variables you plan to use. In particular, you should carry out unit root tests along the lines described in Chapter 9 for every variable in your analysis.

Time Series Regression when X and Y Are Stationary

When X and Y are stationary, OLS estimation of the ADL(p,q) regression model can be carried out in the standard way described in Chapters 4–8. The significance of variables can be tested for using the t-stats and P-values. Such tests can, in turn, be used to select p and q, the number of lags of the dependent and explanatory variables, respectively. You should note, however, that the verbal interpretation of results is somewhat different from the standard case, as elaborated below.

In the case of the AR(p) model in Chapter 9, it proved convenient, both for OLS estimation and interpretation of results, for us to rewrite the model with ΔY as the dependent variable. Similar considerations hold for the ADL(p,q), which can be rewritten as:

$$\Delta Y_t = \alpha + \delta t + \rho Y_{t-1} + \gamma_1 \Delta Y_{t-1} + \ldots + \gamma_{p-1}\Delta Y_{t-p+1} + \theta X_t + \omega_1 \Delta X_t + \ldots + \omega_q \Delta X_{t-q+1} + e_t.$$

It should be emphasized that this model is the same as that in the original form of the ADL(p,q); it has merely undergone a few algebraic manipulations. Just as we had two different variants of the AR(p) model in Chapter 9, we now have two variants of the ADL(p,q) model. As before, we use new Greek letters for the coefficients in the regression to distinguish them from those in the original variant of the ADL(p,q) model.[2] This model may look complicated, but it is still nevertheless just a regression model.

As discussed in Chapter 9, macroeconomic time series are often highly correlated with their lags. This implies that the original form of the ADL model frequently runs into multicollinearity problems. With the rewritten form we will typically not encounter such problems. Most importantly, as we shall see, it has a further benefit, one that lies in the interpretation of the coefficients. For these reasons we will work mainly with this second variant of the ADL(p,q) model.

In Chapter 6, we discussed how to interpret regression coefficients, placing special emphasis on *ceteris paribus* conditions. Recall that we made statements of the form: "The coefficient measures the influence of lot size on the sales price of a house, *ceteris paribus*." In the ADL(p,q) model, such an interpretation can still be made but it is not that commonly done. How then can we interpret the coefficients in the ADL model? The most common way is through the concept of a *multiplier*. You are probably familiar with this idea since it is very common in the social sciences; economists, for instance, use a multiplier when they measure the effect of a change in government spending on national income. In the present context, this concept is a little more complicated because we have to specify a timing for the effect.

It is common to focus on the *long run* or *total multiplier*, which is what we will do here. To motivate this measure, suppose that X and Y are in an equilibrium or steady state, i.e. are not changing over time. All of a sudden, X changes by one unit, affecting Y, which starts to change, eventually settling down in the long run to a new equilibrium value. The difference between the old and new equilibrium values for Y can be interpreted as the long run effect of X on Y and is the long run multiplier. This multiplier is often of great interest for policymakers who want to know the eventual effects of their policy changes in various areas.

It is worth stressing that the long run multiplier measures the effect of a *permanent* change in X. That is, the story in the previous paragraph had X being at some value, then X changed permanently to a new level one unit higher than the original value. The long run multiplier measures the effect of this sort of change. In some cases, you might be interested in the effect of a temporary change in X (X starts at some original level, then increases by one unit for one period before going back to the original level the next). The long run multiplier does not measure the effect of this type of change. We can use the traditional "marginal effect" interpretation of regression coefficients for such temporary changes. The example in Chapter 8, which discussed the effect of safety training on accident losses, illustrates some ways of reporting the effect of a temporary change in the explanatory variable. (There we were interested in the effect of increasing safety training in one particular month on accident losses. We did not discuss the effect of increasing safety training permanently.)

It can be shown (although we will not prove it here),[3] that the long run multiplier for the ADL(p,q) model is:

$$-\frac{\theta}{\rho}.$$

In other words, only the coefficients on X_t and Y_{t-1} in the rewritten ADL model matter for long run behavior. This means that we can easily obtain an estimate of the long run multiplier.

It is worth repeating that we are assuming X and Y are stationary. In Chapter 9, we discussed how $\rho = 0$ in the AR(p) model implied the existence of a unit root. The ADL model is not the same as the AR model, but to provide some rough intuition, note that if $\rho = 0$ then the long run multiplier is infinite. In fact, it can be shown that for the model to be *stable*, then we must have $\rho < 0.$[4] In practice, if X and Y are stationary, this condition will be satisfied.

Example: The Effect of Computer Purchases on Sales

Over the last decade, companies have been purchasing more computers under the assumption that this will improve work force productivity. The purpose of this example is to investigate this assumption empirically. Data set COMPUTER. XLS contains data collected by a company for 98 months on their computer purchases and a variable reflecting the productivity of their sales force. In particular, the dependent and explanatory variables are:

- Y = the percentage change in sales relative to the previous month.
- X = the percentage change in computer purchases relative to the previous month.

The means of these two variables are 0.30% and 0.01% per month, indicating that this company has not increased spending on computers by much *on average*. Note, however, that this average hides wide variation. In some months computer spending increased considerably, while in other months it decreased. Assuming that both variables are stationary, we can estimate an ADL(2,2) model using OLS. Remember that, if the variables in a model are stationary, then the standard regression quantities (for example, OLS estimates, P-values, confidence intervals) can be calculated in the same way as in Chapters 4–8. Table 10.1 contains the results of this procedure.

Using the formula for the long-run multiplier, we can see that its OLS estimate is $-(0.125/-0.120) = 1.042$. There are different ways of expressing this informa-

Table 10.1 ADL(2,2) with deterministic trend model.

	Coefficient	Standard error	t-stat	P-value	Lower 95%	Upper 95%
Intercept	−0.028	0.041	−0.685	0.495	−0.110	0.054
Y_{t-1}	−0.120	0.013	−9.46	4.11E–15	−0.145	−0.095
ΔY_{t-1}	0.794	0.031	25.628	7.41E–43	0.733	0.856
X_t	0.125	0.048	2.605	0.011	0.030	0.221
ΔX_t	0.838	0.044	19.111	2.96E–33	0.750	0.925
ΔX_{t-1}	0.002	0.022	0.103	0.918	−0.041	0.046
time	0.001	0.001	0.984	0.328	−0.001	0.002

tion verbally (remember that the dependent and explanatory variables are measured as percentage changes):

- On average, computer purchases in this company have been increasing by 0.01% per month and sales by 0.30% per month. If the company decides that its computer budget should increase by 1.01% in each month (increase by one unit from 0.01 to 1.01), then in the long run sales should start increasing by 1.342% per month (the initial 0.30 plus the long run multiplier of 1.042).[5]
- The long run multiplier effect of computer purchases on sales is 1.042%.
- If X permanently increases by 1%, the equilibrium value of Y will increase by 1.042%.

The statistical information, though, indicates that this might not be a good model, because some of the explanatory variables are not significant (for example, the P-values for the coefficients on ΔX_{t-1} and the time trend both imply insignificance at the 5% level). This raises the issue of lag length selection in the ADL(p,q) model. We will not discuss this topic here, other than to note that the strategy for selecting q in the distributed lag model (see Chapter 8) and the strategy for selecting p in the AR(p) model (see Chapter 9) can be combined. There is no general convention about whether you should first select p, then q, then decide whether the deterministic trend should be included, or make another ordering (for example, select q, then p then the trend or select q then the trend then p, and so forth). As long as you are careful, you will not be led too far wrong in selecting a good model.

Exercise 10.1

Use the variables Y = percentage change in sales and X = percentage change in computer purchases in data set COMPUTER.XLS to decide whether the model estimated in the table above is a good one. In particular:

(a) Establish whether Y and X really do not have unit roots as was assumed in the example.
(b) Beginning with an ADL(3,3) model with deterministic trend, perform statistical tests to choose suitable lag lengths. Were good choices for p and q made in the example? Should we have included a deterministic trend?
(c) If you found the variables do not have unit roots and made different choices from p and q than the ones in the example, calculate the long run multiplier and compare to the result in the example.

Exercise 10.2

Data set COMPUTE1.XLS contains variables of the same form as COMPUTER. XLS, however for a company in a different industry.

(a) Repeat the analysis of Exercise 10.1 using the data in COMPUTE1.XLS. That is, verify that Y and X are stationary and then test to find a suitable ADL(p,q) specification.
(b) Calculate the long run multiplier for the model estimated in (a).

Time Series Regression when Y and X Have Unit Roots: Spurious Regression

For the remainder of this chapter, we will assume that Y and X have unit roots. In practice, of course, you would have to test whether this was the case using the Dickey–Fuller test of the previous chapter. We begin by focusing on the case of regression models without lags, then proceed with models similar to the ADL(p,q) model.

Suppose we are interested in estimating the following regression:

$$Y_t = \alpha + \beta X_t + e_t.$$

If Y and X contain unit roots, then OLS estimation of this regression can yield results that are completely wrong. For instance, even if the true value of β is 0, OLS can yield an estimate, $\hat{\beta}$, which is very different from zero. Statistical tests (using the t-stat or P-value) may indicate that β is not zero. Furthermore, if $\beta = 0$, then the R^2 should be zero. In fact, the R^2 will often be quite large.

To put it another way: *if Y and X have unit roots then all the usual regression results might be misleading and incorrect.* This is the so-called *spurious regression problem*. We do not have the statistical tools to prove that this problem occurs,[6] but it is important to stress the practical implication. With the one exception of cointegration that we note below, *you should never run a regression of Y on X if the variables have unit roots.*

Time Series Regression when Y and X Have Unit Roots: Cointegration

The one time where you do not have to worry about the spurious regression problem occurs when Y and X are *cointegrated*. This case not only surmounts the spurious regression problem but also provides some nice economic intuition. Cointegration has received a great deal of attention recently in the economics literature so it is worthwhile to discuss the topic in detail here.

Some intuition for cointegration can be obtained by considering the errors in the above regression model: $e_t = Y_t - \alpha - \beta X_t$. Written in this way, it is clear that the errors are just a linear combination of Y and X. However, X and Y both exhibit nonstationary unit root behavior such that you would expect the error to also exhibit nonstationary behavior. (After all, if you add two things with a certain property together the result generally tends to have that property.) The error does indeed usually have a unit root. Statistically, it is this unit root in the error term that causes the spurious regression problem. However, it is possible that the unit roots in Y and X "cancel each other out" and that the resulting error is stationary. In this special case, called *cointegration*, the spurious regression problem vanishes and it is valid to run a regression of Y on X. To summarize: *if* Y *and* X *have unit roots, but some linear combination of them is stationary, then we can say that* Y *and* X *are cointegrated.*[7]

The intuition behind cointegration is clearest for the case where $\alpha = 0$ and $\beta = 1$. Keep this in mind when you read the following statements. Remember also that variables with unit roots tend to exhibit trend behavior (for example they can be increasing steadily over time and therefore can become very large).

- If X and Y have unit roots then they have stochastic trends. However, if they are cointegrated, the error does not have such a trend. In this case, the error will not get too large and Y and X will not diverge from one another; Y and X, in other words, will trend together. This fact motivates other jargon used to refer to cointegrated time series. You may hear references to them as either having *common trends* or *cotrending*.
- If we are talking about an economic model involving an equilibrium concept, e is the equilibrium error. If Y and X are cointegrated then the equilibrium error stays small. However, if Y and X are not cointegrated then the equilibrium error will have a trend and departures from equilibrium become increasingly large over time. If such departures from equilibrium occur, then many would hesitate to say that the equilibrium is a meaningful one.
- If Y and X are cointegrated then there is an equilibrium relationship between them. If they are not, then no equilibrium relationship exists. (This is essentially just a restatement of the previous point.)
- In the real world, it is unlikely that an economic system will ever be in precise equilibrium since shocks and unexpected changes to it will always occur. However, departures from equilibrium should not be too large and there should always be a tendency to return to equilibrium after a shock occurs. Hence, if an economic model that implies an equilibrium relationship exists between Y and X is correct then we should observe Y and X as being cointegrated.
- If Y and X are cointegrated then their trends will cancel each other out.

To summarize: if cointegration is present, then not only do we avoid the spurious regression problem but we also have important economic information (for example, that an equilibrium relationship exists or that two series are trending together).

Example: Cointegration between the Prices of Two Goods

Economic theory suggests that similar goods should be close substitutes for each other and therefore their prices should be cointegrated. As an example, ORANGE. XLS contains time series data for 181 months on the prices of regular oranges and organic oranges in a certain market.[8] These are two closely related products, but many consumers are willing to pay somewhat more for organic oranges. We might expect the prices of these two goods to be cointegrated, because the difference in prices between the two cannot increase too much.

Many people are willing to pay slightly more for organic products but if the premium becomes too large they will switch to regular oranges. For instance, many consumers may be willing to pay an extra 20 pence per pound to receive the supposed health benefits but not 40 pence per pound. Thus, if the price of organic products rises relative to regular products too much, many people will stop buying organic products and their price will fall. On the other hand, if the price of organic oranges falls to roughly the same price as regular oranges, few would probably eat regular oranges. In this case, the price of regular oranges would drop.

In short, although the prices of these two products will fluctuate due to the vagaries of supply and demand, market forces will always keep the price difference between the two goods roughly constant. This is the intuition behind cointegration.

Figure 10.1 plots these two series and provides strong visual evidence that the prices of these two types of oranges are indeed cointegrated. That is, even though the prices of organic oranges are higher than regular ones, the general trend behavior in the two variables looks quite similar.

There are many other examples of cointegration, especially in macroeconomics. Short-term and long-term interest rates, for example, may not move precisely together in the short run but it is unlikely that they will deviate too much in the long run. If long-term interest rates are significantly higher than short-term rates, then traders will buy long term and sell short term, forcing the former down and the latter up. This example implies cointegration. Two prominent economic theories that imply the presence of cointegration between macroeconomic variables are the theory of purchasing power parity and the permanent income hypothesis. Even theories of money demand have been used to justify cointegration findings. All in all, cointegration is an important concept for macroeconomists.

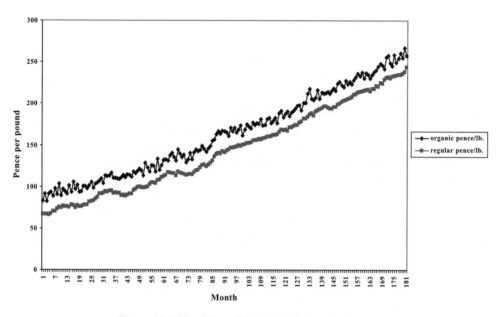

Figure 10.1 The Prices of Regular and Organic Oranges.

Estimation and testing with cointegrated variables

As mentioned above, if Y and X are cointegrated, then the spurious regression problem does not apply; consequently, we can run an OLS regression of Y on X and obtain valid results. Furthermore, *the coefficient from this regression is the long run multiplier*. Thus, insofar as interest centers on the long run multiplier, then estimation with cointegrated variables is very easy.

Before using results from this so-called *cointegrating regression*, it is important to verify that Y and X are in fact cointegrated. Remember that if they are not cointegrated, then the spurious regression problem holds and the results you obtain can be completely meaningless. An examination of time series plots like Figure 10.1, can be quite informative, but remember that visual examinations of graphs should not be considered substitutes for a statistical test.

Many tests for cointegration exist and some computer software packages allow you to perform very sophisticated procedures at a touch of the button. Spreadsheets like Excel do not allow you to carry out these tests. Fortunately, using the regression capabilities of these spreadsheet packages coupled with some data manipulation, we can carry out at least one test for cointegration called the Engle–Granger test. A more sophisticated cointegration test, called the Johansen test, is described in Chapter 11. In many cases, the Johansen test performs better than the Engle–Granger test.

However, the Johansen test is more complicated and cannot easily be carried out using a spreadsheet such as Excel.

The test for cointegration described here is referred to as the Engle–Granger test, after the two econometricians who developed it. It is based on the regression of Y on X. Remember that, if cointegration occurs, then the errors from this regression will be stationary. Conversely, if cointegration does not occur, then the errors will have a unit root. Given the close relationship between the errors and the residuals,[9] it is reasonable to examine the properties of the residuals in order to investigate the presence of cointegration. In Chapter 9 we discussed testing for a unit root in a time series variable. Here, we test for a unit root in the *residuals* using the same techniques. In particular, the test for cointegration involves the following steps:

1. Run the regression of Y on X and save the residuals.
2. Carry out a unit root test on the residuals (without including a deterministic trend).
3. If the unit root hypothesis is rejected then conclude that Y and X are cointegrated. However, if the unit root is accepted then conclude cointegration does not occur.

It is worthwhile to stress that the Engle–Granger test is based on a unit root test, so that the problems described at the end of Chapter 9 will arise. In other words, although the cointegration test is based on the t-statistic from a regression (in this case, one involving the residuals from a preliminary regression), you cannot use the P-value printed out by nonspecialist packages like Excel. The correct critical values are published in many places (and are slightly different from the critical values for the Dickey–Fuller test). If you are going to do a great deal of work with time series data it is a good idea for you to spend the time to learn more about cointegration testing and look up these correct critical values. However, for many purposes it is acceptable to use the same rules of thumb recommended in Chapter 9.

Note that, when testing for a unit root in the residuals we typically do not include a deterministic trend. If such a trend were included it could mean the errors could be growing steadily over time. This would violate the idea of cointegration (the idea that the system always returns to equilibrium and, hence, that errors never grow too big).

In light of these considerations, when carrying out the unit root test on the residuals (see Step 2 above), use −2.89 as a critical value against which to compare the t-statistic. If the t-statistic on ρ in the unit root regression involving the residuals is more negative than −2.89, conclude that the errors do not have a unit root and hence that Y and X are cointegrated.

Note also that in the Dickey–Fuller test, we test the hypothesis that $\rho = 0$ (the null hypothesis is the unit root). In the cointegration test, we use the Dickey–Fuller methodology but cointegration is found if we *reject* the unit root hypothesis for the residuals. In other words, the null hypothesis in the Engle–Granger test is "no cointegration" and we conclude "cointegration is present" only if we reject this hypothesis.

It is also worth stressing that, as the Engle–Granger test is based on the Dickey–Fuller test, it suffers from the difficulties noted at the end of Chapter 9. That is, the Engle–Granger test has low power and can be misleading if structural breaks occur in the data.

Example: Cointegration between the Prices of Two Goods (Continued)

Let us suppose that the two price series both have unit roots. If we run a regression of Y = the price of organic oranges on X = the price of regular oranges using the data in ORANGE.XLS we obtain the following fitted regression model:

$$\hat{Y}_t = 20.686 + 0.996X_t$$

The strategy above suggests that we should next carry out a unit root test on the residuals, u_t, (which computer packages like Excel allow you to create) from this regression. The first step in doing this is to correctly select the lag length using the sequential strategy outlined in Chapter 9. Suppose we have done so and conclude that an AR(1) specification for the residuals is appropriate. The Dickey–Fuller strategy suggests we should regress Δu_t on u_{t-1}. We obtain the results shown in Table 10.2.

Our rule of thumb says that we should compare the t-stat, for the coefficient on u_{t-1}, which is −14.5, to a critical value of −2.89. The former is more negative than the latter so we reject the unit root hypothesis and conclude that the residuals do not have a unit root. In other words, we conclude that two price series are indeed cointegrated.

We have found cointegration so we do not need to worry about the spurious regression problem. Hence, we can proceed to an interpretation of our coefficients without worrying that the OLS estimates are meaningless. The fact that

Table 10.2 AR(1) using the errors from the cointegrating regression.

	Coefficient	Standard error	t-stat	P-value	Lower 95%	Upper 95%
Intercept	0.024	0.292	0.083	0.934	−0.552	0.600
u_{t-1}	−1.085	0.075	−14.500	5.8E–32	−1.233	−0.938

$\hat{\alpha} = 20.69$ in the original regression of Y on X reflects the premium of roughly 20 pence per pound that consumers are willing to pay for organic over regular oranges. Furthermore, the long run multiplier is 0.996. This indicates that, in the long run, an increase in the price of regular oranges by one pence would cause an increase in the price of organic oranges of 0.996 pence.

Exercise 10.3

Use the data in ORANGE.XLS to complete the previous example. In particular:

(a) Do a Dickey–Fuller test to verify that both orange price series have unit roots.

(b) Do a sequential test to verify that the Dickey–Fuller test on the residuals was done correctly. That is, is an AR(1) model for the residuals appropriate?

Exercise 10.4

Excel file LONGGDP.XLS contains annual data on real GDP per capita for four of the largest English-speaking countries (USA, UK, Canada and Australia) for the years 1870–1993.[10] Investigate whether there are common movements or trends between GDP in these different countries. In particular, you should go through the following steps to answer this question:

(a) Plot all the data in one time series graph and discuss your results. (For example, does GDP seem to be trending in all countries? Do there appear to be common trend patterns across countries?)

(b) Carry out unit root tests on the time series. Discuss your findings.

(c) For the time series that have unit roots, carry out cointegration tests. Begin by carrying out cointegration tests between different combinations of two countries (for example, first do USA and the UK, then USA and Canada, and so forth). Does GDP seem to be cointegrated between any pair of countries?

(d) In this chapter on cointegration, we have focused on the case considered in part (c), namely, where there are only two variables. Using $Y =$ USA and the other countries as explanatory variables, test for cointegration among *all* the time series. Discuss your results.

Exercise 10.5

Use the data on Y = personal income and X = personal consumption in INCOME. XLS.

(a) Use Dickey–Fuller tests to verify that Y and X have unit roots.
(b) Run a regression of Y on X and save the errors.
(c) Carry out a unit root test on the residuals using an AR(1) model.
(d) Carry out a unit root test on the residuals using an AR(2) model.
(e) Carry out a unit root test on the residuals using an AR(3) model.
(f) What can you conclude about the presence of cointegration between Y and X?[11]

Time Series Regression when Y and X Are Cointegrated: The Error Correction Model

In empirical applications, it is often vital to establish that Y and X are cointegrated. As emphasized above, cointegration can be related to the idea of Y and X trending together or bearing an equilibrium relationship to each other. A second important task is to estimate the long run multiplier or the long run influence of X on Y. Both cointegration testing and estimation of the long run multiplier can be done using the regression of Y on X. Accordingly, in many empirical projects you may never need to move beyond this simple regression. However, in some cases, you may be interested in understanding short run behavior in a manner that is not possible using only the regression of Y on X. In such cases, we can estimate an *error correction model* (or ECM for short).

An important theorem, known as the *Granger Representation Theorem*, says that if Y and X are cointegrated, then the relationship between them can be expressed as an ECM. In this section, we will assume Y and X are cointegrated. Error correction models have a long tradition in time series econometrics, and the Granger Representation Theorem highlights their popularity. In order to understand the properties of ECMs let us begin with the following simple version:

$$\Delta Y_t = \varphi + \lambda e_{t-1} + \omega_0 \Delta X_t + \varepsilon_t,$$

where e_{t-1} is the error obtained from the regression model involving Y and X. That is, $e_{t-1} = Y_{t-1} - \alpha - \beta X_{t-1}$ and ε_t is the error in the ECM model. Note that, if we know e_{t-1}, then the ECM is just a regression model (although we introduce some new Greek letters to make sure that the coefficients and error in this model do not become confused with those in other regression models). That is, ΔY_t is the dependent variable and e_{t-1} and ΔX_t are explanatory variables. Furthermore, we assume that $\lambda < 0$.[12]

To aid in interpreting the ECM, consider the implications of ΔY_t being its dependent variable. As emphasized throughout this book, the regression model attempts to use explanatory variables to explain the dependent variable. With this in mind, note that the ECM says that ΔY depends on ΔX—an intuitively sensible point (changes in X cause Y to change). In addition, ΔY_t depends on e_{t-1}. This latter aspect is unique to the ECM and gives it its name.

Remember that e can be thought of as an equilibrium error. If it is nonzero, then the model is out of equilibrium. Consider the case where $\Delta X_t = 0$ and e_{t-1} is positive. The latter implies that Y_{t-1} is too high to be in equilibrium (Y_{t-1} is above its equilibrium level of $\alpha + \beta X_{t-1}$). As $\lambda < 0$ the term λe_{t-1} will be negative and so ΔY_t will be negative. In other words, if Y_{t-1} is above its equilibrium level, then it will start falling in the next period and the equilibrium error will be "corrected" in the model; hence the term "error correction model."[13] In the case where $e_{t-1} < 0$ the opposite will hold (Y_{t-1} is below its equilibrium level, hence $\lambda e_{t-1} > 0$, which causes ΔY_t to be positive, triggering Y to rise in period t).

In sum, the ECM has both long run and short run properties built into it. The former properties are embedded in the e_{t-1} term (remember β is still the long run multiplier and the errors are from the regression involving Y and X). The short run behavior is partially captured by the equilibrium error term, which says that, if Y is out of equilibrium, it will be pulled towards it in the next period. Further aspects of short run behavior are captured by the inclusion of ΔX_t as an explanatory variable. This term implies that, if X changes, the equilibrium value of Y will also change and that Y will also change accordingly. All in all, the ECM has some very sensible properties that are closely related to economic equilibrium concepts.

The ECM also has some nice statistical properties that mean that we do not have to worry about the spurious regression problem. Y and X both have unit roots; hence ΔY and ΔX are stationary. Furthermore, since Y and X are cointegrated, the equilibrium error is stationary. Hence, the dependent variable and all explanatory variables in the ECM are stationary. This property means that we can use OLS estimation and carry out testing using t-statistics and P-values in the standard way described in Chapter 5.

The only new statistical issue in the ECM arises due to the inclusion of e_{t-1} as an explanatory variable. The errors in a model are not directly observed. This raises the issue of how they can be used as an explanatory variable in a regression. Some sophisticated econometric techniques have been developed to estimate the ECM but the simplest thing to do is merely to replace the unknown errors by the residuals from the regression of Y on X (replace e_{t-1} by u_{t-1}). That is, a simple technique based on two OLS regressions proceeds as follows:

- Step 1: run a regression of Y on X and save the residuals.
- Step 2: run a regression of ΔY on ΔX *and the residuals from Step 1 lagged one period.*

It should be emphasized that before carrying out this two-step estimation procedure for the ECM, *you must verify that* Y *and* X *have unit roots and are cointegrated using the Dickey–Fuller and Engle–Granger tests.*

So far we have discussed the simplest error correction model. In practice, just as the ADL(p,q) model has lags of the dependent and explanatory variables, the ECM may also have lags.[14] It may also have a deterministic trend. Incorporating these features into the ECM yields:

$$\Delta Y_t = \varphi + \delta t + \lambda e_{t-1} + \gamma_1 \Delta Y_{t-1} + \ldots + \gamma_p \Delta Y_{t-p} + \omega_0 \Delta X_t + \ldots + \omega_q \Delta X_{t-q} + \varepsilon_t.$$

This expression is still in the form of a regression model and can be estimated using the two-step procedure described above. The adjustment to equilibrium intuition also holds for this model. The decisions on whether to include a deterministic trend and on which precise values for p and q are appropriate can be made using t-statistics and P-values in the same manner as for the ADL model. In fact, the ECM is closely related to the ADL model in that it is a restricted version of it.

Example: Cointegration between the Prices of Two Goods (Continued)

In the previous part of this example, we found that the variables, Y = price of organic oranges and X = the price of regular oranges, were cointegrated. This suggests that we can estimate an error correction model. To do so, we begin by running a regression of Y on X and saving the residuals (which was done in the previous part of the example). The residuals, u_t, can then be included in the following regression (in lagged form):

$$\Delta Y_t = \varphi + \lambda u_{t-1} + \omega_0 \Delta X_t + \varepsilon_t$$

Table 10.3 gives results from OLS estimation of this model.

The statistical information can be interpreted in the standard way. We can say that (with the exception of the intercept) all the coefficients are strongly statistically significant (because their P-values are much less than 0.05).

We noted before that $\hat{\beta} = 0.996$ and this is the estimate of the long run multiplier. The point estimates in the table of λ and ω_0 summarize the short run properties. To aid in interpretation note that all variables in the model are measured in pence. The coefficient on u_{t-1} of −1.085 measures how much Y responds to equilibrium errors. This coefficient is negative, so positive errors tend to cause ΔY to be negative and hence Y to fall. In particular, an equilibrium error of 1 pence tends to cause Y to fall by 1.085 pence in the next period, *ceteris paribus*.

Table 10.3 Simple error-correction model.

	Coefficient	Standard error	t-stat	P-value	Lower 95%	Upper 95%
Intercept	−0.023	0.342	−0.068	0.946	−0.700	0.654
u_{t-1}	−1.085	0.075	−14.458	8.69E–32	−1.233	−0.937
ΔX_t	1.044	0.182	5.737	4.11E–08	0.685	1.403

This is a very quick adjustment to an equilibrium error! The coefficient on $\Delta X_t = 1.044$. Imagine, in other words, what would happen if X were to remain unchanged for some time ($\Delta X = 0$) but then suddenly were to change by 1 pence. The ECM implies that Y would instantly change by 1.044 pence. In other words, the price of organic oranges responds very quickly to price changes in regular oranges. Perhaps since oranges are perishable, grocers will almost immediately react to price changes in regular oranges in order to make sure that their organic oranges do not remain unsold.

Exercise 10.6

Use the data in ORANGE.XLS to check the previous example. In particular, does the ECM have enough lags of both ΔX and ΔY?

Exercise 10.7

Use the data on $Y =$ consumption and $X =$ personal income from INCOME. XLS. Assume (perhaps incorrectly) that Y and X are cointegrated.

(a) Estimate an error correction model. Begin with a model containing a deterministic trend and $p = q = 4$ and then carry out statistical tests to find an appropriate ECM.

(b) Discuss your results. Pay particular attention to your estimate of λ and discuss what it tells you about the speed of adjustment to equilibrium.

Time Series Regression when Y and X Have Unit Roots but Are NOT Cointegrated

You may encounter instances where unit root tests indicate that your time series have unit roots, but the Engle–Granger test indicates that the series are not cointegrated. That is, the series may not be trending together and may not have an equilibrium relationship. *In these cases, you should not run a regression of* Y *on* X *due to the spurious regression problem.* The presence of such characteristics suggests that you should rethink your basic model and include other explanatory variables. Instead of working with Y and X themselves, for example, you could difference them. (Remember that if Y and X have one unit root, then ΔY and ΔX should be stationary.)

In this case, you could work with the *changes* in your time series and estimate the ADL model using the techniques described at the beginning of this chapter. In other words, you may wish to estimate the original ADL model, but with changes in the variables:

$$\Delta Y_t = \alpha + \delta t + \phi_1 \Delta Y_{t-1} + \ldots + \phi_p \Delta Y_{t-p} + \beta_0 \Delta X_t + \ldots + \beta_q \Delta X_{t-q} + e_t$$

For most time series variables, this specification should not suffer from multicollinearity problems. Alternatively, you may wish to estimate the second variant of the ADL model based on the differenced data. But if you are working with the differences of your time series and then use the variant of the ADL that involves differencing the data you end up with second differenced data:

$$\Delta^2 Y_t = \alpha + \delta t + \rho \Delta Y_{t-1} + \gamma_1 \Delta^2 Y_{t-1} + \ldots + \gamma_{p-1} \Delta^2 Y_{t-p+1} +$$
$$\theta \Delta X_t + \omega_1 \Delta^2 X_t + \ldots + \omega_q \Delta^2 X_{t-q+1} + e_t,$$

where $\Delta^2 Y_t = \Delta Y_t - \Delta Y_{t-1}$. OLS estimation and testing can be done in either of these models in a straightforward way. Whatever route is chosen, it is important to emphasize that the interpretation of regression results will likewise change.

More specifically, let us suppose $Y = $ exchange rates and $X = $ interest rates. If Y and X are cointegrated, or if both are stationary, we can obtain an estimate of the long run effect of a small change in interest rates on exchange rates. If Y and X are neither stationary nor cointegrated and we estimate either of the two preceding equations, we can obtain an estimate of the long run effect of *a small change in the change of interest rates on the change in exchange rates.* This may or may not be a sensible thing to measure depending on the particular empirical exercise.

Note that, in the example at the beginning of this chapter on the effect of computer purchases on sales, the variables were already in percentage changes. If we had begun with $Y = $ sales and $X = $ computer purchases we would have found they had unit roots but were not cointegrated. Hence, we would have run into the spurious regressions problem. This was why we worked with percentage changes.

Exercise 10.8

Excel data set WP.XLS contains annual data from 1857–1987 on X = wages and Y = the consumer price index in the UK.[15] It is commonly thought that wage pressures are a prime cause of inflation. You wish to investigate this claim by carrying out a time series analysis on the data. In particular,

(a) Construct a time series plot of wages and prices. Do they both seem to be trending? Do they seem to be trending together?
(b) Carry out unit root tests on X and Y. You should find evidence that they both have unit roots.
(c) Carry out a cointegration test on X and Y. You should find evidence that they are *not* cointegrated.
(d) Difference the data to obtain ΔX and ΔY. Repeat parts (a) and (b) with these new variables. You should find that they do not have unit roots.
(e) Specify and estimate an ADL(p,q) model using the new variables, ΔX and ΔY. Discuss your results. Note that the change in the log of a price level is inflation. That is, ΔX and ΔY can be interpreted as wage and price inflation, respectively.

Chapter Summary

1. If all variables are stationary, then an ADL(p,q) model can be estimated using OLS. Statistical techniques are all standard.
2. A variant of the ADL model is often used to avoid potential multicollinearity problems and provide a straightforward estimate of the long run multiplier.
3. If all variables are nonstationary, great care must be taken in the analysis due to the spurious regression problem
4. If all variables are nonstationary but the regression error is stationary, then cointegration occurs.
5. If cointegration is present, the spurious regression problem does not occur.
6. Cointegration is an attractive concept for economists because it implies that an equilibrium relationship exists.
7. Cointegration can be tested using the Engle–Granger test. This test is a Dickey–Fuller test on the residuals from the cointegrating regression.

8. If the variables are cointegrated then an error correction model can be used. This model captures short run behavior in a way that the cointegrating regression cannot.

9. If the variables have unit roots but are not cointegrated you should not work with them directly. Rather you should difference them and estimate an ADL model using the differenced variables. The interpretation of these models can be awkward.

Endnotes

1. Formally, we should call this the ADL(p,q) *with deterministic trend* model. However, we will omit the latter phrase for the sake of simplicity. In practice, you will find that the deterministic trend is often insignificant and will be omitted from the model anyway. Note also that some textbooks abbreviate "autoregressive distributed lag" as ARDL instead of ADL.

2. The coefficients involving the lags of the dependent variable, ρ, γ_1, ... , γ_{p-1} are exactly the same functions of φ_1, ... , φ_p as in Chapter 9. The $q + 1$ coefficients θ, ω_1, ... , ω_q are similar functions of β_0, β_1, ... , β_q.

3. Deriving the long run multiplier from an ADL model is not difficult and you should try it as an exercise. Here are some hints. Assume that the model has been in equilibrium for a long time and that equilibrium values of X and Y are given by X^* and Y^*, respectively. Now assume X is increased permanently to $X^* + 1$ and work out what happens to Y.

4. "Stable" is a statistical term that we will not formally define in this book. It can, however, be interpreted in a common-sense way: If a model is stable, it implies that the time series variables will not be exploding or stochastically trending over time. In essence, it is a very similar concept to stationarity.

5. It is worth emphasizing that 1.042 is an estimate of the long run multiplier. A confidence interval could be calculated but this would involve derivations beyond the scope of this book.

6. You may think that the spurious regression problem occurs as a result of an omitted variable bias when lags are left out of an ADL model. But there is more to it than this. Even when no lags belong in the model, the spurious regression problem arises.

7. To motivate the word "cointegration," note that if X and Y have unit roots, then it is common jargon to say that they are *integrated*. Adding the word "co" to emphasize that the unit roots are similar or common in X and Y yields "cointegration."

8. Organic oranges are grown without the use of chemical pesticides and fertilizers. Many feel that such oranges are healthier than regular oranges.

9. Remember that the errors are deviations from the true regression line while residuals are deviations from the estimated regression line (see Chapter 4). Our notation for OLS residuals is u_t.

10. Note that each of these time series is an index (with 1913 = 100). If you look at the data, you will see, for example, that the value of the data for the UK is 64.85 in 1870. The fact that the variables are indices means that we *cannot* interpret the value of each observation as saying, for instance, that GDP per capita in the UK was £64.85 in 1870. We can, however, interpret changes in the series as GDP growth rates. More importantly for cointegration analysis, the trend in the index for each country accurately reflects trend behavior in GDP per capita.

11. If you have done this question correctly, you will find that cointegration does seem to be present for some lag lengths but not for others. This is a common occurrence in practical applications, so do not be dismayed by it. Economic theory and time series plots of the data definitely indicate that cointegration should occur between Y and X. But the Engle–Granger test does not consistently indicate cointegration. One possible explanation is that the Engle–Granger and Dickey–Fuller tests are known to have low power.

12. We will not formally prove why this condition must hold except to say that it is a stability condition of the sort discussed in the context of the ADL(p,q) model.

13. This intuition motivates the stability condition $\lambda < 0$, which ensures that equilibrium errors are corrected. If λ is positive then equilibrium errors will be magnified.

14. Note that we do not include more lags of e_{t-1} as explanatory variables due to an implication of the Granger Representation Theorem, which we will not discuss here.

15. These data are logged.

CHAPTER 11

Applications of Time Series Methods in Macroeconomics and Finance

Chapters 8–10 developed several different regression models for time series variables. For many cases, knowledge of these models and the relevant techniques (such as cointegration tests) is enough to allow you to write a report and gain a good basic understanding of the properties of the data. However, in some cases, a knowledge of slightly more sophisticated methods is necessary. Fortunately, many such cases can be shown to be simple extensions of the methods learned in earlier chapters. In this chapter we discuss two important such extensions. First we discuss financial volatility. Next, we discuss methods that involve more than one equation. To motivate why multiple equation methods are important, we begin by discussing *Granger causality* before discussing the most popular class of multiple-equation models: so-called *vector autoregressive* (VAR) models.[1] Vector autoregressions can be used to investigate Granger causality, but are also useful for many other things in economics. Furthermore, an extension of a VAR related to the concepts of cointegration and error correction is discussed in this chapter. This is called the *vector error correction model* (VECM) and it allows us to introduce another popular test for cointegration called the *Johansen test*.

Volatility in Asset Prices

We begin our discussion of volatility in asset prices informally, staying with familiar regression methods. We then discuss a very popular method for estimating financial volatility called *autoregressive conditional heteroskedasticity* (ARCH). The ARCH model shares a great deal of intuition with the regression model (including the AR model), but is not exactly the same as a regression model. Accordingly, methods like OLS cannot be used with ARCH. However, many computer software packages (such as Stata, E-views or Microfit) can estimate ARCH models. So the fact that the theory underlying the estimation of ARCH models is difficult need not preclude your using them in practice. This chapter also discusses some extensions of ARCH models.

Volatility in asset prices: introduction

To provide some intuition, recall our discussion of the random walk model in Chapter 9. We defined the model as:

$$Y_t = Y_{t-1} + e_t$$

or

$$\Delta Y_t = e_t.$$

We then noted that there were good reasons for believing that such a model might be appropriate for measuring economic phenomena like stock prices or exchange rate.

The simple random walk model is a little unreasonable as a description of stock price behavior since stocks do appreciate in value over time. A slightly more realistic model is:

$$\Delta Y_t = \alpha + e_t$$

This model can be interpreted as implying that stock prices, on average, increase by α per period, but are otherwise unpredictable. This is the random walk with drift model, which adds an intercept to the random walk model, thus allowing stock prices to "drift" upwards over time (if $\alpha > 0$). Equivalently, it says that stock returns are on average α but are otherwise unpredictable.

In the rest of this section, we will assume that the random walk model for an asset price is the correct one. That is, we will assume that either the asset price follows a pure random walk or that it follows a random walk with drift and that we have taken deviations from the mean. To avoid confusion, we will let Δy_t indicate the series with deviations from means taken ($\Delta y_t = \Delta Y_t - \Delta \bar{Y}$, where $\Delta \bar{Y} = \Sigma \Delta Y_t / T$). Remember that taking deviations from the mean implies that there is no intercept in the model (see the appendix to Chapter 4). Thus, even if the asset price is drifting upwards over time we can ignore the drift term and simply write, $\Delta y_t = e_t$.

We have not yet formally defined what we mean by "volatility." The ARCH model (discussed below) provides such a formal definition for volatility. But before looking at the ARCH model, it is useful to discuss volatility more intuitively. One way to think about volatility is to note that it is possible to simply use Δy_t^2 as an estimate of volatility at time t. To motivate this choice, note that high volatility is associated with big changes, either in a positive or in a negative direction. Since any number squared becomes positive, large rises or large falls in the price of an asset will imply Δy_t^2 is positive and large. In contrast, in stable times the asset price will not be changing much and Δy_t^2 will be small. Hence, our measure of volatility will be small in stable times and large in chaotic times.

An alternative motivation for our measure of volatility can be obtained by recalling some material from Chapter 2. There we stressed that variance is a measure of the volatility of a variable. In general, it is common practice to equate the two and use variance as a measure of volatility. But using the variance as a measure of volatility presents problems in the present context. A key point here is that we want to allow the volatility of an asset to change over time. The volatility at time t might be different from that at time $t-1$ or $t+1$, etc. In Chapter 2, we used all observations to provide one estimate of the variance. Here we can use only the observation at time t to provide an estimate of the variance at time t. (In other words, it makes no sense to use data at time $t+1$ to estimate the variance at time t because the variance might be different in the two periods.)

If you:

- note that we can only use one observation to estimate the variance;
- note that we have assumed the data is in deviations from mean form and, hence, has mean zero; and
- use the formula for the variance from Chapter 2

then you obtain Δy_t^2 as an estimate of the variance.[2]

You can calculate this measure of volatility of an asset price quite easily in any spreadsheet or statistical computer package simply by differencing the stock price data, taking deviations from means and then squaring it. Once this is done, you will have a new time series variable—volatility—which you can analyze using the tools introduced earlier. Autoregressive models are commonly used to model "clustering in volatility," which is often present in financial time series data. Consider, for instance, an AR(1) model that uses volatility as the time series variable of interest:

$$\Delta y_t^2 = \alpha + \phi \Delta y_{t-1}^2 + e_t.$$

This model has volatility in a period depending on volatility in a previous period. If, for instance, $\phi > 0$ then if volatility was unusually high last period (for example, if Δy_{t-1}^2 was very large), it will also tend to be unusually high this period. Alternatively, if volatility was unusually low last period (for example, Δy_{t-1}^2 was near zero) then this period's volatility will also tend to be low. In other words, if the volatility is low it will tend to stay low, if it is high it will tend to stay high. Of course, the presence of the error, e_t, means that there can be exceptions to this pattern. But, in general, this model implies that we will tend to observe intervals or clusters in times where volatility is low and intervals where it is high. In empirical studies of asset prices, such a pattern is very common. As an example, recall that in Chapter 2, we plotted the £/$ exchange rate (see Figure 2.1). If you look back at this figure, you can see long spells when the exchange rate changed very little (for example, 1949–67 and 1993–6) and other, longer spells (for example, 1985–92) where it was more volatile.

The previous discussion refers to the AR(1) model, but it can be extended to the AR(p) model. All of the intuition given in Chapter 9 is relevant here. The only difference is that the interpretation relates to the volatility of the series rather than to the series itself. Furthermore, all of the statistical techniques we described in Chapter 9 are relevant here. Provided the series is stationary (for example $|\phi| < 1$ in the AR(1) case), then OLS estimates and P-values can be interpreted in the standard way. Testing for a unit root can be conducted using a Dickey–Fuller test. In short, there is nothing statistically new here.

Example: Volatility in Stock Prices

The file STOCK.XLS contains data on Y = the stock price of a company collected each week for four years ($T = 208$). The data has been logged. Figure 11.1 provides a time series plot of this data.

You can see that the price of this stock has tended to increase over time, although there are several periods when it also fell. The price of the stock was £24.53 per share in the first month, increasing to £30.14 in the 208th month.[3]

Figure 11.2 plots ΔY, the percentage change in Y. Since $100 \times [ln(Y_t) - ln(Y_{t-1})]$ is the percentage change in the stock price, we multiply the first difference of the data used to create Figure 11.1 by 100.

An examination of this figure indicates that the change in stock price in any given week was usually positive, but that there were some weeks when the price fell. In the middle of the period of study (roughly weeks 90–110), there were many large changes (both in a positive and a negative direction). For instance, in weeks

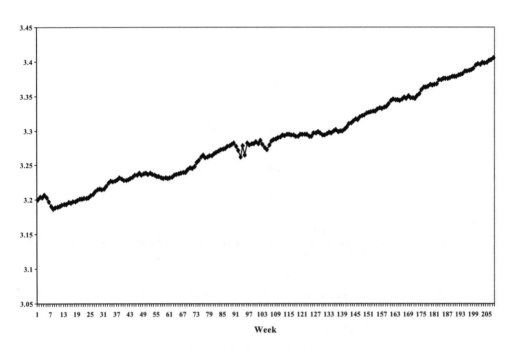

Figure 11.1   Log of Stock Price.

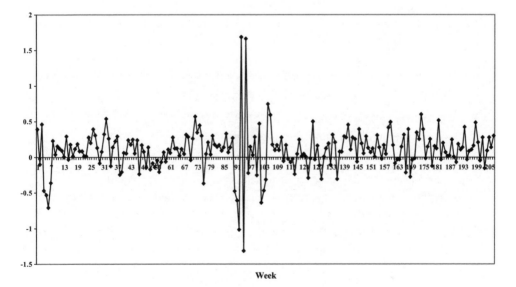

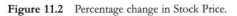

Figure 11.2   Percentage change in Stock Price.

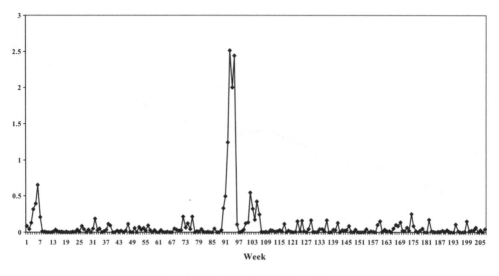

Figure 11.3   Volatility of Stock Price.

94 and 96 the stock price increased by over 1.5%. This is a huge increase in one week. If increases of this magnitude were to keep on occurring for a year, the price of the stock would more than double (a weekly return of 1.5% becomes an annualized return of over 100%). However, in weeks 92, 93 and 95, stock prices fell by almost as much. All in all, the stock price in this middle period was much more volatile than in others.

In order to investigate the volatility properties of stock price in more depth we take deviations from the mean for the observations of the differenced data used to create Figure 11.2 and then square them. That is, we:

1. Calculate the average change in stock price, 0.099%.
2. Subtract this number from every stock price change.
3. Square the result.

Figure 11.3 plots the resulting series which is our measure of volatility.

Note that volatility is the *square* of the stock price and hence cannot be negative. The pattern most evident in Figure 11.3 is the large increase in volatility in weeks 90 to 97 and, to a lesser extent, in weeks 4 to 8 and 101 to 107. This provides visual evidence that the volatility of this stock does indeed seem to vary over time.

Table 11.1 AR(1) Model using volatility as variable of interest.

	Coefficient	Standard error	t-stat	P-value	Lower 95%	Upper 95%
Intercept	0.024	0.015	1.624	0.106	−0.005	0.053
Δy_{t-1}^2	0.737	0.047	15.552	1.74E−36	0.643	0.830

More formal evidence on the pattern of volatility can be found by building an AR(p) model using the techniques of Chapter 9 and volatility as the variable of interest. The sequential testing procedure suggested in that chapter yields the AR(1) model in Table 11.1.

It can be seen that last week's volatility has strong explanatory power for this week's volatility because its coefficient is strongly statistically significant. Furthermore, $R^2 = 0.54$, indicating that 54% of the variation in volatility can be explained by last period's volatility. Consequently, it does seem as if volatility clusters are present. If volatility is high one period, it will also tend to be high the next period.

This information might be of great interest to an investor wishing to purchase this stock. Suppose an investor has just observed that $\Delta y_{t-1} = 0$ and therefore that $\Delta y_{t-1}^2 = 0$. In other words, the stock price changed by its average amount in period $t-1$. The investor is interested in predicting volatility in period t in order to judge the likely risk involved in purchasing the stock. Since the error is unpredictable, the investor ignores it (it is just as likely to be positive as negative). Below is the fitted AR(1) model:

$$\Delta \hat{y}_t^2 = 0.024 + 0.737 \Delta y_{t-1}^2.$$

Since $\Delta y_{t-1}^2 = 0$, the investor predicts volatility in period t to be 0.024. However, had he observed $\Delta y_{t-1}^2 = 1$, he would have predicted volatility in period t to be 0.761 (i.e. 0.024 + 0.737). This kind of information can be incorporated into financial models of investor behavior.

Exercise 11.1

NYSE.XLS contains data on $\Delta Y =$ the percentage change in stock prices each month from 1952 through 1995 on the New York Stock Exchange (NYSE). For those interested in precise details, the data are value-weighted stock returns exclusive of dividends deflated using the consumer price index. Note that these data are already in differenced form but deviations from the mean have not been taken—it is ΔY not Y or Δy.

(a) Make a time series plot of this data and comment on any patterns you observe.

(b) Using the techniques discussed in Chapter 9, comment on the univariate time series properties of ΔY. What does its autocorrelation function look like? If you build an AR(p) model using these data, what is p? Is ΔY stationary? Are stock returns on the NYSE predictable (can past stock returns help you to predict current values)?

(c) Assume that the original series, Y, follows a random walk such that an AR(0) model for ΔY is appropriate (possibly with an intercept). Calculate the volatility of this variable as described in this chapter.

(d) Plot the volatility of this series. Does it appear that volatility clustering is present?

(e) Construct an AR(p) model for the volatility series and discuss its properties. Can past values of volatility on the stock market help you to predict current volatility?

Autoregressive Conditional Heteroskedasticity (ARCH)

The class of ARCH models (including extensions) is probably the most popular one for working with financial volatility. It is most compactly explained by working with the familiar regression model:

$$Y_t = \alpha + \beta_1 X_{1t} + \beta_2 X_{2t} + \ldots + \beta_k X_{kt} + e_t.$$

Note that this general model contains many of the other models with which we have been working. For instance, if $X_{jt} = Y_{t-j}$ (the explanatory variables are lags of the dependent variable) then this is an AR model. Another interesting case we will focus on below occurs if there are no explanatory variables at all ($\alpha = \beta_1 = \ldots = \beta_k = 0$) in which case the ARCH model we will describe shortly simply relates to the dependent variable itself.

If we set this dependent variable to be the demeaned stock returns ($\Delta y_t = \Delta Y_t - \overline{\Delta Y}$), then we will be working with a model of financial volatility analogous to that used in the first half of this chapter.

The ARCH model relates to the variance (or volatility) of the error, e_t. You may wish to review the material in Appendix 2.3 of Chapter 2 if you have forgotten the properties of variances. To simplify notation (and adopt a very common notation in economics), we will let:

$$\sigma_t^2 = \mathrm{var}(e_t).$$

In other words, σ_t^2 will be our notation for volatility, which is defined as the variance of the error. It is this that is crucial in many financial applications (for example, in pricing financial derivatives). Note that we are allowing volatility to vary over time—which is quite important in light of our previous discussion of clustering of volatility.

The ARCH model with p lags (denoted by ARCH(p)) assumes that today's volatility is an average of past errors squared:

$$\sigma_t^2 = \gamma_0 + \gamma_1 e_{t-1}^2 + \ldots + \gamma_p e_{t-p}^2$$

where $\gamma_1, \ldots, \gamma_p$ are coefficients that can be estimated in many statistical software packages. In the case where we have no explanatory variables and the dependent variable is Δy_t, we have

$$\sigma_t^2 = \gamma_0 + \gamma_1 \Delta y_{t-1}^2 + \ldots + \gamma_p \Delta y_{t-p}^2$$

and the ARCH volatility depends on recent values of Δy_t^2—the metric for volatility we were using in the first half of this chapter. This model is closely related to the autoregressive model (which accounts for the "AR" part of the name ARCH) and ARCH models have similar properties to AR models—except that these properties relate to the volatility of the series.

Example: Volatility in Stock Prices (Continued)

With ARCH models we do not need to worry about subtracting the mean off of stock returns as we did in the first part of the chapter (by simply including an intercept in the regression model we are allowing for a random walk with drift). Accordingly, we use the logged stock price data from STOCK.XLS and simply take the first difference to create the variable ΔY_t. If we estimate an ARCH(1) model with ΔY_t as the dependent variable and an intercept in the regression equation, our computer software package produces a table similar to Table 11.2.

The upper part of this table refers to the coefficients in the regression equation. In this case, we have only included an intercept (labeled α in the regression

	Coefficient	P-value	Lower 95%	Upper 95%
Table 11.2 ARCH(1) model using stock returns data.				
ΔY_t				
Intercept	0.105	0.000	0.081	0.129
ARCH				
Lag 1	0.660	0.000	0.302	1.018
Intercept	0.024	0.000	0.016	0.032

equation). The lower part of the table refers to the ARCH equation. We are working with an ARCH(1) model, so the equation includes an intercept (labeled γ_0 in the ARCH equation) and one lag of the errors squares (labeled γ_1 in the ARCH equation and "Lag 1" in the table). The numbers in the table can be read in the same manner as in the tables we reported in earlier regression chapters. That is, the numbers in the column labeled "Coefficient" are estimates of the coefficients (although, in this case, they are not OLS estimates but rather more sophisticated estimates designed for ARCH models). The numbers in the columns labeled "P-value" are P-values for testing the hypothesis that the corresponding coefficient equals zero. In this case, since the P-values are all less than 0.05, we can conclude all the variables (in the regression equation and the ARCH equation) are statistically significant at the 5% level. The final two columns are lower and upper bounds for a 95% confidence interval.

The estimate of γ_1 (the coefficient on the lagged errors squared in the ARCH equation) is 0.660, indicating that volatility this month depends strongly on the errors squared last month. This shows that there is persistence in volatility of a similar degree to that found using the simpler methods in the first half of this chapter. Remember that we previously found that the AR(1) coefficient in a regression involving Δy_t^2 was estimated to be 0.737.

Lag length selection in ARCH models can be done in the same manner as with any time series model. That is, you can simply look at P-values for whether coefficients equal zero (and if they do seem to be zero then variables can be dropped). For instance, if we estimate an ARCH(2) model using the stock return data we obtain Table 11.3.

The coefficient estimates in this table are very similar to those for the ARCH(1) model. However, the coefficient on "Lag 2" (i.e. γ_2) is not significant because its P-value is greater than 0.05. Thus, we have evidence that an ARCH(1) model is adequate and the second lag added by the ARCH(2) model does not add significant explanatory power to the model.

Table 11.3   ARCH(2) model using stock returns data.

	Coefficient	P-value	Lower 95%	Upper 95%
ΔY_t				
Intercept	0.109	0.000	0.087	0.131
ARCH				
Lag 1	0.717	0.000	0.328	1.107
Lag 2	−0.043	0.487	−0.165	0.079
Intercept	0.025	0.000	0.016	0.033

For many purposes (for example, pricing financial derivatives), an estimate of σ_t^2 is required for every time period. We will not discuss how software packages produce this but note only that this is provided by them.

Many extensions of the ARCH model are used by financial analysts. For instance, the computer package Stata lists seven different variants of the ARCH model with acronyms like GARCH, SAARCH, TARCH, AARCH, NARCH and NARCHK. Another popular alternative model, which is not in the ARCH class is called *stochastic volatility*. If you are doing a great deal of work on financial volatility, you should do further study to learn more about these models. Here we will only introduce the most popular of these extensions: generalized ARCH or GARCH. This takes the ARCH model and adds on lags of the volatility measure itself (instead of just adding lags of squared errors). Thus, a GARCH model with (p,q) lags is denoted by GARCH(p,q) and has a volatility equation of:

$$\sigma_t^2 = \gamma_0 + \gamma_1 e_{t-1}^2 + \ldots + \gamma_p e_{t-p}^2 + \lambda_1 \sigma_{t-1}^2 + \ldots + \lambda_q \sigma_{t-q}^2.$$

The properties of the GARCH model are similar to the ARCH model. For instance, the coefficients can be interpreted in a similar fashion to AR coefficients and related to the degree of persistence in volatility. However, it can be shown that the GARCH model is much more flexible, much more capable of matching a wide variety of patterns of financial volatility.

Example: Volatility in Stock Prices (Continued)

If we estimate a GARCH(1,1) model with our stock return data, we obtain the results in Table 11.4.

The numbers in this table can be interpreted in the same manner as for the ARCH tables. Here, however, we have an extra row labeled "GARCH Lag 1", which contains results for λ_1 (the lagged volatility). It can be seen that this coefficient is insignificant because its P-value is greater than 0.05. Thus, for this data set, the extension to a GARCH(1,1) model does not seem necessary. The ARCH(1) model does perfectly well.

Table 11.4   GARCH(1,1) Model using stock returns data.

	Coefficient	P-value	Lower 95%	Upper 95%
ΔY_t				
Intercept	0.109	0.000	0.087	0.131
ARCH				
ARCH Lag 1	0.714	0.000	0.327	1.101
GARCH Lag 1	−0.063	0.457	−0.231	0.104
Intercept	0.026	0.000	0.015	0.038

Exercise 11.2

NYSE.XLS contains data on ΔY = the percentage change in stock prices each month from 1952 through 1995 on the New York Stock Exchange (NYSE).

(a) Estimate ARCH(p) models for various values of p. Is there volatility clustering in this data (i.e. does an ARCH model beat a simpler model where there is constant volatility which means $\gamma_1 = \ldots = \gamma_p = 0$)? Which value of p is preferable?

(b) For your preferred choice of p, make a time series plot of volatility (plot a graph of σ_t^2).

(c) Repeat parts (a) and (b) using a GARCH(p,q). Does your graph of volatility look the same with ARCH and GARCH models?

Granger Causality

In this book we have referred to causality quite a bit; however, mostly through warnings about interpreting correlation and regression results as reflecting causality. For instance, in Chapter 3 we discussed an example where alcohol drinking and lung cancer rates were correlated with one another, even though alcohol drinking does not cause lung cancer. Here correlation did not imply causality. In fact, it was cigarette smoking that caused lung cancer, but a correlation between cigarette smoking and alcohol drinking produced an apparent relationship between alcohol and lung cancer.

In our discussion of regression we were on a little firmer ground because we attempted to use economic reasoning and common sense in labeling one variable the dependent variable and the others the explanatory variables. In many cases, because the latter "explained" the former it was reasonable to talk about X "causing" Y. For instance, in our house price example in Chapters 4, 5, 6 and 7, the price of the house was said to be "caused" by the characteristics of the house (for example, number of bedrooms, number of bathrooms). However, in our discussion of omitted variable bias in Chapter 6, it became clear that multiple regressions could provide a misleading interpretation of the degree of causality present if important explanatory variables were omitted. Furthermore, there are many regressions in which it is not obvious which variable causes which. For instance, in Chapter 10 (Exercise 10.8), you ran a regression of $Y =$ wage inflation on $X =$ price inflation. It is possible that price inflation causes wage inflation (X causes Y), since workers will demand higher wage settlements if prices are rising rapidly. However, one could also argue that Y causes X, since wage increases will eat into company profits unless they raise prices. So wage inflation could cause price inflation. In other words, the causality could run in either direction—or both! Hence, when using the word "cause" with regression or correlation results a great deal of caution has to be taken and common sense has to be used.

However, with time series data we can make slightly stronger statements about causality simply by exploiting the fact that time does not run backward. That is, if event A happens before event B, then it is possible that A is causing B. However, it is not possible that B is causing A. In other words, events in the past can cause events to happen today. Future events cannot.

These intuitive ideas can be investigated through regression models incorporating the notion of *Granger causality*. The basic idea is that a variable X *Granger-causes* Y if past values of X can help explain Y. Of course, if Granger causality holds this does not guarantee that X causes Y. This is why we say "Granger causality" rather than just "causality". Nevertheless, if past values of X have explanatory power for current values of Y, it at least suggests that X might be causing Y.

Granger causality is only relevant with time series variables. To illustrate the basic concepts we will consider Granger causality between two variables (X and Y) which are both stationary. A nonstationary case, where X and Y have unit roots but are cointegrated, will also be mentioned below.

Granger causality in a simple ADL model

We have assumed that X and Y are stationary, so the discussion of Chapter 10 suggests an ADL model is appropriate. Suppose that the following simple ADL model holds:

$$Y_t = \alpha + \phi_1 Y_{t-1} + \beta_1 X_{t-1} + e_t.$$

This model implies that last period's value of X has explanatory power for the current value of Y. The coefficient β_1 is a measure of the influence of X_{t-1} on Y_t. If $\beta_1 = 0$, then past values of X have no effect on Y and there is no way that X could Granger-cause Y. In other words, if $\beta_1 = 0$ then X does not Granger-cause Y. An alternative way of expressing this concept is to say that "if $\beta_1 = 0$ then past values of X have no explanatory power for Y beyond that provided by past values for Y." Since we know how to estimate the ADL and carry out hypothesis tests, it is simple to test for Granger causality. That is, OLS estimation of the above regression can be conducted using any standard spreadsheet or econometric computer package, and the P-value for the coefficient on X_{t-1} examined for significance. If β_1 is statistically significant (for example, P-value < 0.05) then we conclude that X Granger-causes Y. Note that the null hypothesis being tested here is $H_0: \beta_1 = 0$ which is a hypothesis that Granger causality *does not occur*. So we should formally refer to the test of $\beta_1 = 0$ as a test of *Granger noncausality*, but we will adopt the more common informal terminology and just refer to this procedure as a *Granger causality test*.

Granger causality in an ADL model with p and q lags

Of course, the above ADL model is quite restrictive in that it incorporates only one lag of X and Y. In general, we would want to select lag lengths using the methods described in Chapter 10 to work with an ADL(p,q) model of the form:[4]

$$Y_t = \alpha + \delta t + \phi_1 Y_{t-1} + \ldots + \phi_p Y_{t-p} + \beta_1 X_{t-1} + \ldots + \beta_q X_{t-q} + e_t.$$

Here X Granger-causes Y if *any or all of $\beta_1, \ldots, \beta_q$ are statistically significant*. In other words, if X at any time in the past has explanatory power for the current value of Y, then we say that X Granger-causes Y. We are assuming X and Y do not contain unit roots, so OLS regression analysis can be used to estimate this model. The P-values of the individual coefficients can be used to determine whether Granger causality is present. If you were using the 5% level of significance, then if any of the P-values for the coefficients $\beta_1, \ldots, \beta_q$ were less than 0.05, you would conclude that Granger causality is present. If none of the P-values were less than 0.05 then you would conclude that Granger causality is not present.

The strategy outlined above is a useful one that can be carried out quite simply in Excel or any other statistical software package. You are likely to obtain reliable evidence about whether X Granger-causes Y by following it. Note, however, that there is formally a more correct—also more complicated—way of carrying out this test. Recall that the null hypothesis tested is formally one of Granger noncausality. That is, X does not Granger-cause Y if past values of X have no explanatory power for the current value of Y. Appropriately, then, we want to test the hypothesis H_0: $\beta_1 = \beta_2 = \ldots = \beta_q = 0$ and conclude that X Granger-causes Y only if the hypothesis is rejected. Note that this test is slightly different from the one proposed in the previous paragraph. That is, a joint test of $\beta_1 = \beta_2 = \ldots = \beta_q = 0$ is not exactly the same as q individual tests of $\beta_i = 0$ for $i = 1, \ldots, q$. We have not discussed how to carry out tests to determine whether several coefficients are jointly equal to zero. For readers interested in such joint tests, the appendix to this chapter offers some practical advice.

However, if you choose to follow the simpler strategy outlined above then you should note the following: *if you find any or all of the coefficients* $\beta_1, \ldots, \beta_q$ *to be significant using t-statistics or the P-values of individual coefficients, you may safely conclude that X Granger-causes Y. If none of these coefficients is significant, it is probably the case that X does not Granger-cause Y. However, you are more likely to be wrong if you conclude the latter than if you had used the correct joint test of Granger noncausality.*

Example: Does Wage Inflation Granger-Cause Price Inflation?

Annual data from 1855–1987 on UK prices and wages is contained in the file WP.XLS, introduced in Exercise 10.8. If you have done that exercise you will recall that both the log of wages and prices appear to have unit roots but are not cointegrated. However, the differences of these series are stationary and can be nicely interpreted as inflation rates (wage and price inflation).

We will use this data set to investigate whether past wage inflation causes price inflation. There is good reason to think that this may indeed be the case. After all, if wages are increasing, companies will have an incentive to increase prices to stop their profit margins from falling.

Table 11.5 contains results from OLS estimation of the regression of ΔP = price inflation on four lags of itself, four lags of ΔW = wage inflation and a deterministic trend.

Table 11.5   ADL model using price inflation as the dependent variable.

	Coefficient	Standard error	t-stat	P-value	Lower 95%	Upper 95%
Intercept	−0.751	0.710	−1.058	0.292	−2.156	0.654
ΔP_{t-1}	0.822	0.170	4.850	3.81E–6	0.486	1.158
ΔP_{t-2}	−0.041	0.186	−0.222	0.825	−0.409	0.326
ΔP_{t-3}	0.142	0.186	0.762	0.448	−0.227	0.511
ΔP_{t-4}	−0.181	0.175	−1.035	0.303	−0.526	0.165
ΔW_{t-1}	−0.016	0.143	−0.114	0.909	−0.299	0.267
ΔW_{t-2}	−0.118	0.143	−0.823	0.412	−0.402	0.166
ΔW_{t-3}	−0.042	0.143	−0.292	0.771	−0.324	0.241
ΔW_{t-4}	0.038	0.142	0.266	0.791	−0.244	0.319
Time	0.030	0.011	2.669	0.009	0.0077	0.052

An examination of the P-values in this table indicates that only the deterministic trend and last period's price inflation have explanatory power for present inflation. All of the coefficients on the lags of wage inflation are insignificant. Contrary to our expectations, then, wage inflation does not seem to Granger-cause price inflation.[5]

Causality in both directions

In many cases, it is not obvious which way causality should run. For instance, should past wage inflation cause price inflation or should the reverse hold? In such cases, when causality may be in either direction, it is important that you check for it. If Y and X are the two variables under study, in addition to running a regression of Y on lags of itself and lags of X (as above), you should also run a regression of X on lags of itself and lags of Y.

Note that it is possible to find that Y Granger-causes X and that X Granger-causes Y. In the case of complicated economic models, such bidirectional causality is quite common and even reasonable. Think, for instance, of the relationship between interest rates and exchange rates. It is reasonable, from a macroeconomic perspective, to say that interest rate policy may affect future exchange rates. However, it is also equally reasonable to think that exchange rates may also affect future interest rate policy (for example, if the exchange rate is perceived to be too high now the central bank may be led to decrease interest rates in the future).

Example: Does Price Inflation Granger-Cause Wage Inflation?

In the previous example we used data set WP.XLS to investigate whether wage inflation Granger-causes price inflation. We found that it did not. However, it is possible that causality runs in the opposite direction—that is, that price inflation may actually cause wage inflation. After all, workers and unions often look at past inflation and adjust their wage demands accordingly.

Table 11.6 contains results from OLS estimation of the regression of ΔW = wage inflation on four lags of itself, four lags of ΔP = price inflation and a deterministic trend.

Here we do find evidence that price inflation Granger-causes wage inflation. In particular, the coefficient on ΔP_{t-1} is highly significant, indicating that last year's price inflation rate has strong explanatory power for wage inflation.

Table 11.6   ADL model using wage inflation as the dependent variable.

	Coefficient	Standard error	t-stat	P-value	Lower 95%	Upper 95%
Intercept	−0.609	0.835	−0.730	0.467	−2.262	1.044
ΔW_{t-1}	0.053	0.168	0.312	0.755	−0.280	0.386
ΔW_{t-2}	−0.040	0.169	−0.235	0.814	−0.374	0.294
ΔW_{t-3}	−0.058	0.168	−0.348	0.728	−0.391	0.274
ΔW_{t-4}	0.036	0.167	0.215	0.830	−0.295	0.367
ΔP_{t-1}	0.854	0.200	4.280	3.83E−5	0.459	1.249
ΔP_{t-2}	−0.217	0.218	−0.993	0.323	−0.649	0.215
ΔP_{t-3}	0.234	0.219	1.067	0.288	−0.200	0.668
ΔP_{t-4}	−0.272	0.205	−1.323	0.188	−0.678	0.135
Time	0.046	0.013	3.514	0.001	0.020	0.072

Exercise 11.3

In the previous examples using the data set WP.XLS, we have set $p = q = 4$ (four lags of both wage and price inflation). Using price inflation as the dependent variable and the sequential testing procedure outlined in Chapter 10 select optimal values for p and q. Discuss whether wage inflation causes price inflation using the ADL(p,q) model you have selected. Repeat the analysis using wage inflation as the dependent variable.

Exercise 11.4

Excel file LONGGDP.XLS contains annual data on real GDP per capita for four of the world's largest English-speaking countries (USA, UK, Canada and Australia) for the years 1870–1993.

(a) Take differences to obtain time series of the growth in GDP per capita for each of the four countries.
(b) Investigate where GDP growth in any country Granger-causes GDP growth in any other country. For instance, does GDP growth in the US Granger-cause GDP growth in the UK? Does it in Canada?

This brief discussion of Granger causality has focused on two variables, X and Y. However, there is no reason why these basic techniques cannot be extended to the case of many variables. For instance, if we had three variables, X, Y and Z and if we were interested in investigating whether X or Z Granger-cause Y, we would simply regress Y on lags of Y, lags of X and lags of Z. If say, the lags of Z were found to be significant and the lags of X not, then we could say that Z Granger-causes Y, but X does not.

Granger causality with cointegrated variables

Testing for Granger causality among cointegrated variables is very similar to the method outlined above. It is common to work with a variant of the error correction model (ECM) introduced in Chapter 10:

$$\Delta Y_t = \varphi + \delta t + \lambda e_{t-1} + \gamma_1 \Delta Y_{t-1} + \ldots + \gamma_p \Delta Y_{t-p} + \omega_1 \Delta X_{t-1} + \ldots + \omega_q \Delta X_{t-q} + \varepsilon_t.$$

As noted in Chapter 10, this is essentially an ADL model except for the presence of the term λe_{t-1}. Remember that $e_{t-1} = Y_{t-1} - \alpha - \beta X_{t-1}$, an estimate of which can be obtained by running a regression of Y on X and saving the residuals. Intuitively, X Granger-causes Y if past values of X have explanatory power for current values of Y. Applying this intuition to the ECM, we can see that past values of X appear in the terms $\Delta X_{t-1}, \ldots, \Delta X_{t-q}$ and e_{t-1}. This implies that X does not Granger-cause Y if $\omega_1 = \ldots = \omega_q = \lambda = 0$. Chapter 10 discussed how we can use two OLS regressions to estimate ECMs, and then use their P-values or confidence intervals to test for causality. Thus, t-statistics and P-values can be used to test for Granger causality in the same way as the stationary case. Also, the F-tests described in the appendix to this chapter can be used to carry out a formal test of H_0: $\omega_1 = \ldots = \omega_q = \lambda = 0$.

In the previous paragraph we described how to test whether X Granger-causes Y. Testing whether Y Granger-causes X is achieved by reversing the roles that X and Y play in the ECM. One interesting consequence of the Granger representation theorem is worth noting here: If X and Y are cointegrated then some form of Granger causality must occur. That is, either X must Granger-cause Y or Y must Granger-cause X (or both).

Exercise 11.5

Use the data on $Y =$ consumption and $X =$ personal income from INCOME. XLS. Assume (perhaps incorrectly in light of Exercise 10.5) that Y and X are cointegrated. Test whether Y Granger-causes X. Test whether X Granger-causes Y.

Vector Autoregressions

Our discussion of Granger causality naturally leads us to the topic of vector autoregressions or VARs. Before discussing their popularity and estimation we will first define what a VAR is. Initially, we will assume that all variables are stationary. If the original variables have unit roots then we assume that differences have been taken such that the model includes the changes in the original variables (which do not have unit roots). The end of this section will consider the extension of this case to that of cointegration.

When we investigated Granger causality between X and Y we began with a restricted version of an ADL(p,q) model with Y as the dependent variable. We used it to investigate if X Granger-caused Y. We then went on to consider causality in the other direction, which involved switching the roles of X and Y in the ADL; in particular, X became the dependent variable. We can write the two equations as follows:

$$Y_t = \alpha_1 + \delta_1 t + \phi_{11} Y_{t-1} + \ldots + \phi_{1p} Y_{t-p} + \beta_{11} X_{t-1} + \ldots + \beta_{1q} X_{t-q} + e_{1t}$$

and

$$X_t = \alpha_2 + \delta_2 t + \phi_{21} Y_{t-1} + \ldots + \phi_{2p} Y_{t-p} + \beta_{21} X_{t-1} + \ldots + \beta_{2q} X_{t-q} + e_{2t}.$$

The first of these equations can be used to test whether X Granger-causes Y; the second, whether Y Granger-causes X. Note that now the coefficients have subscripts indicating which equation they are in. For instance, α_1 is the intercept in the first equation, and α_2 the intercept in the second. Furthermore, the errors now have subscripts to denote the fact that they will be different in the two equations.

These two equations comprise a VAR. A VAR is the extension of the autoregressive (AR) model to the case in which there is more than one variable under study. Remember that the AR model introduced in Chapter 9 involved one dependent variable, Y_t, which depended only on lags of itself (and possibly a deterministic trend). A VAR has more than one dependent variable (Y and X) and, thus, has more than one equation (one where Y_t is the dependent variable and one where X_t is). Each equation uses as its explanatory variables lags of *all the variables under study* (and possibly a deterministic trend).

The two equations above constitute a VAR with two variables. For instance, you can see that in the first equation Y depends on p lags of itself and on q lags of X. The lag lengths, p and q, can be selected using the sequential testing methods introduced in Chapter 9. However, especially if the VAR has more than two variables, many different lag lengths need to be selected (one for each variable in each equation). In light of this, it is common to set $p = q$ and use the same lag length for every variable in every equation. The resulting model is known as a VAR(p) model. The following VAR(p) has three variables, Y, X and Z:

$$Y_t = \alpha_1 + \delta_1 t + \phi_{11} Y_{t-1} + \ldots + \phi_{1p} Y_{t-p} + \beta_{11} X_{t-1} + \ldots + \beta_{1p} X_{t-p} + \delta_{11} Z_{t-1} + \ldots + \delta_{1p} Z_{t-p} + e_{1t}$$

$$X_t = \alpha_2 + \delta_2 t + \phi_{21} Y_{t-1} + \ldots + \phi_{2p} Y_{t-p} + \beta_{21} X_{t-1} + \ldots + \beta_{2p} X_{t-p} + \delta_{21} Z_{t-1} + \ldots + \delta_{2p} Z_{t-p} + e_{2t}$$

$$Z_t = \alpha_3 + \delta_3 t + \phi_{31} Y_{t-1} + \ldots + \phi_{3p} Y_{t-p} + \beta_{31} X_{t-1} + \ldots + \beta_{3p} X_{t-p} + \delta_{31} Z_{t-1} + \ldots + \delta_{3p} Z_{t-p} + e_{3t}.$$

Note that, in addition to an intercept and deterministic trend, each equation contains p lags of all variables in study and VAR(p) models with more than three variables can be obtained in an analogous manner.

We assume that all the variables in the VAR(p) are stationary, so estimation and testing can be carried out in the standard way. That is, you can obtain estimates of coefficients in each equation using OLS. P-values or t-statistics will then allow you to ascertain whether individual coefficients are significant. You can also use the material covered in the appendix of this chapter to carry out more complicated F-tests.

Vector autoregressions are, then, easy to use. However, you may be wondering why we would want to work with such models. One reason has to be Granger causality testing. That is, VARs provide a framework for testing for Granger causality between each set of variables. However, we should also mention deeper reasons why we would want to use them.

Throughout this book, we have stressed the need for care when interpreting correlation or regression results as reflecting causality or influence. Economic theory or common sense can be a big help to you in many cases. In Chapters 4 and 6 we worked through many examples about which we could comfortably say that the regressions reflected causality. For instance, X (population density) caused Y (deforestation) or X (lot size) influenced Y (house price). In both cases it is not plausible for us to say that Y influenced or caused X.

However, there are many instances when neither economic theory nor common sense can provide you with a regression model that can be interpreted as reflecting causality. For instance, does Y (wage inflation) cause X (price inflation)? Or does the opposite happen? Economic theory and common sense tells us that either can happen and that Granger causality tests can shed light on these questions. The field of macroeconomics, in particular, is filled with such examples. Should interest rates cause exchange rates to change or vice versa? Both? Should GDP growth cause interest rates to change? The opposite? Both? The answers are unclear and it is hard to know how to interpret coefficients in a regression of Y_t on X_t.

We have so far ignored the issues of cointegration and the long-run multiplier. However, even if cointegration is present, we have to be careful when interpreting regression results as reflecting causality. For instance, in Chapter 10 we found the prices of Y (organic oranges) and of X (regular oranges) to be cointegrated and the long run multiplier effect of X on Y to be 0.996. These results probably indicate that X influenced Y (i.e. if the price of regular oranges went up by 1 pence, price of organic oranges would probably rise by 0.995 pence in the long run). However, it is unlikely that the price of organic oranges would influence regular oranges because the former make up such a small part of the market. Hence, X influences Y, but Y does not influence X. If we had reversed things and the price of regular oranges was our dependent variable and the price of organic oranges the explanatory variable, we would still have found cointegration and calculated a long run multiplier. But we would be wrong in using it as a measure of the influence of organic orange prices on regular prices.

The issues raised in the previous paragraphs either do not arise at all or do to a far less extent in VAR models. That is, all of the variables we are using to explain the current value of the dependent variable occurred in the past (for example, in the first equation the explanatory variables are all dated $t-1$ or earlier, whereas the dependent variable is Y_t). It is possible that the past might influence the present but it is not possible for the present to influence the past. Hence, in the VAR model, the explanatory variables might influence the dependent variable but there is no possibility that the dependent variable influences the explanatory variable. Problems of interpretation that arise with the regression of Y_t on X_t do not arise in the VAR case.[6]

One of the controversial things about VARs is that they are *atheoretical*; that is, they do not draw heavily on economic theory. Theory is limited to selecting the variables in the VAR. Consider, for instance, the relationship between interest rates, the price level, money supply and real GDP. Macroeconomic theorists have created many sophisticated models of this relationship. The IS-LM model extended for inflation is perhaps the best known, but many others exist. Whereas the macroeconomic theorist would like this theory to influence empirical work, the VAR practitioner does not draw on it at all. A VAR model states: "Interest rates, price level, money supply and real GDP are related. We model this relationship as implying only that each variable depends on lags of itself and all other variables." There is no real link between the *empirical* VAR and a *theoretical* macroeconomic model (for example, IS-LM).

The VAR user would defend the VAR by noting its excellent forecasting performance. We will discuss this trait in greater detail below but you should merely note now that this constitutes a strong reason for using them. In many cases, VARs have been shown to have better forecasting ability than sophisticated macroeconomic models. The fact that simple regression-based methods using a computer spreadsheet can often outperform complicated macroeconomic models that are created and maintained by specialists in government or the private sector, is a strong motivation for using VARs.

Example: A VAR(1) with RMPY Variables

Economists often use such important macroeconomic variables as: R = the interest rate, M = the money supply, P = the price level and Y = real GDP. Due to the symbols used, models using these variables are sometimes informally referred to as RMPY models (pronounced "rumpy"). The file RMPY.XLS contains quarterly data on the variables for the US from 1947Q1 through 1992Q4. To be precise:

- R is the three-month Treasury bill rate
- M is the money supply (M2) measured in billions of dollars
- P is the price level measured by the GDP deflator (a price index with 1987 = 1.00)
- Y is real GDP measured in billions of 1987 dollars.

Before carrying out an analysis using time series data you must conduct unit root tests. Remember that, if unit roots are present but cointegration does not occur, then the spurious regression problem exists. In this case, you should work with differenced data. Alternatively, if unit roots exist and cointegration does occur then you will have important economic information that the series are trending together.

In the present case, tests indicate that we cannot reject the hypotheses that unit roots exist in all variables and that cointegration does not occur. In order to avoid the spurious regression problem, we work with differenced data. In particular, we take logs of each series, then take differences of these logged series, then multiply them by 100. This implies that we are working with percentage changes in each variable (for example, a value of 1 implies a 1% change). Thus:

- ΔR is the percentage change in the interest rate
- ΔM is the percentage change in the money supply
- ΔP is the percentage change in the price level (inflation)
- ΔY is the percentage change in GDP (GDP growth).

Table 11.7 presents results from OLS estimation of a VAR(1). Note that this table is in a slightly different format from previous ones. Since there are four variables in our VAR (i.e. ΔR, ΔM, ΔP and ΔY), there are four equations to estimate. We have put results for all equations in one table. Each equation regresses a dependent variable on one lag of all the variables in the VAR. To save space, we have included only the OLS estimate and P-value of each coefficient.

Table 11.7 The RMPY VAR(1) using ΔR, ΔM, ΔP and ΔY as dependent variables.

	Dependent variable ΔR		Dependent variable ΔM		Dependent variable ΔP		Dependent variable ΔY	
	Coefficient	P-value	Coefficient	P-value	Coefficient	P-value	Coefficient	P-value
Intercept	−3.631	0.162	0.335	0.001	0.161	0.138	0.495	0.005
ΔR_{t-1}	0.222	0.003	−0.013	2.0E−5	0.010	0.002	3.8E−4	0.940
ΔM_{t-1}	3.391	0.007	0.749	1.E−33	0.121	0.021	0.283	9.3E−4
ΔP_{t-1}	1.779	0.228	0.061	0.303	0.519	1.E−14	−0.117	0.242
ΔY_{t-1}	3.224	0.004	−0.032	0.480	−0.039	0.407	0.309	7.0E−5
Time	−0.056	0.011	3.4E−4	0.695	0.002	0.048	−0.003	0.035

If we examine the significant coefficients (those with P-value less than 0.05), some interesting patterns emerge. First, in every equation, the lag of the dependent variable is significant. That is, in the equation with ΔR_t as the dependent variable, ΔR_{t-1} provides significant explanatory power. In the equation with ΔM_t as the dependent variable, ΔM_{t-1} provides significant explanatory power, and so forth.

Secondly, the results for the four equations demonstrate some interesting patterns of Granger causality. In the equation with ΔR as the dependent variable, we can see that both GDP growth and money growth Granger-cause interest-rate changes. In other words, past values of GDP and money growth have explanatory power for current interest rate changes. In the case of the $\Delta R/\Delta M$ (interest rate/ money supply) relationship, the equation with ΔM as the dependent variable shows that the causality flows in both directions because interest-rate changes also

Granger-cause money growth. However, interest rate changes do not Granger-cause GDP growth. The Granger-causality results in respect to inflation are particularly interesting since it can be seen that inflation does not Granger-cause any other variable, but that both ΔR and ΔM Granger-cause inflation.

A macroeconomist could use these results to address theoretical questions of interest (for example, whether inflation is purely a monetary phenomenon, whether monetarist or Keynesian views of the economy are supported, whether the real economy is affected by inflation) but it is beyond the scope of this book to discuss them in detail.

Exercise 11.6

Use the data on R, M, P and Y in RMPY.XLS.

(a) Test for unit roots in each of the variables.
(b) Test for cointegration among the variables.
(c) Use the data on ΔR, ΔM, ΔP and ΔY in RMPY.XLS. Test for a unit root in each of the variables.

Lag length selection in VARs

The results in the previous example are based on a VAR(1). That is, we set $p = 1$ and used one lag of each variable to explain the dependent variable. In general, of course, we might want to set p to values other than one. The literature on lag length selection in VARs is voluminous and most of the criteria suggested are too complicated to be easily calculated using a spreadsheet such as Excel. However, more sophisticated computer software packages do automatically calculate many criteria for lag length. For instance, Stata calculates several *information criteria* with names like *Akaike's information criterion (AIC)*, the *Schwarz Bayes information criterion (SBIC)* and the *Hannan–Quinn information criterion (HQIC)*. A full explanation of these would require concepts beyond those covered in this book. However, for use in practice, all you need to know is that these can be calculated for VARs for every lag length up to pmax (the maximum possible lag length that is reasonable). You then select the lag length that yields the smallest value for your information criterion.[7]

In addition, the *t*-stats and P-values we have used throughout this book provide useful information on lag length. This is illustrated in the following example.

Example: A VAR(2) with RMPY Variables

In the previous example, we used data on ΔR, ΔM, ΔP and ΔY to estimate a VAR(1). Table 11.8 repeats the analysis using a VAR(2).

Several of the coefficients on variables two periods ago are significant. For instance, ΔR_{t-2} is significant in the equation with ΔR_t as the dependent variable. This indicates that the VAR(1) used in the previous example was not appropriate.

To give you an idea of the costs of using an incorrect model, take a careful look at the equation with ΔY as the dependent variable. Recall that in the VAR(1) model, we concluded that inflation did not Granger-cause GDP growth. However, the VAR(2) indicates that inflation does Granger-cause GDP growth. The relationship between GDP growth and the inflation rate is the source of much controversy in modern macroeconomics, so the cost of incorrectly using a VAR(1) is quite large.

Table 11.8 The RMPY VAR(2) using ΔR, ΔM, ΔP and ΔY as dependent variables.

	Dependent variable ΔR		Dependent variable ΔM		Dependent variable ΔP		Dependent variable ΔY	
	Coefficient	P-value	Coefficient	P-value	Coefficient	P-value	Coefficient	P-value
Interc.	−4.000	0.103	0.261	0.017	0.113	0.311	0.513	0.006
ΔR_{t-1}	0.315	1.9E−5	−0.017	3.6E−7	0.009	0.004	0.002	0.670
ΔM_{t-1}	2.824	0.106	0.655	8.E−15	0.086	0.280	0.310	0.019
ΔP_{t-1}	3.049	0.061	−0.020	0.785	0.366	1.6E−6	0.074	0.545
ΔY_{t-1}	3.696	4.6E−4	−0.051	0.270	−0.010	0.835	0.270	0.001
ΔR_{t-2}	−0.346	4.5E−6	0.003	0.298	−0.001	0.795	−0.010	0.085
ΔM_{t-2}	−2.201	0.213	0.157	0.045	0.025	0.755	−0.094	0.480
ΔP_{t-2}	1.164	0.457	0.095	0.170	0.282	1.0E−4	−0.233	0.049
ΔY_{t-2}	1.085	0.303	0.036	0.445	−0.046	0.334	0.153	0.054
Time	−0.045	0.029	−2.E−4	0.798	0.001	0.209	−0.003	0.104

Exercise 11.7

Using the results in the previous table, discuss Granger causality among all the variables in the model.

Exercise 11.8

Use the variables ΔR, ΔM, ΔP and ΔY from RMPY.XLS.

(a) Beginning with $p\max = 5$, select an appropriate lag length for a VAR.
(b) Using your result from (a), discuss Granger causality among the variables ΔR, ΔM, ΔP and ΔY.

Exercise 11.9

Excel file LONGGDP.XLS, as you will recall, contains annual data on real GDP per capita for four of the largest English-speaking countries (USA, UK, Canada and Australia) for the years 1870–1993. Take differences to obtain time series of the growth in GDP per capita for each of the four countries. Construct a VAR using these data.

Forecasting with VARs

We have said very little in the book so far about forecasting, despite the fact that this is an important activity of economists. There are two main reasons for omitting the topic. Firstly, the field of forecasting is enormous. Given the huge volume of research and issues to consider, it is impossible to do justice to the field in a book like this.[8] Second, basic forecasting using the computer is either very easy or very hard, depending on the computer software you have. To be precise, many computer packages have forecasting facilities that are simple to use. Once you have estimated a model (for example, a VAR or an AR), you can forecast simply by clicking on an appropriate option. In other words, many computer packages can allow you to undertake basic forecasting without a deep knowledge of the topic. However, spreadsheets such as Excel typically do not have forecasting capabilities for the models used in this book. It is possible to calculate forecasts but it is awkward, involving extensive typing of formulae.

In light of these issues, we will offer only a brief introduction to some of the practical issues and intuitive ideas relating to forecasting. All our discussion will relate to forecasting with VARs but it is worth noting that the ideas also relate to forecasting with univariate time series models. After all, an AR model is just a VAR with only one equation.

Forecasting is usually done using time series variables. The idea is that you use your observed data to predict what you expect to happen in the future. In more technical terms, you use data for periods $t = 1, \ldots, T$ to forecast periods $T+1$, $T+2$, and so forth.

To provide some intuition for how forecasting is done, consider a VAR(1) involving two variables, Y and X:

$$Y_t = \alpha_1 + \delta_1 t + \phi_{11} Y_{t-1} + \beta_{11} X_{t-1} + e_{1t}$$

and

$$X_t = \alpha_2 + \delta_2 t + \phi_{21} Y_{t-1} + \beta_{21} X_{t-1} + e_{2t}.$$

You cannot observe Y_{T+1} but you want to make a guess of what it is likely to be. Using the first equation of the VAR and setting $t = T + 1$, we obtain an expression for Y_{T+1}:

$$Y_{T+1} = \alpha_1 + \delta_1(T+1) + \phi_{11} Y_T + \beta_{11} X_T + e_{1T+1}.$$

This equation cannot be used directly to obtain Y_{T+1} since we don't know what e_{1T+1} is. In words, we do not know what unpredictable shock or surprise will hit the economy next period. Furthermore, we do not know what the coefficients are. However, if we ignore the error term (which cannot be forecast) and replace the coefficients by OLS estimates we obtain a forecast which we denote by $\hat{Y}_{T+1}$:

$$\hat{Y}_{T+1} = \hat{\alpha}_1 + \hat{\delta}_1(T+1) + \hat{\phi}_{11} Y_T + \hat{\beta}_{11} X_T.$$

If you are working in a spreadsheet such as Excel, note that everything in the formula for $\hat{Y}_{T+1}$ can be taken from either the original data or from the output from the regression command. It is conceptually easy just to plug in all the individual numbers (the OLS estimates of the coefficients and Y_T, X_T and $T+1$) into a formula to calculate $\hat{Y}_{T+1}$. A similar strategy can be used to obtain $\hat{X}_{T+1}$. You can see how, in practice, calculating these forecasts in this way can be awkward and time consuming. Hence, if you plan on doing more forecasting, we stress that it is preferable to avoid spreadsheets such as Excel and work with sophisticated econometrics computer packages.

The previous paragraph described how to forecast one period into the future. We can use the same strategy for two periods, provided that we make one extension. In the one period case, we used X_T and Y_T to create $\hat{Y}_{T+1}$ and $\hat{X}_{T+1}$. In the two period case, $\hat{Y}_{T+2}$ and $\hat{X}_{T+2}$ depend on Y_{T+1} and X_{T+1}. But since our data only runs until period T, we do not know what Y_{T+1} and X_{T+1} are. Consequently, we replace Y_{T+1} and X_{T+1} by $\hat{Y}_{T+1}$ and $\hat{X}_{T+1}$. That is, we use the relevant equation from the VAR, ignore the error, replace the coefficients by their OLS estimates and replace past values of the variables that we do not observe by their forecasts. In a formula:

$$\hat{Y}_{T+2} = \hat{\alpha}_1 + \hat{\delta}_1(T+2) + \hat{\phi}_{11} \hat{Y}_{T+1} + \hat{\beta}_{11} \hat{X}_{T+1}.$$

The above equation can be calculated in a spreadsheet, although somewhat awkwardly. $\hat{X}_{T+2}$ can be calculated in a similar manner using the formula:

$$\hat{X}_{T+2} = \hat{\alpha}_2 + \hat{\delta}_2(T+2) + \hat{\phi}_{21}\hat{Y}_{T+1} + \hat{\beta}_{21}\hat{X}_{T+1}.$$

We can use the general strategy of ignoring the error, replacing coefficients by OLS estimates and replacing lagged values of variables that are unobserved by forecasts, to obtain forecasts for any number of periods in the future for any VAR(p).

The previous discussion demonstrated how to calculate point estimates of forecasts. Of course, in reality, what actually happens is rarely identical to your forecast. In Chapter 5, we discussed a similar issue. There we pointed out that OLS provides estimates only of coefficients, and that these will not be precisely correct. For this reason, in addition to OLS estimates, we also recommended that you present confidence intervals. These reflect the level of uncertainty about the coefficient estimate. When forecasting, confidence intervals can also be calculated, and these can be quite informative. It is increasingly common for government agencies, for instance, to present confidence intervals for their forecasts. For instance, a central banker might make a statement of the form: "My forecast of inflation next year is 1.8%. I am 95% confident that it will be between 1.45% and 2.15%." Many computer packages automatically provide confidence intervals and, thus, you do not need to know their precise formula when forecasting. If you are using a spreadsheet, the formula is fairly complicated and it would be awkward to calculate, which is why we do not present it here.

Example: A VAR(2) with RMPY Variables (Continued)

In this example, we consider forecasting using the data on ΔR, ΔM, ΔP and ΔY from RMPY.XLS. As above, we use a VAR(2), recalling that we have data on these variables from 1947Q2 through 1992Q4. A common practice is to withhold some data with which to compare forecasts. Here we use data from 1947Q2 through 1991Q4 to estimate the VAR(2). We forecast from 1992Q1 through 1992Q4, and then compare our forecasts for the year 1992 to what actually happened in 1992. Doing so will give us some idea of the forecast performance of our model.

Table 11.9 contains the forecasts and actual observations for 1992 for inflation and GDP growth.

To aid in interpretation, note that all figures are percentage changes over the quarter. For example, the forecast for inflation for 1992Q2 of 0.731, translates

Table 11.9 Forecasts of inflation and GDP growth for 1992 using a RMPY VAR(2).

	ΔP forecast	ΔP actual	ΔY forecast	ΔY actual
1992Q1	0.626	0.929	-0.019	0.865
1992Q2	0.731	0.689	0.220	0.698
1992Q3	0.862	0.289	0.275	0.838
1992Q4	0.940	0.813	0.271	1.393

into a 2.96% annual inflation rate. The table indicates that the VAR(2) did reasonably well at forecasting inflation, except for 1992Q3, when actual inflation was unusually low. The forecasting performance for GDP growth is not quite as good, with our VAR consistently predicting slower growth than had actually occurred.

Exercise 11.10

It is recommended that you do this question and others involving forecasting only if you have access to an econometrics computer package that is capable of doing forecasts. If you are working with a spreadsheet such as Excel this question will be difficult.

Use the variables ΔR, ΔM, ΔP and ΔY from RMPY.XLS.

(a) In the previous example, we used a VAR(2). Using a VAR(p) for various values of p (for example, $p = 1, 3, 4$) construct forecasts for the year 1992. Do any of the VARs you worked with produce better forecasts than in the table above?

(b) In the previous example, data from 1947Q2 through 1991Q4 was used to estimate the VAR, which was then used to forecast from 1992Q1 through 1992Q4. Redo the above example using data from 1947Q2 through 1990Q4 to forecast 1991Q1 through 1992Q4 (forecast for 2 years instead of 1).

(c) Try forecasting for longer and longer periods. For instance, in (b) you forecasted for 2 years. Now try 3 years, 4 years, 5 years, and so forth. Discuss your results. Do your results suggest that VARs are better at forecasting a short period ahead than a long period?

Exercise 11.11

Using the data in Exercise 11.9 and the VAR constructed therein, carry out a forecasting exercise for GDP growth for the four included countries. Experiment with various forecast horizons. Does the VAR forecast well?

Vector autoregressions with cointegrated variables

In the preceding discussion of VARs we assumed that all variables are stationary. If some of the original variables have unit roots and are *not* cointegrated, then the ones with unit roots should be differenced and the resulting stationary variables should be used in the VAR. This covers every case except the one where the variables have unit roots and are cointegrated.

Recall that in this case in the discussion of Granger causality, we recommended that you work with an ECM. The same strategy can be employed here. In particular, instead of working with a vector autoregression (VAR), you should work with a vector error correction model (VECM). Like the VAR, the VECM will have one equation for each variable in the model. In the case of two variables, Y and X, the VECM is:

$$\Delta Y_t = \varphi_1 + \delta_1 t + \lambda_1 e_{t-1} + \gamma_{11}\Delta Y_{t-1} + \ldots + \gamma_{1p}\Delta Y_{t-p} + \omega_{11}\Delta X_{t-1} + \ldots + \omega_{1q}\Delta X_{t-q} + \varepsilon_{1t}$$

and

$$\Delta X_t = \varphi_2 + \delta_2 t + \lambda_2 e_{t-1} + \gamma_{21}\Delta Y_{t-1} + \ldots + \gamma_{2p}\Delta Y_{t-p} + \omega_{21}\Delta X_{t-1} + \ldots + \omega_{2q}\Delta X_{t-q} + \varepsilon_{2t}.$$

As before, $e_{t-1} = Y_{t-1} - \alpha - \beta X_{t-1}$. Note that the VECM is the same as a VAR with differenced variables, except for the term e_{t-1}. An estimate of this error correction variable can be obtained by running an OLS regression of Y on X and saving the residuals. We can then use OLS to estimate ECMs, and P-values and confidence intervals can be obtained. Lag length selection and forecasting can be done in a similar fashion to the VAR, with the slight added complication that forecasts of the error correction term, e_t, must be calculated. However, this is simple using OLS estimates of α and β and replacing the error, e_t, by the residual u_t. Furthermore, many computer packages such as Stata or Microfit will do estimation, testing and forecasting in VECMs automatically.

Of course, as with any of the models used in this chapter, you should always do unit root tests to see if your variables are stationary or not. If your variables have unit roots, then it is additionally worthwhile to test for cointegration. In the previous chapter, we introduced a test for cointegration based on checking whether there is a unit root in the residuals from the cointegrating regression. However, there is a more popular cointegration test called the *Johansen test*. To explain this test would require a discussion of concepts beyond the scope of this book. However, if you have a software package (e.g. Stata) which does the Johansen test, then you can use it in practice. Accordingly, we offer a brief intuitive description of this test.

The first thing to note is that it is possible for more than one cointegrating relationship to exist if you are working with several time series variables (all of which you have tested and found to have unit roots). To be precise, if you are working with M variables, then it is possible to have up to $M-1$ cointegrating relationships (and thus up to $M-1$ cointegrating residuals included in the VECM). For instance, in the following example we will investigate cointegration among three variables: consumption, assets and income. As we shall see below, there probably is just one cointegrating relationship between these variables. That is, c, a and y all have unit roots, but $c_t - \alpha - \beta_1 a_t - \beta_2 y_t$ is stationary. However, in theory it would have been possible for there to be two cointegrating relationships (for example, if $c_t - y_t$ and $a_t - y_t$ were both stationary). Thus, it is often of interest to test, not simply for whether cointegrating is present or not, but for the number of cointegrating relationships.

The Johansen test can be used to test for the number of cointegrating relationships using VECMs. For reasons we will not explain, the "number of cointegrating relationships" is referred to as the "cointegrating rank." The details of the Johansen test statistic are quite complicated. However, like any hypothesis test, you can compare the test statistic to a critical value and, if the test statistic is greater than the critical value, you reject the hypothesis being tested. Fortunately, many software packages (such as Stata) will calculate all these numbers for you. We will see how this works in the following example.

Before working through this example, note that when you do the Johansen test you have to specify the lag length and the deterministic trend term. We have discussed the former before. That is, lag length can be selected using hypothesis testing procedures or information criteria as described above. With VECMs it is possible simply to put an intercept and/or deterministic trend in the model (as we have done in the equations above—see the terms with coefficients φ and δ on them). However, it is also possible to put an intercept and/or deterministic trend actually in the cointegrating residual (for example, if you say $c_t - \alpha - \beta_1 a_t - \beta_2 y_t$ is the cointegrating residual you are putting an intercept into it). The Johansen test varies slightly depending on the exact configuration of deterministic terms you use, so you will be asked to specify these before doing the Johansen test.

Example: Consumption, Aggregate Wealth and Expected Stock Returns

In an influential paper in the *Journal of Finance* in 2001, "Consumption, aggregate wealth and expected stock returns," Lettau and Ludvigson present financial theory arguing that consumption, assets and income should be cointegrated and the cointegrating residual should be able to predict excess stock returns. They then present empirical evidence in favor of their theory. We will not repeat the theory (nor will we consider the forecasting aspect of their paper). However, we stress that their work uses the tools we have been developing in this chapter: testing for cointegration and estimation of a VECM. We will investigate the presence of cointegration here using US data from 1951Q4 through 2003Q1 on c, which is consumption (formally it is the log of real per capita expenditures on nondurables and services excluding shoes and clothing); a, which is our measure of assets (formally it is the log of a measure of real per capita household net worth including all financial and household wealth as well as consumer durables); and y, which is the log of after-tax labor income. These data are available in CAY.XLS.

Unit root tests indicate that all of these variables have unit roots. If we do the Johansen test using a lag length of one and restricting the deterministic term to allow for intercepts only (no deterministic trends such as those with coefficients δ in the previous equations are allowed for), we get the results in the Table 11.10 (using Stata).

Table 11.10   Johansen test for cointegration using CAY data.

Rank	Trace statistic	5% critical value
0	37.27	29.68
1	6.93	15.41
2	0.95	3.76

How should you interpret this table? Note first that "Trace Statistic" is the name of the test statistic used in the Johansen test and "Rank" indicates the number of cointegrating relationships with Rank = 0 indicating that cointegration is not present. With the Johansen test, the hypothesis being tested is always a certain cointegrating rank with the alternative hypothesis being that cointegrating rank is greater than the hypothesis being tested.

If we compare the trace statistic to its critical value we can see, for Rank = 0, that the test statistic is greater than the 5% critical value. This means we can reject the hypotheses that Rank = 0 at the 5% level of significance (in favor of the hypothesis that Rank ≥1). Thus, the Johansen test indicates that cointegration is present. However, if we look at the row with Rank = 1 we see that the test statistic is less than the critical value. Thus, we can accept the hypothesis that Rank = 1 (and are not finding evidence in favor of Rank ≥2). Thus, we are finding evidence that Rank = 1 (with this evidence, the information in the last row of the table is not relevant). As expected by Lettau and Ludvigson, we are finding evidence that one cointegrating relationship exists in this data set.

Armed with the information that one cointegrating relationship seems to exist, you can then (following Lettau and Ludvigson) calculate the cointegrating residual and investigate whether this has predictive power for expected stock returns. Alternatively, you could use this information to specify a VECM with one cointegrating relationship (and, thus, one error correction term).

Exercise 11.12

For this question, use the data on regular and organic orange prices in ORANGE. XLS.

(a) Starting with $p$max = 4, select a lag length for the VECM and estimate each equation using OLS.

(b) Using the VECM from part (a), carry out a forecasting exercise. Experiment with various forecast horizons. Does the VAR forecast well?

Exercise 11.13

Use the data on Y = consumption and X = personal income from INCOME. XLS.

(a) Assume (perhaps incorrectly in light of Exercise 10.5) that Y and X are cointegrated. Repeat the steps in Exercise 11.11 to carry out a forecasting exercise.

(b) Now assume that Y and X have unit roots but are not cointegrated. Construct a VAR using differenced data (ΔY and ΔX) and carry out a forecasting exercise.

(c) Compare results from part (a) and (b). What effect does assuming (possibly incorrectly) cointegration have on forecasting performance?

Chapter Summary

1. Many time series variables, particularly asset prices, seem to exhibit random walk behavior. For this reason, it is hard to predict how they will change in the future. However, such variables often do exhibit predictable patterns of volatility.
2. The square of the change in an asset price is a measure of its volatility.
3. Standard time series methods can be used to model the patterns of volatility in asset prices. The only difference is that volatility of the asset price is used as the variable of interest rather than the asset price itself.
4. ARCH models are a more formal way of measuring volatility. They contain two equations. One is a standard regression equation. The second is a volatility equation, where volatility is defined as being the (time varying) variance of the regression error.
5. ARCH models share similarities with AR models, except that the "AR" part relates to the volatility equation.
6. There are many extensions of ARCH, of which GARCH is the most popular.
7. ARCH and GARCH models can be estimated using many common statistical software packages (but are hard to work with using a spreadsheet).
8. X Granger-causes Y if past values of X have explanatory power for Y.
9. If X and Y are stationary, standard statistical methods based on an ADL model can be used to test for Granger causality.
10. If X and Y have unit roots and are cointegrated, statistical methods based on an ECM can be used to test for Granger causality.
11. Vector autoregressions have one equation for each variable being studied. Each equation chooses one variable as the dependent variable. The explanatory variables are lags of all the variables under study.
12. Vector autoregressions are useful for forecasting, testing for Granger causality or, more generally, understanding the relationships between several series.
13. If all the variables in the VAR are stationary, OLS can be used to estimate each equation and standard statistical methods can be employed (for example, P-values and t-statistics can be used to test for significance of variables).
14. If the variables under study have unit roots and are cointegrated, a variant on the VAR called the Vector error correction model, or VECM, should be used.
15. The Johansen test is a very popular test for cointegration. It is included in many software packages.

Appendix 11.1: Hypothesis Tests Involving More than One Coefficient

In Chapters 5 and 6 we discussed the F-statistic, which was used for testing the hypothesis $R^2 = 0$ in the multiple regression model:

$$Y = \alpha + \beta_1 X_1 + \beta_2 X_2 + \ldots + \beta_k X_k + e$$

We discussed how this was equivalent to testing H_0: $\beta_1 = \ldots = \beta_k = 0$ (i.e. whether all the regression coefficients are jointly equal to zero). We also discussed testing the significance of individual coefficients using t-statistics or P-values.

However, we have no tools for testing intermediate cases (for example, in the case $k = 4$, we might be interested in testing H_0: $\beta_1 = \beta_2 = 0$). Such cases arose in our discussion of Granger causality (for example, we had a regression model with four lags of price inflation, four lags of wage inflation and a deterministic trend and we were interested in testing whether the coefficients on the four lags of wage inflation were all zero). The purpose of this appendix is to describe a procedure and a rough rule of thumb for carrying out these kinds of tests.

The F-statistic described in Chapter 5 is more properly referred to as *an* F-statistic since it is only one of an enormous class of test statistics that take their critical values from statistical tables for the F-distribution. In this book, as you know by now, we have provided little statistical theory and do not describe how to use statistical tables. However, if you plan to do much work in Granger causality testing, you are well-advised to study a basic statistics or econometrics book to learn more about the statistical underpinnings of hypothesis testing.

To understand the basic F-testing procedure we introduce a distinction between *unrestricted* and *restricted* regression models. That is, most hypotheses you would want to test place restrictions on the model. Hence, we can distinguish between the regression with the restrictions imposed and the regression without. For instance, if the unrestricted regression model is:

$$Y = \alpha + \beta_1 X_1 + \beta_2 X_2 + \beta_3 X_3 + \beta_4 X_4 + e$$

and you wish to test the hypothesis H_0: $\beta_2 = \beta_4 = 0$, then the restricted regression model is:

$$Y = \alpha + \beta_1 X_1 + \beta_3 X_3 + e.$$

The general strategy of hypothesis testing is that a test statistic is first calculated and then compared to a critical value. If the test statistic is greater than the critical value (in an absolute value sense) then you reject the hypothesis; otherwise, you accept the hypothesis. In short, there are always two components to a hypothesis testing procedure: a test statistic and a critical value.

Table 11.11 Critical values for F-test if $T-k$ is large.

Significance level	$J=2$	$J=3$	$J=4$	$J=5$	$J=10$	$J=20$
5%	3.00	2.60	2.37	2.21	1.83	1.57
1%	4.61	3.78	3.32	3.02	2.32	1.88

Here the test statistic is usually called the F-statistic and is given by:

$$f = \frac{\left(R_U^2 - R_R^2\right)/J}{R_U^2/(T-k)}$$

where R_U^2 and R_R^2 are the R_S^2 from the unrestricted and restricted regression models, respectively. J is the number of restrictions (for example, $J=2$ in our example since $\beta_2 = 0$ and $\beta_4 = 0$ are two restrictions). T is the number of observations and k, the number of explanatory variables in the unrestricted regression.

Note that the F-statistic can be obtained by running the unrestricted and restricted regressions (for example, regress Y on X_1, X_2, X_3 and X_4 to get R_U^2, then regress Y on X_1 and X_3 to get R_R^2) and then calculating the above formula using a spreadsheet or calculator. Many specialist econometric packages will calculate the F-statistic for you automatically if you specify the hypothesis being tested.

Obtaining the critical value with which to compare the F-statistic is a more complicated. Formally, the critical value depends on $T-k$ and J. Table 11.11 contains critical values which you may use as a rough rule of thumb if $T-k$ is large.

For instance, if you have a large number of observations, are testing $J=2$ restrictions ($\beta_2 = 0$ and $\beta_4 = 0$), and you want to use the 5% level of significance, then you will use a critical value of 3.00 with which to compare the F-statistic.

To aid in interpretation, note that the case $J=1$ has not been included since testing only one restriction is something that the t-statistic already does. Note also that the critical values always become smaller as the number of restrictions increases. This fact can be used to approximate critical values for values of J that are not included in Table 11.11.

For instance, the critical value for testing $J=7$ restrictions will lie somewhere between the critical values for the restrictions $J=5$ and $J=10$ given in the table. In many cases, knowing that the correct critical value lies between two numbers will be enough for you to decide whether to accept or reject the hypothesis. Consequently, even though Table 11.11 does not include every possible value for J, you may be able to use it if J differs from those above.

Formally, the critical values in the previous table are correct if $T-k$ is equal to infinity. The correct critical values for $T-k>100$ are quite close to these. To give you an

Table 11.12 Critical values for F-test if $T-k$ is 40.

Significance level	$J=2$	$J=3$	$J=4$	$J=5$	$J=10$	$J=20$
5%	3.23	2.92	2.69	2.53	2.08	1.84
1%	5.18	4.31	3.83	3.51	2.80	2.37

idea of how bad an error may be made if $T-k<100$, examine Table 11.12, which gives the correct critical values if $T-k=40$.

As you can see, these critical values are all somewhat larger than those given in the table for $T-k$ equal to infinity. You may want to use these if your value for $T-k$ is about 40. However, we also report them here to get some idea of the error that may result if you use the large sample critical values. For instance, if $J=2$, $T-k=40$ and you obtain an F-statistic of 4 then using either table is fine: both state that the hypothesis should be rejected at the 5% level of significance. However, if the F-statistic were 3.1 you would incorrectly reject it using the large sample table.

In summary, you can safely use the methods and tables given in this appendix in the following cases:

If your sample size is large relative to the number of explanatory variables (e.g. $T-k>100$) the large sample table above is fine.

- If $T-k$ is approximately 40 the $T-k=40$ table is a safe choice.
- If $T-k$ is neither large, nor approximately 40, you are still safe using $T-k=40$ table, *provided your test statistic is not close to the critical value and provided $T-k$ is not extremely small (for example $T-k<10$).*

Generally speaking, so long as you have either a large number of data points or your data do not fall into one of these "borderline" cases you should not be led astray by using the methods outlined in this appendix.

Example: Granger Causality with Price and Wage Inflation Data

In the body of this chapter, we carried out Granger causality tests using price and wage inflation data. We found that wage inflation did not Granger-cause price inflation, but that price inflation did Granger-cause wage inflation. Here, we will investigate whether these conclusions still hold by carrying out the correct F-tests for Granger causality.

Consider first whether wage inflation Granger-causes price inflation. In the body of the chapter we use the following unrestricted model where $Y=$ price inflation and $X=$ wage inflation:

$$Y_t = \alpha + \delta t + \phi_1 Y_{t-1} + \ldots + \phi_4 Y_{t-4} + \beta_1 X_{t-1} + \ldots + \beta_4 X_{t-4} + e_t.$$

$T = 128^9$ and $k = 9$ ($p = q = 4$ plus we have the deterministic trend in the model). OLS estimation of this model yields $R_U^2 = 0.616$.

The hypothesis that Granger causality does not occur is $H_0: \beta_1 = \ldots = \beta_4 = 0$ which involves four restrictions; hence $J = 4$. The restricted regression model is:

$$Y_t = \alpha + \delta t + \phi_1 Y_{t-1} + \ldots + \phi_4 Y_{t-4} + e_t.$$

OLS estimation of this model yields $R_R^2 = 0.613$.

Using these numbers we calculate that the F-statistic is 0.145. $T - k = 119$ and is large, so we can compare 0.145 to a critical value of 2.37. Since $0.145 < 2.37$ we cannot reject the hypothesis at the 5% level of significance. Accordingly, we accept the hypothesis that wage inflation does not Granger-cause price inflation.

To test whether price inflation Granger-causes wage inflation we repeat the steps above except that wage inflation becomes the dependent variable and price inflation the explanatory variable. If we use OLS to estimate the restricted and unrestricted regressions, we obtain $R_U^2 = 0.605$ and $R_R^2 = 0.532$. Note that the other elements in the formula for the F-statistic do not change. Plugging these numbers into the equation for the F-statistic yields $f = 33.412$, which is much larger than either the 1% or 5% critical values. In this case, we can safely reject the hypothesis that $\beta_1 = \ldots = \beta_4 = 0$ and conclude that price inflation does Granger-cause price inflation.

Note that the findings that wage inflation does not Granger-cause price inflation but that price inflation does Granger-cause wage inflation, are exactly the same as given in the body of the chapter.

Endnotes

1. The notation "VAR" for "vector autoregression" is the standard one in empirical economics. However, financial economists use VAR to denote "value-at-risk," which is a different concept altogether.
2. In deriving this result we have ignored the $N - 1$ term in the denominator in the formula introduced in Chapter 2. You should simply note that it is not important here. In some formulas for the variance, $N - 1$ is replaced by N. Here, $N = 1$ so we can just ignore it.
3. This follows from the fact that $\ln(24.53)$ is 3.200 and $\ln(30.14)$ is 3.406.
4. Note that the variable X_t has been omitted from this ADL(p,q) model This is because Granger causality tests seek to determine whether past, not current, values of X can explain Y. If we

were to include X_t we would be allowing for contemporaneous causality and all the difficulties noted previously in this book about interpreting both correlations and regressions as reflecting causality would hold. You may also be wondering why we are using this ADL(p,q) model as opposed to the variant in which ΔY_t is the dependent variable (see Chapter 10). The reason is that it is easier to interpret Granger causality in this basic ADL(p,q) model as implying coefficients are equal zero. We could have covered all the material in this section using our previous ADL(p,q) variant.

5. This conclusion is based on an examination of the individual P-values for each coefficient. The joint test of $\beta_1 = \ldots = \beta_4 = 0$ is detailed in the appendix and supports the conclusion that wage inflation does not Granger-cause price inflation.

6. A more formal way of expressing the ideas in this paragraph is that VARs do not suffer from problems of *simultaneity*. This topic is discussed briefly in Chapter 12 in the section called "Problems that Call for the Use of Multiple Equation Models."

7. This statement is true in Stata (and most financial econometrics textbooks and software packages). However, confusingly, some statisticians define information criteria as being the negative of that used by Stata. With this definition, you would select the lag length that yields the largest value for the information criterion. So please be careful when using information criteria and read the manual or help facilities of your computer software.

8. One introductory text is Philip Hans Franses, *Time Series Models for Business Economics and Forecasting*, Cambridge University Press.

9. Remember that differencing variables and including lagged variables in a regression decreases the number of observations, which is why $T = 128$ rather than $T = 133$.

CHAPTER 12

Limitations and Extensions

Regression and its related techniques are quite powerful in that they are suited to the practical solution of a wide variety of economic problems. Nevertheless, if they were perfectly suited to solving every problem, econometricians and statisticians who seek to develop new tests, models and estimators would find themselves out of a job!

This chapter briefly introduces some limitations of OLS regression methods and appropriate extensions designed to deal with them. As will be seen, some cases do not imply so much that OLS is the wrong method as that better estimators exist and should be used. In other cases the use of OLS is strictly erroneous and should be avoided.

It is quite important to distinguish between these two cases—cases where the use of OLS represents the second-best option versus cases where its use is just plain wrong. Further study is required to identify and understand how to carry out empirical work in these different cases, especially those where OLS should never be used.

It is not the purpose of this chapter to develop methods for dealing with every problem case. A thorough treatment of all of these cases would fill several textbooks— well beyond the introductory scope of this book. Rather, it seeks to introduce a few general cases and their terminology so that you will, at a minimum, be able to recognize problem cases when they arise as well as know where to look for further study.

The problems can be loosely grouped into the following three areas, each of which we discuss in turn below:

- problems that occur when the dependent variable has particular forms
- problems that occur when the errors have particular forms
- problems that call for the use of multiple equation models.

If you go beyond the techniques described in previous chapters and learn about the new models and estimators discussed in this chapter, you will quickly realize that it will be difficult to continue using Excel. Fortunately, many other specialized econometrics packages (for example, SHAZAM, PCGIVE, MicroFit, TSP, E-views, Gauss, LIMDEP, Stata and Gretl) on the market have better capabilities. If you plan on doing a great deal of empirical work in the future you should learn how to use one or more of these software packages.

Problems that Occur when the Dependent Variable Has Particular Forms

Consider the simple regression model:

$$Y = \alpha + \beta X + e.$$

In previous chapters we focused a great deal on cases where Y is a real number that can take on any value (for example, sales price of a house, percentage change in forest cover, GDP per capita). However, you may come across cases where the dependent variable has a more restricted form. This form has implications for estimation. Here we list the most common cases.

- *Y is a dummy variable.* This case is discussed at the end of Chapter 7. To summarize, it usually arises when the dependent variable is a choice (for example, to take or not to take public transport, to choose or not to choose a specific occupation). When the dependent variable takes this form, OLS estimation is probably adequate for at least a crude summary of the information in the data but better estimators do exist, including Probit and Logit. Note that in other books, the terminology, *limited dependent variable, qualitative choice, discrete dependent variable or dummy dependent variable* models refer to this case. These are the chapter headings or index entries you should look for in an econometrics textbook if you want to learn more about these kinds of models. Cases where Y is a proportion (Y is a number between 0 and 1) or where many choices exist can also be handled using these sorts of methods.
- *Y is censored.* These cases arise when values of Y below or above a particular cutoff are recorded as that cutoff point. For instance, it is common in income surveys to report every person's income in a survey of household consumption, with the exception of the very richest group of people, which is usually recorded as being over some amount (for example, £100,000). So an individual making £20,000 will be recorded as £20,000, but an individual making £200,000 will be recorded as £100,000. As a second example, suppose that your dependent variable is the *desired* investment level of a firm but that all you can observe is *actual* investment by the firm. If actual invest-

ment cannot be negative, then all firms with a negative level of desired investment will be recorded as having zero investment. If your dependent variable is censored then OLS estimation can be misleading. In statistical jargon, OLS will be biased.[1] The degree of bias will increase with the proportion of observations censored. If only a few of your data points are censored, the use of OLS might be acceptable *but if the proportion of the observations that are censored is high, then OLS should definitely not be used.* In these cases, it is standard practice to use the *tobit* estimator. In econometric textbooks, this case will usually be addressed under the heading of *limited dependent variable* models.

- *Y is a non-negative integer.* This usually arises when the dependent variable is the number of times an event occurs. For instance, Y might measure the number of defects in a production process in a given week. Alternatively, Y might measure the number of patents taken out by a firm in a given year. If the dependent variable has this form, then OLS estimation is probably adequate but better approaches do exist. The phrase *count data model* is what you should look for in textbooks if you are interested in this area of the econometric literature.
- *Y measures a duration.* This case is common in labor economics where the dependent variable is often the time spent in a certain state. For instance, a labor economist might be interested in explaining why some unemployed individuals find work faster than others. In this case, the dependent variable is the duration of unemployment for each individual (the time spent before the individual finds a job). Another common example involves the analysis of industrial actions where the duration of strikes is the dependent variable. In such cases, OLS estimation of a regression is not automatically wrong or misleading. However, other, better models have been developed and probably should be used. The phrase *duration model* is what you should look for in textbooks if you are interested in this area of the econometrics literature.

The four cases listed above are probably the most common in this special category of empirical economic problems. Only in the case of a censored dependent variable will OLS necessarily be misleading. Nevertheless, it would be wise in all such cases for you to do some supplementary reading and consider using a computer software package other than Excel.

Problems that Occur when the Errors Have Particular Forms

We have not said much about the error terms in this book other than to note that they measure the distance between an observation and the regression line. There is a large literature discussing which estimator is the best when different statistical assumptions about the errors are made. Here we will not discuss the underlying statistical theory of these techniques in any detail. Instead, we will introduce just enough intuition and jargon to explain why these problems occur and highlight what words you should look for in an econometrics textbook if you are to do future research in this area.

We will begin by noting that OLS is the most common estimator for the regression model. It is very robust (works well) under many different statistical assumptions. Nevertheless, it is really only optimal if all the errors have, in a sense, the same properties.[2] In other cases, you may obtain more reliable estimates by using a *generalized least squares* (or *GLS*) estimator. By way of providing an intuitive understanding of the GLS estimator, we will begin by considering a problem known as *heteroskedasticity*.

Suppose you are interested in estimating a cross-country growth regression where the dependent variable is the average GDP growth rate in each of N countries. The explanatory variables include the level of education, investment, savings rate, and so on, for each country. Suppose that you include many developed countries (for example, USA, UK, Germany) as well as many less developed countries (such as Sudan, Angola and Haiti). Developed countries tend to have large, well financed government statistical organizations that collect data on GDP (among many other things) and, consequently, GDP tends to be measured with reasonable accuracy. In contrast, less developed countries often lack well financed data-gathering agencies and have large informal or subsistence economies. As a result, official GDP data are often measured inaccurately. What are the implications of this data-collection characteristic for OLS estimation?

First, it implies that the errors, *e*, for the less developed countries may tend be larger than for the developed countries. This phenomenon is known as *heteroskedasticity*.[3] Second, we may wish to attach more weight to the evidence of the developed countries because their data are probably more accurate than comparable data for the less developed countries. This is precisely what the GLS estimator does. In fact, the GLS estimator can be interpreted as the OLS estimator using reweighted data.

If you do more work in econometrics, you will learn precisely what we mean by "reweight." It is sufficient for you merely to note at this stage that OLS is still a good estimator[4] but that GLS is better if heteroskedasticity is present. You can reweight the data and use GLS in Excel but with most data sets this will be awkward and you will be better off using another computer package.

In addition to heteroskedasticity there are other data problems that have similar intuition and implications for the choice of methods in an analysis (OLS is suitable but GLS is better). The best known of these occurs when the errors are *autocorrelated*. The concept of autocorrelation was introduced in Chapter 9. The difference here is that e_t, rather than Y_t, is correlated with lags of itself. If you have correctly specified lag length (p in the AR(p) or p and q in the ADL(p,q)), then autocorrelation of the errors is unlikely to be a problem. However, if it is, then GLS estimation will produce more reliable estimates than will OLS. Excel cannot easily carry out GLS in this case, but most specialist econometrics packages can quite straightforwardly.

The above are all cases where OLS is probably adequate but other estimators are better suited to the application. Yet there is one prominent case where error problems mean that the use of OLS is misleading. This occurs if the error is correlated with the explanatory variables. You will not have much understanding about why this case may cause problems and when it may occur. However, some graphical intuition is given in Figure 12.1, which illustrates a case where the errors are positively correlated with the explanatory variable. The true regression line is marked on the graph with a solid line labeled $Y = \alpha + \beta X$. The positive correlation between X and the errors means that high values of X are associated with high (positive) errors and low values of X, with low (negative) errors. The XY-plot will thus be of the form given in Figure 12.1, with data points lying below the true regression line for low values of X and above it for high values of X. In other words, Figure 12.1 is drawn in such a way that the errors are all negative for low values of X and positive for all high values of X. OLS will fit a line through the data points, ending up as the dotted line shown in Figure 12.1. Given that this dotted line has a different slope and intercept than the true regression line, OLS is clearly inappropriate in this case.

The most common case where the explanatory variables and errors are correlated is the *simultaneous equations* model. This topic will be dealt with in the next section. You should merely note at this stage that if the error is correlated with the explanatory variables *then you should not use OLS*. Instead you should learn about and use *instrumental variables* estimators.

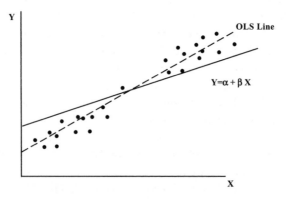

Figure 12.1   OLS when error is correlated with X.

Problems that Call for the Use of Multiple Equation Models

Throughout this book, except for our discussion on VARs and VECMs, we have focused on the one-equation regression model. In practice, it is common to have several dependent variables and, thus, several regression models (sometimes called *systems of equations*). A few examples will serve to illustrate when such applications arise:

- Imagine that you have collected cross-sectional data on the production of a number of firms. In particular, you observe the amount of labor, capital, energy and materials inputs, as well as the price of each input. You are interested in explaining the input choices of firms. Here you have four different dependent variables (labor, capital, energy and materials) all of which depend on the prices of the inputs. You would have a separate regression equation for each dependent variable and, thus, four different equations.
- Imagine that you have time series data on consumption, broken down into its sources (for example, consumption of food, consumption of transport, consumption of housing, consumption of clothing and consumption of durable goods). You are interested in how these various components of consumption depend on the state of the economy. In this case you will have many dependent variables (for example, consumption of food, transport, housing and so forth) and will use macroeconomic variables such as GDP and interest rates as your explanatory variables. Each dependent variable will imply a different regression equation.
- In a finance application, you may be interested in explaining the stock returns of many different firms. In this case, you may have many different dependent variables (the stock return for each firm) dependent on explanatory variables such as the interest rate and so on.
- The vector autoregressive (VAR) model discussed in Chapter 11 is a multiple equation model. In this model, Y depends on lags of itself and on lags of another variable, X. It also has a second equation, in which X is the dependent variable and the latter depends on lags of Y and lags of itself.
- The IS-LM model will be well known to those who have taken macroeconomics. Note that it is based on two equations (IS and LM).
- The model of supply and demand is also a standard one in economics. This model has two equations, one being the supply curve and the other the demand curve.

To anticipate the essential point of this section, it is only the last two of these examples that will cause major problems for OLS estimation.

To understand the issues that arise in multiple equation systems we must introduce a few concepts that you may be familiar with from previous economic training. A variable is *endogenous* if it is determined within the model under study. It is *exogenous* if it is not.

These concepts are closely related to the causality issues raised in Chapter 4. Recall that we stressed that regression is most easily interpreted if the explanatory variable causes the dependent variable (and not the opposite). In other words, the regression model assumes that Y is determined by what happens to X. We did not specify how X was generated. In this case, Y, the dependent variable, is endogenous and X, the explanatory variable, is assumed to be exogenous. Intuitively speaking, as long as your explanatory variables are exogenous, the use of OLS estimation is fine, even if you have many equations. However, if your explanatory variables are endogenous, then you should not carry out OLS estimation.

A few examples should further clarify these ideas:

• In Chapters 6 and 7 we regressed house prices on a variety of house characteristics. House prices, Y, depend on the characteristics of a house, X (for example, houses with more bedrooms tend to have higher prices). However, the characteristics of a house do not depend on the price of a house (if the housing market collapsed and the price of a house dropped, it would not cause the house to have fewer bedrooms or bathrooms). X causes Y but Y does not cause X. X is exogenous and Y is endogenous.

• Firms choose the levels of their inputs based on the prices of the inputs (for example, if wages are low relative to the price of buying new machinery they would tend to hire workers rather than buy new machines). The latter prices determine or cause the input choice. But the input choice of a firm does not affect the price of the inputs. For instance, in competitive markets at least, if the firm hires some extra workers that action will not cause wages to rise. So in a model designed to explain input choice, inputs will be endogenous (determined by the model) but input prices will be exogenous.

• If you solve an IS-LM model, you typically come up with answers for national income and for the interest rate. That is, national income and the interest rate are both determined (or solved) in the model. When econometricians seek to estimate IS-LM models they use these two variables (among others). Note that they are both endogenous (the model determines both).

• In a supply-demand model, equilibrium price and quantity occurs where the supply curve intersects the demand curve. Both the price and the quantity of the good supplied and demanded in a market are determined by the model. Hence both price and quantity are endogenous.

For the rest of this section we will let Y indicate an endogenous variable and X an exogenous variable. If we have more than one of these variables, we will use the notation $Y_1, \ldots, Y_M$ and $X_1, \ldots, X_K$ to indicate M endogenous and K exogenous variables. Following is a quick taxonomy of possible cases:

- The regression model $Y = \alpha + \beta_1 X_1 + \ldots + \beta_K X_K + e$ has been discussed in detail in this book. OLS estimation of this model can be carried out with ease.[5]
- If you have a system of equations of the following form:

$$Y_1 = \alpha_1 + \beta_{11} X_1 + \ldots + \beta_{1K} X_K + e_1$$
$$Y_2 = \alpha_2 + \beta_{21} X_1 + \ldots + \beta_{2K} X_K + e_2$$

....

....

$$Y_M = \alpha_M + \beta_{M1} X_1 + \ldots + \beta_{MK} X_K + e_M,$$

simply carry out OLS one equation at a time. Note that this model assumes that all equations have exactly the same explanatory variables (for example, the amount of each input depends on the prices of all the inputs). If the equations have different explanatory variables (the amount of each input depends only on its own price for instance), then a better estimator than OLS is the *seemingly unrelated regression equations* or *SURE* estimator. Note, though, that OLS is an adequate second best estimator.

- If you are working with the following model:

$$Y_1 = \alpha + \beta Y_2 + e,$$

or, more generally,

$$Y_1 = \alpha_1 + \gamma_{12} Y_2 + \ldots + \gamma_{1M} Y_M + \beta_{11} X_1 + \ldots + \beta_{1K} X_K + e_1$$
$$Y_2 = \alpha_2 + \gamma_{21} Y_1 + \ldots + \gamma_{2M} Y_M + \beta_{21} X_1 + \ldots + \beta_{2K} X_K + e_2$$

....

....

$$Y_M = \alpha_M + \gamma_{M1} Y_1 + \ldots + \gamma_{M,M-1} Y_{M-1} + \beta_{M1} X_1 + \ldots + \beta_{MK} X_K + e_M.$$

then the use of OLS can yield misleading results and should be avoided.

To summarize, if your explanatory variables are exogenous then it is acceptable to use OLS (even in multiple equation models). If the explanatory variables are endogenous, however, OLS is not a suitable estimator (even in a single equation model).

The last model above is called the *simultaneous equations model* and it has received a great deal of attention in the econometrics literature. It is beyond the scope of this book to discuss this model in detail. Nevertheless, it is worthwhile to motivate briefly why the problem with OLS occurs through the consideration of a representative example.

Consider the simplest version of the standard supply and demand model in economics. The demand curve is given by:

$$Q^D = \alpha_D + \beta_D P,$$

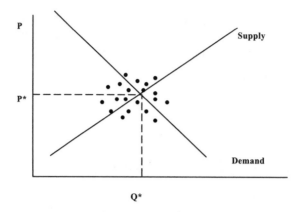

Figure 12.2   Observed data in a model of supply and demand.

which states that the quantity demanded of a good, Q^D, depends on its price, P. The supply curve tells how the quantity supplied by firms, Q^S, also depends on price:

$$Q^S = \alpha_S + \beta_S P.$$

The solid lines in Figure 12.2 plot the supply and demand curves. The point at which they intersect determines the equilibrium price and quantity, P^* and Q^*. In other words, price and quantity are determined in the model and are endogenous.

What would happen if price and quantity data were obtained (for example, from a market for a certain product each week for several weeks) and a regression of quantity on price run?

We would obtain OLS estimates of the intercept and slope, say, $\hat{\alpha}$ and $\hat{\beta}$. But what would $\hat{\alpha}$ and $\hat{\beta}$ be estimates of? Already you may spot the problem in using OLS: we don't know if $\hat{\alpha}$ and $\hat{\beta}$ will be estimates of α_D and β_D (the demand curve) or of α_S and β_S (the supply curve).[6] In practice, OLS will probably estimate neither the supply curve nor the demand curve.

Further intuition for the failure of OLS can be found by looking at Figure 12.2. P^* and Q^* are the equilibrium price and quantity. Suppose we observe the price and quantity in a market for this good many times (for example, every week for a year). In the real world, we are likely never to be precisely in equilibrium and small errors will occur. That is, the actual price and quantity observed each week will not be exactly P^* and Q^* every time. So the observed data points will probably be in a cloud around the equilibrium in the manner plotted in Figure 12.2. Imagine trying, as OLS does, to fit a straight line through those points. Intuitively it is clear that the line that is fitted will not necessarily bear any relationship to either the supply or demand curve.

More formally, we can demonstrate that when either some or all explanatory variables are endogenous, the regression error will be correlated with explanatory variables and the use of OLS is erroneous (see the discussion on Figure 12.1 above). If you run into this case, you should do further study and learn about simultaneous equations models and instrumental variable estimation.

Chapter Summary

In summary, although the OLS estimator is a powerful tool that can be used for a wide variety of data sets, it is not perfect for every situation. There are some cases when the use of OLS is not the best choice, but it may nevertheless be adequate. Yet, there are also cases when its use is completely misleading. Below is a summary list of both of these types of cases.

Cases when OLS is Second Best

1. The dependent variable is a dummy variable, a duration or a count (an integer).
2. The errors are heteroskedastic or autocorrelated (these concepts are explained more fully in the chapter).
3. The data have many dependent variables and thus many equations but all the explanatory variables are exogenous.

Cases when OLS is Misleading and Should be Avoided

1. The dependent variable is censored.
2. The errors are correlated with the explanatory variables.
3. One or more of the explanatory variables is endogenous.
4. You have many dependent variables and thus many equations but some of the explanatory variables are endogenous.

Endnotes

1. *Bias* is a statistical term that will not be formally defined here. Informally speaking, if you use an *unbiased* estimator in many applications then your estimate may be high or low in any one application, but on average it will be correct. In contrast, *biased* estimators will, on average, be wrong, and should be avoided.

2. In statistical jargon, OLS is the best of all estimators (in a certain class) if the errors are independent of one another and are all drawn from the same distribution. If this distribution is Normal then an even stronger case can be made for the optimality of the OLS estimator.

3. Formally, heteroskedasticity occurs if the standard deviation of the errors differs across observations.

4. In statistical language, OLS and GLS are both unbiased estimators; however, GLS is more efficient than OLS.

5. Of course, if the error or dependent variable problems discussed in the previous part of this chapter are present, then OLS may have to be modified along the lines of the previous discussion. This qualification holds for the following cases as well.

6. To introduce even more econometric jargon, this is an example of an *identification problem*.

Appendix A: Writing an Empirical Project

This appendix offers general guidelines on writing an empirical paper or project. This discussion is followed by several project topics on which you may wish to work in order to gain a deeper understanding of the techniques described in this book. The data are available on the web site associated with this book (except for the final project topic, which uses data from a different web site).

Description of a Typical Empirical Project

Economists engage in research in a wide variety of areas today. Undergraduate and graduate students, academic economists, policymakers working in the civil service and central banks, professional economists working in private sector banks or industry—all may need to write reports that involve analyzing economic data. Depending on the topic and intended audience, the form of these reports can vary widely, so that there is no one correct format for an empirical paper. With this in mind, we provide common elements of economic reports below as a guideline for future empirical work. Note, however, that, in the context of your own undergraduate projects or careers, it may not be necessary for you to include all of these elements in your report.

1. *Introduction.* Most reports begin with an introduction that briefly motivates and describes the issue being studied and summarizes the main empirical findings. The introduction should be written in simple nontechnical language, with statistical and economic jargon kept to a minimum. A reader who is not an expert in the field should be able to read and understand the general issues and findings of the report or paper.

2. *Literature review.* This should summarize related work that others have done. It should list and very briefly describe other papers and findings that relate to yours.

3. *Economic theory.* If the report is academic in nature and involves a formal theoretical model then it is often described in this section. For policy reports you may not need to include a formal mathematical model but this section allows you to describe the economic or institutional issues of your work in more detail. This section can be more technical than the preceding ones and will typically include some mathematics and economic jargon. In short, you can address this section solely to an audience of experts in your field.

4. *Data.* In this section you should describe your data, including a detailed discussion of their sources.

5. *The model to be estimated.* In this section you should discuss how you use the data to investigate the economic theory outlined in section 3. The exact form of this section might vary considerably, depending on the topic and on the intended audience. For instance, you may want to argue that a particular regression is of interest for the study, that a certain variable will be the dependent variable and that other variables will be the explanatory variables. Similarly, in a macroeconomic time series exercise, you may wish to argue that your economic theory implies that your variables should be cointegrated and that, for this reason, a test of cointegration will be carried out. In short, it is in this section that you should justify the techniques used in the next section.

6. *Empirical results.* This section is typically the heart of any report. In it you should describe your empirical findings and discuss how they relate to the economic issue(s) under investigation. It should contain both statistical and economic information. By "economic" information we refer, for example, to coefficient estimates or to a finding of cointegration between two variables and what these findings may imply for economic theory. In contrast, "statistical" information may include: results from hypothesis tests that show which coefficients are significant; a justification for choice of lag length; an explanation for deleting insignificant explanatory variables; a discussion of model fit (for example, the R^2 or outliers) and so forth. This information will largely be presented in tables and graphs. It is common for papers to begin with some simple graphs (for example, a time series plot of the data) and then follow with a table of descriptive statistics (for example, the mean, standard deviation, minimum/maximum of each variable and a correlation matrix). Another table might

include results from a more formal statistical analysis, such as OLS coefficient estimates, together with t-statistics (or P-values), R^2s and F-statistics for testing the significance of the regression as a whole.

7. *Conclusion.* This should briefly summarize the issues addressed in the paper, specifically, its most important empirical findings.

General Considerations

The following contains a discussion of a few of the issues that you should keep foremost
in your mind while carrying out an empirical project. In particular, it discusses what
constitutes good empirical science and how you should present your results.

The first thing worth stressing is that there are no right or wrong empirical results.
*Empirical results are what they are and you should not be disappointed if they do not show what you
had hoped they would.* In an ideal world, a researcher comes up with a new theory then
carries out empirical work that supports this new theory in a statistically significant way.
The real world very rarely approaches this ideal.

In the real world, explanatory variables that you expect to be statistically significant
often aren't significant. Variables you expect to be cointegrated often aren't cointegrated. Coefficients you expect to be positive often turn out to be negative. These
results are obtained all the time—even in the most sophisticated of studies. They should
not discourage you! Instead, you should always keep an open mind. *A finding that a theory
does not seem to work is just as scientifically valid as a finding that a theory does work.*

Furthermore, empirical results are often unclear or confusing. For instance, a statistical test might indicate one thing whereas another might indicate the opposite. Likewise,
an explanatory variable that is significant in one regression might be insignificant in
another regression. There is nothing you can do about this, except to report your results
honestly and try (if possible) to understand why such conflicts or confusions are
occurring.

It is rare for economists to completely falsify their results. Often, however, they may
be tempted to do slightly dishonest things in order to show that results are indeed as
economic reasoning anticipated. For instance, it is common for a researcher to run a
large number of regressions with many different explanatory variables. On the whole,
this is a very wise thing—a sign that the researcher is exploring the data in detail and
from a number of angles. However, if researchers present only the regression that supports a particular theory and not the other regressions that discredit it, they are intentionally misleading the reader. Always avoid this temptation to misrepresent your
results!

On the issue of how results should be presented, we cannot stress enough the importance of clarity and brevity. Whether it is a good thing or a bad thing, it is undoubtedly

the case that university lecturers, civil servants, policymakers and employers are busy people who do not want to spend a lot of time reading long, poorly organized and verbose reports.

One key skill that writers of good reports show is selectivity. For example, you may have many different coefficient results and tests statistics from your various regression runs. An important part of any report is to decide what information is important and what is unimportant to your readership. Select only the most important information for inclusion in your report and—as always—report honestly and openly the results that you obtain.

Project Topics

The following are several project topics that you may wish to undertake.

Project 1: the equity underpricing puzzle

Background

Investors and financial economists are interested in understanding how the stock market values a firm's equity (shares). In a fundamental sense, the value of a firm's shares should reflect investors' expectations of the firm's future profitability. However, data on expected future profitability are nonexistent. Instead, empirical financial studies must use measures such as current income, sales, assets and debt of the firm as explanatory variables.

In addition to the general question of how stock markets value firms, a second question has also received considerable attention from financial economists in recent years. By way of motivating this question, note that most of the shares traded on the stock market are old shares in existing firms. However, many old firms will issue some new shares in addition to those already trading—these are referred to as "seasoned equity offerings" or SEOs. Furthermore, some firms that have not traded shares on the stock market in the past may decide to now issue such shares (for example, a computer software firm owned by one individual may decide to "go public" and sell shares in order to raise money for future investment or expansion). Such shares are called "initial public offerings" or IPOs. Some researchers have argued on the basis of empirical evidence that IPOs are undervalued relative to SEOs.

In this project, you are asked to empirically investigate these questions using the following data set.

Data

Excel file EQUITY.XLS contains data on $N = 309$ firms who sold new shares in the year 1996 in the US. Some of these are SEOs and some are IPOs. Data on the following variables is provided. All variables except SEO are measured in millions of US dollars.

- *VALUE* = the total value of all shares (new and old) outstanding just after the firm issued the new shares. This is calculated as the price per share times the number of shares outstanding.
- *DEBT* = the amount of long-term debt held by the firm.
- *SALES* = total sales of the firm.
- *INCOME* = net income of the firm.
- *ASSETS* = book value of the assets of the firm (what an accountant would judge the firm's assets to be worth).
- *SEO* = a dummy variable that equals 1 if the new share issue is an SEO and equals 0 if it is an IPO.

Project 2: the determinants of economic growth

Background

Barro (1991) used regression methods to investigate which factors could explain why some countries grew more than others. Since then there have been dozens of other papers which investigate this issue using other data sets, variables or statistical methods. The purpose of this project is to use regression methods and the data set described below to investigate the determinants of economic growth.

Data

Excel file GROWTH.XLS contains data on $N = 72$ countries on the following variables. All of the variables are either averages over 1960–92 or for some year in that period:

- GDP growth = average growth in GDP per capita;
- primary school = proportion of population with at least primary school education;
- life expectancy = life expectancy;
- GDP 1960 = level of per capita GDP in 1960 (in US dollars);
- investment = investment in machinery and equipment;
- higher education = proportion of population with higher education;
- war dummy = 1 if country has experienced a war in 1960–92, = 0 if not.

Note that the data set used in this project is part of a data set used in a paper that uses more sophisticated statistical methods: Fernandez, Ley and Steel (2001). This paper describes the data in more detail and also tells you where to get the complete data set.

Project 3: wage-setting behavior

Background

This project allows you to investigate wage-setting behavior using time series data. The general issue of interest in such analyses is how wages depend on macroeconomic factors such as the price level, GDP and variables reflecting employment and the labor force. An empirical analysis of such data must involve a discussion of issues such as unit roots and cointegration.

Data

Excel file WAGE.XLS contains annual UK data from 1855 through 1987. The natural logarithm of all variables has been taken. Data on the following variables are provided:

- W = the log of nominal wages;
- P = the log of consumer price index;
- GDP = the log of real GDP;
- E = the log of total employment;
- L = the log of total potential labor force.

Further background

In addition to the general issue of wage-setting behavior, economic interest often focuses on functions of the variables provided here. If you remember the properties of the logarithm operator, such as $\ln(A/B) = \ln(A) - \ln(B)$ and $\ln(1 + A) \approx A$, you can derive the following relationships:

- the log of real wages = $W - P$;
- the log of productivity per worker = $GDP - E$;
- the log of the unemployment rate $\approx L - E$;
- log of the share of wages in $GDP = W - P - GDP + E$.

You might be interested in investigating whether the relationships above are cointegrating relationships. In Chapter 11, we considered estimating the cointegrating regression using OLS techniques—something you may want to explore in your project. You may also wish to use the relationships above to tell you what the coefficients in the cointegrating regression might be. For instance, if the log of real wages equation above is a cointegrating relationship, then the regression of W on P should be:

$$W_t = P_t + e_t.$$

In other words, $\alpha = 0$ and $\beta = 1$. You can either estimate the regression of W on P (as in Chapter 11), or impose $\alpha = 0$ and $\beta = 1$ and see whether these values imply cointegration. In this project, I suggest that you consider using both strategies. That is, you can either estimate a regression using OLS and then test the residuals for a unit root or you can impose a possible cointegrating relationship and then test the residuals for a unit root.

The previous material does not focus directly on the issue of wage-setting behavior. You may want to do other tests or estimate other regressions in addition to (or instead of) the things suggested above.

Project 4: consumption, wealth and income

Background

This project uses the data set CAY.XLS, which contains US data from 1951Q4 through 2003Q1 on the variables: consumption (c), assets (a) and income (y). Such so-called cay relationships have received a great deal of attention in the recent empirical finance literature. Lettau and Ludvigson (2001) presented financial theory arguing that the cay variables should be cointegrated and the cointegrating residual should be able to predict excess stock returns. They then present empirical evidence in favor of their theory. In a subsequent paper, using the cay data, Lettau and Ludvigson (2004) presented further empirical work involving cointegration testing and VECMs.

This project topic asks you to use the techniques associated with unit roots, cointegration testing and VECMs. You are free to push the project in several directions. The following are a few examples of the types of issues/questions you may wish to focus your project on.

The conclusions of Lettau and Ludvigson are based on a finding that these variables are cointegrated. Investigate this in more detail using different lag lengths and different treatments of the deterministic terms. Confirm the original finding of Lettau and Ludvigson that all variables have unit roots.

Estimate a VECM and interpret the results. Which explanatory variables are good for predicting which variables? Use VECM methods to address Granger causality issues.

Project 5: financial volatility

This project uses data from Franses and Van Dijk (2000). This book has a web site containing a rich collection of data sets from several countries on stock prices and exchange rates, which you can download (see http://www.few.eur.nl/few/people/ djvandijk/nltsmef/nltsmef.htm, accessed 3 November 2008). In particular, stock price indices from Amsterdam (EOE), Frankfurt (DAX), Hong Kong (Hang Seng), London (FTSE100), New York, (S&P 500), Paris (CAC40), Singapore (Singapore All Shares) and Tokyo (Nikkei) are provided. The exchange rates are the Australian dollar, British pound, Canadian dollar, German DeutschMark, Dutch guilder, French franc, Japanese yen and the Swiss franc, all expressed as number of units of the foreign currency per US dollar. The sample period for the stock indexes runs from 6 January 1986 until 31 December 1997, whereas for the exchange rates the sample covers the period from 2 January 1980 until 31 December 1997.

Investigate financial volatility using this data with ARCH and GARCH models. Do stock returns appear to exhibit volatility? Do exchange rates?

There are many other things you can do using these data, depending on your interests. For example, an issue much studied by financial researchers is whether volatility in financial markets differs depending on the frequency a financial market is observed. For instance, stock markets might be more volatile when observed every day than when observed monthly. You could investigate this issue using this data set. Note that it is available at a daily frequency. When you work with weekly data you can use data every Wednesday. For monthly frequency use the last day of each month.

References

Barro, R. (1991) Economic growth in a cross section of countries. *Quarterly Journal of Economics*, **106** (2), 407–43.

Fernandez, C., Ley, E. and Steel, M. (2001) Model uncertainty in cross-country growth regressions. *Journal of Applied Econometrics*, **16**, 563–76.

Franses, P.H. and Van Dijk, D. (2000) *Nonlinear Time Series Models in Empirical Finance*, Cambridge University Press, Cambridge.

Lettau, M. and Ludvigson, S.C. (2001) Consumption, aggregate wealth and expected stock returns. *Journal of Finance*, **56**, 815–49.

Lettau, M. and Ludvigson, S.C. (2004) Understanding trend and cycle in asset values: reevaluating the wealth effect on consumption. *American Economic Review*, **94** (1), 276–99.

Appendix B: Data Directory

Data file	Content	Data type	Chapter
ADVERT.XLS	Sales and advertising expenditure	Cross-sectional, $N = 84$ companies	Chapters 4 and 5
CAY.XLS	Consumption, assets and income	Time series, $T = 206$ quarters	Appendix A
COMPUTE1.XLS	Percentage change in computer purchases and employee productivity	Time series, $T = 98$ months	Chapter 10
COMPUTER.XLS	Percentage change in computer purchases and employee productivity	Time series, $T = 98$ months	Chapter 10
CORMAT.XLS	Artificial variables labeled Y, X and Z	Cross-sectional, $N = 20$	Chapter 3
EDUC.XLS	Education spending, GDP growth	Time series, 1910 through 1995, $T = 86$ years	Chapter 8
ELECTRIC.XLS	Cost of electricity production, output produced and price of inputs	Cross-sectional, $N = 123$ companies	Chapters 4, 5, and 6
EQUITY.XLS	Firm share value, debt, sales, income, assets, SEO dummy	Cross-sectional, $N = 309$ companies	Appendix A

Data file	Content	Data type	Chapter
EX34.XLS	Artificial variables labeled Y, $X1$, $X2$ and $X3$	Cross-sectional, $N = 20$	Chapter 3
EX46.XLS	Artificial variables labeled Y and X	Cross-sectional, $N = 50$	Chapter 4
EXRUK.XLS	UK pound/US dollar exchange rate	Time series, January 1947 through October, 1996, $T = 598$ months	Chapter 2
FIG51.XLS	Artificial variables labeled X and Y	Cross-sectional, $N = 5$	Chapter 5
FIG52.XLS	Artificial variables labeled X and Y	Cross-sectional, $N = 100$	Chapter 5
FIG53.XLS	Artificial variables labeled X and Y	Cross-sectional, $N = 100$	Chapter 5
FIG54.XLS	Artificial variables labeled X and Y	Cross-sectional, $N = 100$	Chapter 5
FIG95.XLS	Artificial variable labeled "b = 0 series"	Time series, $T = 100$	Chapter 9
FIG96.XLS	Artificial variable labeled "b = 0.8 series"	Time series, $T = 100$	Chapter 9
FIG97.XLS	Artificial variable labeled "b = 1 series"	Time series, $T = 100$	Chapter 9
FIG98.XLS	Artificial variable labeled "trend stat"	Time series, $T = 100$	Chapter 9
FOREST.XLS	Forest loss, population density, pasture change, cropland change	Cross-sectional, $N = 70$ countries	Chapters 2, 3, 4, 5 and 6
GDPPC.XLS	Real GDP per capita	Cross-sectional, $N = 90$ countries	Chapters 2 and 5
GROWTH.XLS	GDP growth and explanatory variables	Cross-sectional, $N = 72$ countries	Appendix A
HPRICE.XLS	Housing prices and housing characteristics (e.g. lot size, no. of bedrooms)	Cross-sectional, $N = 546$ houses	Chapters 3, 4, 5, 6 and 7
INCOME.XLS	Log of US personal income and consumption	Time series, 1954Q1 through 1994Q4, $T = 164$ quarters	Chapters 2, 9, 10 and 11
LONGGDP.XLS	Real GDP per capita for Australia, US, UK, Canada	Time series, 1870 through 1993, $T = 124$ years	Chapters 10 and 11
NYSE.XLS	Changes in stock price	Time series, January 1952 through December 1995, $T = 528$ months	Chapter 11

Data file	Content	Data type	Chapter
ORANGE.XLS	Prices of regular oranges and organic oranges	Time series, $T = 181$ months	Chapters 10 and 11
RMPY.XLS	Monthly Treasury Bill rate, price level, money supply, GDP and logged changes of all variables	Time series, 1947Q1 through 1992Q4, $T = 184$ quarters	Chapter 11
SAFETY.XLS and SAFETY1.XLS	Company accident losses, hours spent in safety training	Time series, $T = 60$ months	Chapter 8
STOCK.XLS	Logged stock price data	Time series, $T = 208$ weeks	Chapter 11
WAGE.XLS	Log of UK nominal wages, consumer price index, real GDP, total employment, total potential labor force	Time series, 1855 through 1987, $T = 133$ years	Appendix A
WAGEDISC.XLS	Employee occupation data (e.g. salary, education, experience, sex)	Cross-sectional, $N = 100$ employees	Chapter 7
WP.XLS	Log of UK Wages and Consumer Price Index	Time series, 1857 through 1987, $T = 131$ years	Chapters 10 and 11

User Note

The web site accompanying this book contains a variety of time series and cross-sectional data in Excel file format ("xls").

Index